P9-CKY-039

DATE DUE

PRINTED IN U.S.A.

CULTURE, GENDER, RACE, AND U.S. LABOR HISTORY

CULTURE, GENDER, RACE, AND U.S. LABOR HISTORY

Edited by
Ronald C. Kent, Sara Markham,
David R. Roediger, and Herbert Shapiro

Contributions in Labor Studies, Number 39

GREENWOOD PRESS
Westport, Connecticut • London

RIVERSIDE C C LIBRARY

Library of Congress Cataloging-in-Publication Data

Culture, gender, race, and U.S. labor history / edited by Ronald C.
    Kent . . . [et al.].
            p.   cm. — (Contributions in labor studies, ISSN 0886-8239 ;
    no. 39)
        Includes bibliographical references and index.
        ISBN 0-313-28828-3 (alk. paper)
        1. Labor—United States—History.   2. Working class—United
    States—History.   3. Labor movement—United States—History.
    4. Women—Employment—United States—History.   5. Afro-Americans—
    Employment—History.   I. Kent, Ronald Charles.   II. Series.
    HD8066.C78   1993
    331'.0973—dc20   92-35921

British Library Cataloguing in Publication Data is available.

Copyright © 1993 by Ronald C. Kent, Sara Markham, David R. Roediger, and
Herbert Shapiro

All rights reserved. No portion of this book may be
reproduced, by any process or technique, without the
express written consent of the publisher.

Library of Congress Catalog Card Number: 92-35921
ISBN: 0-313-28828-3
ISSN: 0886-8239

First published in 1993

Greenwood Press, 88 Post Road West, Westport, CT 06881
An imprint of Greenwood Publishing Group, Inc.

Printed in the United States of America

∞™

The paper used in this book complies with the
Permanent Paper Standard issued by the National
Information Standards Organization (Z39.48-1984).

10 9 8 7 6 5 4 3 2 1

RIVERSIDE CC LIBRARY

The editors and authors dedicate this volume to Professor Philip S. Foner. Shoulder to shoulder Professor Foner has stood with the progressive currents of the history profession; the Abraham Lincoln Brigade; and the labor, civil rights, and civil liberties movements throughout the world. He has supported blacklisted friends, students, and colleagues. Professor Foner's personal courage, his dedication to his research, and his engagement with local and world communities continue to inspire us. His scholarship has advanced the study of culture, gender, race, and U.S. labor history. We who have read his prodigious volume of books and who have come to know Professor Foner as an historian, editor, and activist honor him and wish him many more years of intellectual creativity.

> Courage yet, my brother or my sister!
> Keep on—Liberty is to be subserv'd whatever occurs;
> That is nothing that is quell'd by one or two failures, or any number
>   of failures
> Or by the indifference or ingratitude of the people, or by any
>   unfaithfulness,
> Or the show of the tushes of power, soldiers, cannon, penal statutes.
>
> What we believe in waits latent forever through all the continents,
> Invites no one, promises nothing, sits in calmness and light, is positive
>   and composed, knows no discouragement,
> Waiting patiently, waiting its time.*

* Walt Whitman, "To a Foil'd European Revolutionaire" (1856), quoted in Whitman's *Leaves of Grass*, ed. Emory Holloway (Garden City, N.Y.: Doubleday, 1926, 309–310).

Contents

Acknowledgments

We are indebted to many individuals who have contributed substantive ideas, incisive criticism, and creative, financial, moral, and logistical support toward the final publication of this volume. The editors would like to thank: Dexter Arnold, Sandra Bloomfield, the Board of Curators of the State Historical Society of Wisconsin, Julian Chazin and Mildred Chazin, Robert Chrisman, David Clarenbach, Henry Foner, Laura Foner, Philip S. Foner, Allen Highman, Daryl Holter, Kay Houston, Adam David Kent, Lillian Knuttel, Vitalina Koval, Marie Laberge, Lakeside Press Printers of Madison, Wisconsin, Mark Lapitsky, Staughton Lynd, Connie Meier, R. David Myers, Laurie Ellen Neustadt, Kim Peterson, Norm Stockwell, Laurie Wermter, and local union members of AFSCME Local 2412 in Madison, Wisconsin. If we have omitted any person, we apologize for our oversight; we thank each and every one heartily.

Finally, we wish to thank Cynthia Harris, Jude Grant, and Elisabeth Bruno of Greenwood Press for their editorial assistance and dedicated patience. The editors and authors alone, however, are responsible for the final content of the volume.

Introduction

The studies contained in this volume were presented at a conference in Madison, Wisconsin, in late 1990, sponsored by the International Labor History Association and the State Historical Society of Wisconsin. Responding to a call for papers in the areas of culture, African American history, women and labor history, and U.S. labor history, the authors contributed investigations remarkable for their original content, impressive in their documentation, and significant because they offer multifaceted approaches[1] in historical discourse while illuminating dissident moments in the past.

The scholars here assembled demonstrate both a regard for the "old" school of labor history, with its focus on working-class institutions, as well as more than a passing nod to the "new" tendencies of labor history that have reflected since the 1960s diverse concerns about culture, race, ethnicity, gender, community, and rank-and-file empowerment and experience.[2] In short, readers will find engaging studies in this rich area of historical inquiry, and they may indeed discover aspects inviting further examination and rethinking.

In the first section on U.S. labor history, historians elucidate new features of labor biography and working-class party politics. Selecting "one of the most underappreciated of Gilded Age labor leaders," Robert R. Montgomery evaluates George Edwin McNeill's central role in bridging the traditions of U.S. radicals and immigrant European socialists. By situating McNeill as an active figure in the nineteenth-century U.S. labor movement, Montgomery uncovers the dynamic interplay of individual engagement with the social forces of the day, assessing McNeill's involvement in abolitionism, the eight-hour movement in Massachusetts, the

International Workingmen's Association, the Workingmen's Party of the United States, the International Labor Union, and the Knights of Labor. Taking up another neglected topic, John Sherman relates the uneven efforts of the Socialist Party to free Eugene Debs during 1919–1921. He examines the amnesty campaigns in a broadly drawn context of initial internal party opposition, the red scare, local union and other allied support, the hostility of the *New York Times*, different organizational forms of the campaign, and the leadership work of women, including Harriot Stanton Blatch. Turning to "history long overlooked or glossed over," Allen Ruff focuses on the left wing of the Socialist Party, particularly the development of the Proletarian Party. Integrating in his analysis political biography, trends in Michigan labor, and international communism, Ruff depicts an organization that stressed educational activity in specific U.S. conditions, becoming in 1920 the "first tendency to be purged from the foundling Communist Party."

Feminist scholars have called for approaches that draw on the strengths of women's history and of "old" and "new" labor history to articulate the relationships among gender, class, family, community, and the question of power.[3] The section on women and U.S. labor history presents two studies that further advance this nexus of research. Suggesting the future need to explore community-based, working-class, and feminist organizational strategies, Rochelle Gatlin turns to the recent past, analyzing the strengths and weaknesses of Union W.A.G.E., 1972–1982, an organization of "mainly white, working-class women," including unionized, unpaid, and nonunionized women workers. Based in the San Francisco Bay community, Union W.A.G.E. sought to "infuse class consciousness into the women's movement and feminism into the labor movement." Gatlin investigates its role in rank-and-file union activities, E.R.A. campaigns, debates over reproductive rights, cases of sexual harassment and assault experienced by women hotel workers, and the 1980 San Francisco hotel workers' strike. Strike activity also attracts the critical attention of Jennifer Bosch, as she reconstructs the life of Ellen Gates Starr, cofounder of Hull House. Starr, inspired by the philosophy of William Morris and John Ruskin, became a conscientious participant in immigrant workers' efforts to improve their working conditions in Chicago. Bosch brings to light interconnected dimensions of class, gender, ethnicity, union solidarity, and power relations in her rendering of Starr's life.

In African American historiography, scholars have evaluated the dynamics of labor relations in the South, as they concretely affected and were affected by Black workers.[4] The two studies in the section on African American history enrich this scholarship, lending new evidence to the record of African American life and work during Reconstruction, particularly the African American quest for rights as agricultural laborers and for acquisition of land. Eric Foner explores the contributions and limitations of Black labor's attempts to realize the full potential of Reconstruction. By focusing on Black labor conventions held during 1867–1872 in Georgia, South Carolina, and Alabama, Foner documents the organizational forms of empowerment pursued by African Americans and the multi-component constraints of power, including the "ideological barriers," with which they contended. He reveals intriguing details such as Black labor's call of welcome to immigrants, especially to those arriving from China, and the call for Black women to withdraw from field labor. Elizabeth Ann Sharpe reaches a similar conclusion concerning the elusive nature of Reconstruction reforms as she maintains in her study that the "legacy" of "dire poverty and economic retardation" of Black Mississippi today is "rooted" in the post–Civil War failure to redistribute land. Sharpe shows how slavery was transformed into wage labor, and into peonage and sharecropping in Mississippi between 1861 and 1877. She places in sharp relief one example of Black economic empowerment in Davis Bend, Mississippi, where African American laborers successfully conducted a collective experiment in economic democracy, albeit of short duration.

Scholars addressing the interconnections between culture and the working class have explored the meanings and implications of leisure, of mass, dominant, alternative, and workers' culture.[5] The four studies in the section on culture elucidate developments in an alternative public sphere and illustrate the difficulties encountered in such efforts to call into question prevailing cultural norms. Gloria Garrett Samson examines the workers' education movement of the 1920s, whose "radical intent," she maintains, has been overlooked as scholars have treated this cultural movement either as "an idealistic failure" or "an anachronistic oddity." Tracing the movement's development from its founding by Jewish and women workers in 1899 to the 1920s, Samson exposes how the visionary workers' education movement was ultimately undermined by the AFL hierarchy and the Cold War, redirected by institutional labor studies departments, and further diffused in its potential to attract workers in their leisure time by the rise of mass cultural pursuits—movies, radio, and spectator sports.

Focusing specifically on radio, Nathan Godfried argues the need to examine the "dialectical relationship between the dominant media structure and its challengers." He assesses the growth of corporate broadcasting in the United States and the struggle of the Socialist Party to establish and sustain an alternative radio station, with the support of such allies as the

International Ladies Garment Workers' Union, the American Civil Liberties Union, the *Jewish Daily Forward*, and the *Nation*. Godfried reveals the flaws in the "dual radio strategy" pursued by the Socialist Party as it concurrently sought coverage of its perspective by dominant NBC radio. Horst Ihde investigates the literary portrayal of sailors' experiences in R. H. Dana's *Two Years before the Mast*, evaluating Dana's work in the context of economic and social developments of the nineteenth century, the patterns of previous travel writing, the dominant traditions of romanticism, and the rising tendencies of realism. Although U.S. literature had seldom focused previously on the realities of maritime labor, R. H. Dana's novel inspired the work of many subsequent sailor-writers, including Herman Melville. Morris U. Schappes contributes to the growing body of first-person accounts concerning the Cold War period in the United States as he recalls the effects of redbaiting on academic life at City College of New York and the principled efforts of left-wing scholars to resist the Rapp-Coudert Committee and its cultural inquisition.

What unifies the essays in this volume is their recollection of dissident historical moments, when individuals and collectives attempted to change perceived reality, to confront injustices in the general polity, and to seek alternative paths to a shared future. Some individuals and groups paid a dear price for their independent paths, suffering personal and organizational setbacks; others achieved limited success. The unconventional and compelling projects they strove to hew out of existing conditions invite our critical attention.

NOTES

The editors would like to thank Dexter Arnold for his careful reading and constructive suggestions. For a more extensive listing of references to the topical areas addressed in this volume, see the Selected Bibliography.

1. See J. Carroll Moody and Alice Kessler-Harris, eds., *Perspectives on American Labor History. The Problems of Synthesis* (DeKalb, IL, 1990); Howard Kimeldorf, "Bringing Unions Back In (Or Why We Need a New Old Labor History)," *Labor History*, 32:1 (Winter 1991); "The Limits of Union-Centered History: Responses to Kimeldorf," a collection of articles by Michael Kazin, Alice Kessler-Harris, David Montgomery, Bruce Nelson, and Daniel Nelson, *Labor History* 32:1 (Winter 1991); Ava Baron, "Gender and Labor History: Learning from the Past, Looking to the Future," in *Work Engendered: Toward a New History of American Labor*, ed. Ava Baron (Ithaca, NY, 1991).

2. For a discussion of "old" and "new" labor history, cf. Howard Kimeldorf and the responses; J. Carroll Moody and Alice Kessler-Harris; David Montgomery, "To Study the People: The American Working Class," *Labor History* 21

(1980); James R. Green, "Preface," *The World of the Worker: Labor in Twentieth-Century America* (New York, 1980); Herbert Gutman, *Work, Culture and Society in Industrializing America: Essays in American Working Class and Social History* (New York, 1977) and *Power and Culture: Essays on the American Working Class*, ed. Ira Berlin (New York, 1987); David Brody, "The Old Labor History and the New," *Labor History* 20 (1979); Milton Cantor, ed., *American Workingclass Culture: Explorations in American Labor and Social History* (Westport, CT, 1979); Thomas A. Krueger, "American Labor Historiography, Old and New: A Review Essay," *Journal of Social History* 4:3 (Spring 1971).

3. For a discussion of women's labor history compare: Alice Kessler-Harris, "A New Agenda for American Labor History. A Gendered Analysis and the Question of Class," in J. Carroll Moody and Alice Kessler-Harris; Ruth Milkman, ed., *Women, Work and Protest: A Century of U.S. Women's Labor History* (Boston, MA, and London, England, 1985); Ava Baron, *Work Engendered*; Joan Scott, "On Language, Gender, and Working Class History," *International Labor and Working-Class History*, 31 (Spring 1987).

4. See Philip S. Foner and Ronald L. Lewis, eds., *The Black Worker: A Documentary History from Colonial Times to the Present*, 8 vols. (Philadelphia, PA, 1978–84); Gerald D. Jaynes, *Branches without Roots: Genesis of the Black Working Class in the American South, 1862–1882* (New York, 1986); Jacqueline Jones, *Labor of Love, Labor of Sorrow: Black Women, Work and the Family from Slavery to the Present* (New York, 1985); Gary M. Fink and Merl E. Reed, eds., *Essays in Southern Labor History* (Westport, CT, 1977); John Bracey, ed., *Black Workers and Organized Labor* (Belmont, CA, 1971); W. E. B. Du Bois, *Black Reconstruction* (New York, 1935).

5. Recent studies on culture and the working class include, "Scholarly Controversy: Mass Culture," *International Labor and Working-Class History* 37 (Spring 1990); "Response to Controversy: Mass Culture," *International Labor and Working-Class History* 38 (Fall 1990); Harmut Keil and John Jentz, eds., *German Workers in Chicago. A Documentary History of Working-Class Culture from 1850 to World War I* (Urbana and Chicago, IL, 1988); David Roediger and Philip S. Foner, *Our Own Time* (Westport, CT, 1989); Richard J. Altenbaugh, *Education for Struggle: The American Labor Colleges of the 1920s and 1930s* (Philadelphia, PA, 1990); Milton Cantor; James Murphy, *The Proletarian Moment: The Controversy over Leftism in Literature* (Chicago, IL, 1991).

Part 1 U.S. Labor History: Movements and Leaders

1 "To Fight This Thing Till I Die": The Career of George Edwin McNeill

Robert R. Montgomery

> Self-renunciation, the renunciation of life and of all human needs, is its principle thesis, the less you eat, drink and buy books; the less you go to the theatre, the dance hall, the public house; the less you think, love, theorize, sing, paint, fence, etc. . . . The less you are, the less you express your own life, the greater is your alienated life.
> —Karl Marx, "The Meaning of Human Requirements"

> The true idea of an increase in wages is to bring men [*sic*] into relations which will remind them of what they ought to have and make them feel through their pride or ambition, or more worthy motives, that it must be had.
> —George Edwin McNeill, "A Labor Oasis," the *Labor Standard* (18 November 1876).

George Edwin McNeill remains one of the most underappreciated of Gilded Age labor leaders. He was a catalyst for the interpenetration of native U.S. radicalism and European socialism that underlay the emergence of both the American Federation of Labor (AFL) and the Knights of Labor (K of L). Historians influenced by the "Wisconsin School" of John R. Commons dichotomize the two traditions. Those writing in the shadow of the late Herbert Gutman have focused their research on the antiindustrial ethos of immigrant communities, while David Montgomery and his students have concentrated on the social relations of production within the factory. If the Commons school bifurcates the institutional history of the U.S. labor movement, the "new labor" historians place less stress on institutional forms while emphasizing social/shop floor relations. A figure such as George McNeill presents interpretive problems for either school.

McNeill played as important a role in his way in shaping the labor movement of the late nineteenth-century United States as that of Samuel Gompers or Terence Powderly. While Gompers and Powderly personified the national labor organizations of the 1880s and 1890s, McNeill was a pivotal figure in linking native labor reformers, seeking a theory of labor organization, with immigrant socialists seeking to apply Marx's theory to U.S. conditions.

Between 1863 and 1890 McNeill was at the epicenter of the struggles over the direction of the labor movement, led strikes in Massachusetts textile factories, and was a ubiquitous force in the reciprocal processes of differentiation and synthesis that drove the labor movement toward increasingly more distinct forms of ideology and organization. Closer attention to McNeill's career can sharpen our picture of the late nineteenth-century labor movement as a dynamic process, with flesh and blood agents as its moving force.

BIOGRAPHY

Uncharacteristically modest for men of his time and type, McNeill seldom wrote of himself. He left a monumental history of the U.S. labor movement, but no autobiography. In 1877 his close associate, George Gunton, penned a biographical sketch for the *New York Labor Standard*. By combining Gunton's sketch and McNeill's own spotty reminiscences with inferences drawn from his 1906 obituary, the broad contours of the man can be brought into focus. Despite its skeletal form—nothing of his father's occupation, or about his mother—the frame is particularly intriguing. It provides context for situating George McNeill at the nodal point of his career—his collaboration with J. P. McDonnell from 1876 to 1880. This collaboration marked a decisive transition in McNeill's life and shaped his views on the ends and means of labor organization through the 1880s.

George McNeill was born in Amesbury, Massachusetts, in 1836. His father cast one of the sixteen votes for William Lloyd Garrison for governor. John Greenleaf Whittier was a neighbor and frequent house guest. At fourteen, McNeill went to work in the Amesbury Woolen Factory, carding, spooling, and spinning from 5:30 A.M. until 7 P.M. When the overseer revoked the traditional twenty-minute lunch break, McNeill led a walkout that lasted six months. He was fired at its conclusion and never returned to the Amesbury mills. Outraged at his experience, the fifteen-year-old McNeill said, "I hereby swear to fight this thing till I die."

Early in 1852, McNeill began visiting a neighbor's shoemaking shop, to read the local newspaper to the cobbler as he worked. In return, the cobbler taught him to stitch shoes. McNeill earned enough to pay for one year's education at a private school.

Gunton described McNeill's move to Boston in 1854, "where he found the workshop discipline more monarchial than in the country." He left shoemaking and "worked at nearly all kinds of labor, mostly in newspaper offices, where he apprenticed as a printer, and began to read labor literature." A committed abolitionist, McNeill never identified himself with the conventional political parties. In 1857, he personally created the first labor ticket in Boston by selecting names of workers from the candidate lists, and printing them up as a separate ticket which he distributed at the polls. His refusal to support Republican candidates, which distinguishes McNeill from most other labor abolitionists, most likely had its roots as early as the Amesbury mills strike. In *The Labor Movement* McNeill wrote that the "strong Whig" town of Amesbury sent a Democrat to the State House in 1852, who introduced a ten-hour bill.[1] Yet there is no indication that McNeill ever voted Democratic. The refusal of the young abolitionist to vote Democratic, no matter how prolabor the candidate, is easily understood. So also is his antipathy to the Republicans, whom he viewed as nouveau Whigs—at least as far as labor was concerned.

Despite his abolitionist history, which included attending a Wendell Phillips speech attacked by "violent mobs of well dressed young aristocrats," McNeill did not fight in the Civil War. Perhaps his later illness, which drove him home from Paterson to Boston and lasted for two years, was chronic and active in the early 1860s.

In 1864, the printers of the Boston Typographical Union struck and began their own paper, the *Daily Evening Voice*. McNeill formed "Voice Clubs" to discuss the articles and to encourage subscribers and advertisers. According to Gunton, "The files of the *Voice* are replete with reports of enthusiastic mass meetings addressed by Geo. E. McNeill." At the paper's death in 1867, the publishers presented him with one of the only two existing complete sets of the *Voice*.

An early member of Ira Steward's Grand Eight-Hour League, McNeill eventually became president. Through the influence of the Boston Grand Eight-Hour League, E. H. Rogers of Chelsea and John Carruthers of Lynn were elected to the Massachusetts legislature in 1866. Their petition for a Commission on the Hours of Labor led to a law banning employment of children under ten years of age; required three months schooling for children under fifteen as a condition of employment; limited hours of children under fifteen to sixty hours per week; and created an office of special deputy constable to supervise the statute's schooling provisions.[2] General H. K. Oliver, a prominent advocate of universal education, was appointed deputy constable.

McNeill formed the New England Labor Reform Association to spread the eight-hour movement. After two years, the Association was captured by Ezra Heywood and devoted itself to advocating, according to Gunton, "free love, abolition of interest, and free banking." Heywood "drove the practical men out of the Reform League," and early in 1869, on advice of Wendell Phillips, the Boston Eight-Hour League was formed. Ira Steward was its first president, followed by McNeill. The Eight-Hour Leaguers considered themselves in a double-edged battle, "having to fight the capitalists on the one hand, and the professed labor men on the other."

The eight-hour men "succeeded in . . . establishing the Massachusetts Bureau of Statistics of Labor in 1869, the first of its kind ever established." General Oliver was appointed chief of the Bureau, with George McNeill as deputy chief. For his secretary McNeill chose Mrs. Mary Steward. The Bureau was a major victory for Massachusetts labor. The persistence of the Boston Eight-Hour League had led to the establishment of a state-funded bureau headed by a radical fighter for education for factory children, assisted by a class-conscious advocate of reduced hours and improved conditions.

Between 1869 and 1872, the Oliver-McNeill Bureau investigated tenement housing conditions, factory safety standards and accident rates, wages and hours of work, the distribution of deposits in savings banks by social class, and holdings of real estate by laborers. It also attempted to define poverty and to document its extent within Massachusetts. The Bureau used questionnaires to ascertain the attitudes of the laborers to their conditions, especially on the matter of the hours of labor. The four reports issued by the Oliver-McNeill Bureau remain a rich description and indictment of the condition of the working class in Massachusetts, 1869–1872. The reports proposed a panoply of reforms, especially the demand for state-empowered factory inspectors and safety legislation.[3]

In his inaugural address of 1873, Governor William B. Washburn charged the Bureau with giving "a false, or partial picture of the relations of labor to capital in our Commonwealth." During the following session the legislature "took into consideration to abolish the Bureau altogether . . . [b]ut decided for fear of public reaction, to giving recommendations for another direction by a change of its officers." In 1873 Carroll Wright replaced the Oliver-McNeill team at the Bureau. Often credited with carrying on the work of the Oliver-McNeill Bureau, Wright actually converted the Bureau from an investigative, advocacy agency to a scientific body employing statistical methods to formulate its data.[4]

In 1877 the *New York Labor Standard* serialized McNeill's "Argument on the Hours of Labor delivered before the Labor Committee of the Massachusetts Legislature." McNeill used the occasion to draft a balance sheet of the efforts of the Bureau.

What had we proposed? McNeill queried:

— The eight-hour day for State workers, and a ten-hour day for all others.
— No wage labor for children under thirteen years of age.
— Uniform, compulsory education for all.
— A factory law and factory inspectors.
— An increase in the powers of the Bureau to legally force employers to answer its questions.

McNeill then asked: As of 1877, what were the results of the Bureau's efforts?

— the eight-hour day not considered at all;
— a ten-hour bill, but only for women and for children under eighteen;
— children ten years old still employable;
— neither compulsory education, as in Germany, nor half-time education, as in England;
— no factory bill or inspectors;
— an antilabor conspiracy law; and
— the existence of the MBLS still insecure[5]

The general tone of the article makes it clear that McNeill still considered the existence of the Bureau an important gain for labor, but realized that the organized power of the employers condemned its reports to gathering dust in the state's archives. By 1877 McNeill argued that only the organized power of an energized labor movement could force the class-oriented reforms advocated by the Oliver-McNeill Bureau. If David Montgomery is correct that the men of the "Boston Eight-Hour League-Boston Trades Assembly-*Daily Evening Voice* clique of labor reformers" harbored naive illusions in the possibilities for legislative reform under radical Republican sponsorship, McNeill leaves little room for doubt that by 1877 the Boston eight-hour men harbored no such illusions.

As early as his appointment to the Bureau by a Republican governor in 1869, McNeill made Eight-Hours the central plank of the newly formed

Massachusetts Labor Reform Party. The party ran E. M. Chamberlin, an eight-hour man, for governor against the Republican William Claflin, who had appointed McNeill to the Bureau of Labor Statistics. The Chamberlin ticket received 15,000 votes. McNeill was both president of the Boston Eight-Hour League and a member of the central committee of the Labor Reform Party for his full four years at the Bureau, never once voting for the governor under whom he held office.

The year 1872 was a watershed year for McNeill and the Boston eight-hour men, who began a transformation in the direction of their work for the next decade. McNeill entered a new phase of personal and political development. Biographical details about McNeill after 1882 become intelligible only after considering the previous decade. The emerging liaison of Yankee mechanics rooted in the native culture of protestantism, abolitionism, and labor republicanism, with emigre Marxists in the immigrant ghettoes of urbanizing centers, requires some prior explication.

YANKEE MECHANICS AND IMMIGRANT MARXISTS

The International Workingmen's Association (IWA) was founded in London in 1864 by French and British trade unionists. Karl Marx, leader of the German socialists' exile community in London, drafted its first platform. The first U.S. delegation to the IWA from the National Labor Union attended the International's Congress in Basel in 1869. The same year the first U.S. section of the IWA was formed by mostly German-speaking trade unionists in New York. By 1872 there were several North American sections. The most prominent were the trade-unionist Section 1, and Section 12, led by Victoria Woodhull and William West. By July 1872 the North American Federation of the IWA held its first national convention. Later that year, the General Council was transferred from London to New York in an attempt by Marx to remove the IWA from the potential control of anarchists led by Mikhail Bakunin. Friedrich Sorge of New York became general secretary of the IWA; Ferdinand Laurell, coworker and mentor of Samuel Gompers, was one of three cigarmakers elected to the General Council.[6]

From its inception in 1869, the North American section of the IWA was politically unstable. Section 1 was dominated by German-speaking followers of Ferdinand Lassalle, a leading German opponent of Marx. The Lassalleans insisted upon the primacy of organizing socialist political parties, which would gain power through electoral politics, if possible; armed struggle, if necessary. Once in possession of political power, socialists would establish a state-controlled banking system to issue credit for producer-owned cooperatives. This was the Lassallean road to the socialist commonwealth. Lassalleans opposed the economic organization of workers into trade unions, because it conflicted with their political agenda and because they adhered to Lassalle's doctrine of the "iron law of wages." The "iron law," a subsistence theory of wages, postulated that if wages rose above the minimum level required to reproduce the worker physically, an increased supply of workers would flow where wages were higher. The resulting competition for jobs would function to return wages to subsistence levels. Consequently, efforts by particular groups of workers to influence the wage rate by trade unionism, strikes, or short-hour demands were doomed to fail by the workings of the "iron law."[7]

Marx and his European followers battled the anarchists on the one hand, who sought to bypass the state entirely, and Lassalleans on the other, who would use it as a vehicle to establish socialism through the credit-monetary system. In North America this conflict was refracted through two mediating forces. Both the Lassalleans in the German-dominated socialist movement, and native anarchists like Victoria Woodhull, William West, and the followers of Ezra Heywood in New England, had a natural propensity to form alliances with middle-class currency reformers. Greenbackism, a movement to boost commodity prices and reduce interest on loan capital by expanding paper money through government issue of currency, persisted from the end of the Civil War through the 1880s. The confrontation with Greenbackism, as both ideology and political movement, constituted a key point of intersection between the New York Marxists and the Boston eight-hour men.

Two documents demonstrate the difficulty the New York Marxists had in responding to the Lassalleans: an 1871 letter from Marx to Fred Bolte, the New York cigarmaker and intimate of Samuel Gompers; and a copy of a pamphlet written by the German Marxist Carl Hillmann in 1873, read and saved by Gompers. In his letter to Bolte, Marx stressed the dialectical relationship between the political and economic dimensions of the class struggle:

The political movement of the working class has, of course, as its final object the conquest of political power for this class, and this requires, of course, a previous organization of the working class developed up to a certain point, which arises from its economic struggles. . . . The attempt in a particular factory or trade, to force a shorter working day out of individual capitalists by strikes is a purely economic movement. The movement to force through an eight hour *law*, however, is a *political* movement, a movement of the *class*. . . . Though these movements presuppose a certain degree of previous organization, they are in turn equally a means of developing this organization.[8]

Marx's repetitive "of course . . . of course" implied that the relationship of the political and the economic movements should be obvious provided the reader's real interest and commitments were to the class struggle, and not to parochial interests, either of the economistic trade union, or the cross-class "party" variety.

The Hillmann document, "Practical Suggestions for Emancipation," argued that trade unions could play a catalytic role in the political emancipation of the working class. Against the Lassalleans—who were "rushing like a storm ten years ahead of the movement which is supposed to include and unite all elements of the working class"—Hillmann contended that trade unions had a "tremendous impact on legislation, and thus on politics." Among the critical functions of the trade unions, according to Hillmann, are: defense against even further deterioration of the working class; elevation of wages to a level where it becomes possible to expand and increase demands, through which the "worker not only combats the plague of hunger, but learns to value shorter hours"; protection from overproduction and trade crises; and finally, to "nurture those most awesome weapons in the hands of the proletariat—statistics and mass discipline—which supported by political agitation and organization, will eventually shatter the bourgeois world and inaugurate the new society." Hillmann urged workers to develop democratically organized local unions with health, death, and travel benefits. National and international trade union organizations could be established atop such a base, which would unify locals through a general constitution and publication of a trade union journal.[9]

Concurrently, the Boston eight-hour men battled the alliance between Ezra Heywood and their old ally, Wendell Phillips. Heywood and Phillips were promoting a labor party ticket based on Greenback currency reform. The eight-hour men fought the reformers, contending that currency, banks, tariffs, and taxes "are not laborers' questions, because they have no appreciable relation to the wage system." The autodidact economist and machinist Ira Steward contended that such issues dealt only with the distribution and division of capital. Labor reformers who fixated on interest rates and currency reform were reinforcing the "wages fund" theory of the capitalist economists. The "wages fund" theory held that wages were determined by the ratio of capital to labor, or more simply, the supply of capital and the demand for labor at a given time. In fighting against "capitalist credit monopolists," currency reformers were telling workers that cheaper credit would expand the supply of capital, increase the demand for labor, and cause wages to rise. Such an outlook was anathema to Steward since it upheld the prevailing idea that capital created wages and determined their rate. Steward argued that the wage rate was a function of the expectations of workers, which depended, in turn, upon the general level of material progress and culture pertaining at a given time.

Steward also held that capital was the product of surplus labor—defined as that portion of the working day the laborer provided the employer gratis. Steward viewed labor participation and currency campaigns like Greenbackism as support to one faction of the capitalist class against a second, with no possibility of gain for the working class. Steward read nothing of Marx's writings until Sorge mailed him the section on the working day from *Das Kapital* in 1877. For his relentless attacks on the Greenbackers, Sorge referred to Ira Steward as "an oasis in the desert of the Currency Reform humbug."[10] By 1872, the Boston eight-hour men were looking for new strategies and routes to their goal of a labor movement centered on the class demand of reduced hours and increased wages. But any hope of a class-conscious labor movement growing from the Massachusetts Labor Reform Party was dashed by the Heywood-Phillips Greenback alliance.

The eight-hour men had been noticed by the New York Marxists who were desperately looking for a native, class-oriented current that would provide a channel out of the ghetto of German Lassalleanism and into the indigenous labor culture of a republican tradition foreign to them. With an obvious glance in the direction of anarcho-bohemians Woodhull and West, IWA Secretary Friedrich Sorge wrote of Steward and McNeill: "They give a refreshing example of the manly [*sic*] bearing of American workers and show progress in the conception of real conditions."[11]

With the renewal of trade union agitation for the eight-hour day in 1871, the IWA's German-speaking sections appropriated Steward's native critique of capitalism. For his part, Steward moved towards the New York Marxists when IWA member Victor Drury pilloried Ezra Heywood's Greenbackism in a New York debate. In September 1871 the IWA men invited Steward to address a mass mobilization of New York workers for the eight-hour day. Invigorated by the New York strike, Steward wrote that these unionists represented "the manhood and conscience, the brains and hope of their class."[12] The New Yorkers adopted the resolutions of the Boston Eight-Hour League and sent representatives to the League's convention in 1872.[13] A copy of the proceedings, including the text of Ira Steward's "Poverty," still resides in the collected papers of J. P. McDonnell.[14]

The first collaboration between the two groups occurred in 1875, when both joined to aid the striking textile operatives in Fall River, Massachusetts. Provoked by wage reductions in the wake of the 1873 financial panic, the Fall River operatives struck for eight weeks. Boston eight-hour men, New York Marxists, and textile operatives throughout the state raised support funds. After two months, the operatives marched to city hall to demand bread for their families. The Massachusetts state militia, called out to suppress the strike, prevented the marchers from reaching their destination. When no investigation followed the incident, Steward wrote, "the Capitalist classes and the State authorities are a unit in all that concerns labor."[15]

Ironically, in February 1874, New York police had violently dispersed a demonstration for unemployed relief in Tompkins Square. One of those clubbed was the Lassallean leader of the carpenters' union, P. J. McGuire. McGuire's experience led him to reassert the Lassallean program of government intervention to protect the working class from the power of the capitalists. Later in 1874, the Lassalleans formed the Social Democratic Workingmen's Association of North America—splitting the IWA. The IWA men, adhering to Marx's position on building trade unions, formed the United Workers of America. For the next two years the split attenuated the U.S. socialist and trade union movements.

In July 1876 the two groups held a unity conference with invitations sent to the Boston Eight-Hour League. The unity conference was a formal victory for the trade union wing. The first principle of the resolution list stated that "political liberty without economical independence is but an empty phrase," and asserted that the new group would "in the first place direct our efforts to the economical question."[16] In a clear repudiation of middle-class political reformers, the new unity group chose the name Workingmen's Party of the United States (WPUS).[17]

The party newspaper's name was changed from *The Socialist* to *Labor Standard*, and J. P. McDonnell, a young trade unionist and former secretary to Marx, was appointed editor. Each issue of the new *Labor Standard* headlined the ten-point program of the WPUS. The first seven points read as though they could have been taken directly from the program of the Boston Eight-Hour League.[18]

The *Labor Standard* immediately published writings of the Boston eight-hour men. The weekly paper featured excerpts from Marx's *Kapital*; articles by Ira Steward, George McNeill, and "Middleton" (George Gunton); labor news; and an editorial by J. P. McDonnell. Steward's political economy, rooted in the labor theory of value and the concept of surplus value, which formed the theoretical basis of the Boston Eight-Hour League, received prominent exposure.[19]

McDonnell, recognizing the usefulness of Steward's ideas, prevailed upon him to compose a hypothetical dialogue between a politician and a worker. The little dialogue neatly summarized Steward's economics:

P: Is it your idea that as much pay can be obtained for eight as for ten hours of labor?

W: Certainly!

P: And those who work ten hours are giving away two hours labor to the employers for nothing?

W: Yes, more than two hours.

P: How much more?

W: We don't know: as the labor we give away, over and above our wages, is enough to make hundreds of millionaires, besides paying for all the wars, taxes, interest, accidents etc.; and having proved that the 12, 14 and 15 hour systems meant giving away from two to five hours labor for nothing, we are going to show that the ten hour system means giving several more hours labor for nothing.[20]

Steward's hypothetical worker went on to answer the rebuttal that reduced hours necessitated reduced wages with a brief course on the labor theory of value. Workers compensated according to the actual value of their product need only labor for short periods to receive their due wage, and the resulting wage rate would allow the workers to fulfill their actual needs. With both increased leisure and consumption, the short-hour worker would be vastly more productive than the overworked, underpaid long-hour worker. Steward's worker replied to overproduction arguments by simply relating the increased productivity of the workers to their increased consumption capacity. Within a month, the excerpt on the normal working day from the first volume of *Kapital* appeared in the *Labor Standard*.

However, Steward's political economy involved more than reducing the hours of labor. George McNeill displayed a more supple ability to draw out and express its implications. In McNeill's rendering, as hours of labor progressively decreased and wages increased, capitalists would be forced to compensate for rising labor costs by increasing the productivity of labor through technological innovation. The increased leisure time would generate a qualitative change in the workers' understanding of their human needs. This transformation would trigger a self-expanding cycle of new consumption requirements, along with stronger demands for higher wages and shorter hours, which would outrun the capitalists' ability to compensate by increasing mechanization. The resulting drop in per-unit productivity would progressively reduce the rate of capitalist profit. As profit rates dropped, capitalists would lose their incentive to accumulate and sell their industries to cooperatives of workers. The cooperative enterprises, not driven by competitive pressures, would be free to balance production and consumption. The process possessed a certain automaticity—once the working class "kicked it off" by acting concertedly to reduce the hours of labor. The eight-hour men had come to appreciate that class organization was a necessary condition for such concerted action. The eight-hour "philosophy" was now clearly linked to the question of organization.

The Steward-McNeill political economy must have seemed utopian to the Marxists. It both lacked the analytical rigor of Marx's theory of crisis and presumed that the capitalist class would react passively to workers eating away at profit rates and force a peaceful change in the ownership of the means of production. However, the third volume of *Kapital*, which articulated the theoretical problems of the tendency of profit rates to fall, and the transformation of values and prices, was not available until 1894. So, in the late 1870s, both groups recognized a remarkable affinity in their respective theories of value. If they differed on the ultimate road to socialism, both groups could agree that the struggle for eight hours and the organization of workers into trade unions were interlinked components of a class-conscious socialist program. When the Greenback press opened a campaign against the *Labor Standard* in the fall of 1876, accusing it of tying workers to the wages system through the eight-hour question, McDonnell fired back:

The eight-hour doctrine is indeed one of the fundamental principles of the Workingmen's Party. . . . The *Labor Standard* favors the eight-hour doctrine because only through a general decrease in the hours of labor can the material, physical and intellectual interests of the working people be advanced. We declare in the language of the European proletariat that a preliminary condition for the early destruction of the wage system . . . is the legal limitation of the working day.[21]

In May 1877 a crisis erupted at the *Labor Standard* when Lassalleans attempted to divorce the *Labor Standard* from the Workingmen's Party. Adolf Strasser intervened to save the *Labor Standard*, and denounced the faction as covert Greenbackers. Meanwhile, McNeill's stature at the *Labor Standard* continued to grow. In August 1877 McNeill was nominated to represent the U.S. labor movement at the International Labor Congress in Europe. In October of that year, the *Labor Standard* nominated "Geo. E. McNeill as Chief-Organizer of a new, Great National Labor Union." The nomination claimed "his name is well known from one end of the Republic to the other." In November, the smoldering conflict within the WPUS exploded in the pages of the *Labor Standard*. McNeill defended the trade union perspective of the newspaper "as the basis of a vigorous labor movement." He accused the Executive Committee of the Workingmen's Party of attempting to control the *Labor Standard*. In his column "Labor Politics," McNeill followed McDonnell, describing the WPUS as a "muddle of financial and industrial reformers, Greenbackers, Social Democrats, Trade Unionists, and Eight-Hour men—all but the last two, opposite in theory and measure." He further accused the "unprincipled elements" of trying to divide the trade unionists against the eight-hour men.[22]

The next issue contained a report on McNeill's address to the new Boston Trades Council advocating that unionized cigarmakers join the Cigar Makers' International Union (CMIU). The correspondent credited McNeill with calling the meeting that formed the Trades Council. The same issue reported that "In Fall River the spinners hold regular meetings and number 600 members. At their last meeting they elected Mr. Geo. E. McNeill to represent them in the Trades Council in Boston."[23] McNeill reported in November that the WPUS in Massachusetts had collapsed into political action in endorsing Greenbackers, especially Wendell Phillips for governor. In the same issue, Ira Steward waxed indignant at the *National Labor Tribune*'s spate of correspondences attacking the eight-hour movement.

The impending split was finally announced by McDonnell, under the heading "Labor Revolution," on December 2, 1877. McDonnell pointed to the confluence of two factors that necessitated the formation of a new organization of the U.S. working class—the collapse of the WPUS into Greenbackism and the "Great Upheaval" on the railroads in the summer of 1877. The sprawling, chaotic rail strike brought two issues to center stage: the emergence of the unskilled and the unorganized workers as an elemental social force, and the total absence of a single centralized organization of labor.

McDonnell's editorial of 23 December 1877, "The Labor Union of the United States," is worth quoting at some length:

It is clear to every thoughtful workingman, skilled or unskilled, organized or unorganized, that the time has arrived for a more perfect system of labor organization. . . . The barriers that have so long existed between skilled and unskilled labor must be broken down forever. . . . The interests of all wage workers are identical and their action must subsequently be harmonious. . . . Those now styled "unskilled laborers" must be organized in one great union so that they may not be used against each other, or against the already organized. . . . There shall no longer be barriers of skill or states or nations between the wage workers of the world.[24]

Early in 1878, McDonnell's project took on organizational form as the International Labor Union. Sorge, McDonnell, Gompers, Adolf Strasser, Adolph Douai, Otto Weydemeyer, and Albert Parsons joined Ira Steward, George McNeill, and George Gunton to launch the ILU as a union of skilled and unskilled, organized and unorganized, around a program of shorter hours and higher wages. As President, McNeill presided over a central committee which drafted a declaration of principles representing a compromise between the two groups. The part describing ultimate aims was drafted by the Eight-Hour wing of the coalition and stated:

The first step towards the emancipation of labor is a reduction of the hours of labor, that the added leisure produced . . . will operate on the natural causes that affect the habits and customs of the people, enlarging wants, decreasing idleness, and increasing wages.

The part dealing with demands resembled the platform of the erstwhile WPUS. The part of the platform dealing with tactics reflected the Marxists, calling for:

The formation of an Amalgamated Union of Laborers so that members of any calling can combine under a central head . . . ; the establishment of a general fund for protective and benefit purposes; The organization of all workingmen in their Trade Unions, the creation of Trade Unions where none exist; and, the National and International Amalgamation of all Labor Unions.[25]

The object of the ILU was to build a mass organization of labor. According to McNeill, "The ILU presents a plan by which the unorganized masses and local unions can become affiliated." McNeill placed special emphasis on organization of "the Negro population of the South." Although intended as an organizational vehicle for all unskilled workers, the vast majority of the eight thousand who joined the ILU in thirteen states were female textile workers. As soon as the ILU made its existence known, unions sprang up in every textile center from Vermont to New Jersey, and strikes followed in short order. The ILU was the storm center for a great textile strike wave from 1878 to 1880, spreading from Clinton and Cohoes, New York, to Fall River, Massachusetts, and from Passaic to Paterson, New Jersey. The great strike of 1878–79 in Fall River was one of the most momentous in U.S. labor history. Five thousand strikers joined the ILU and won higher wages and the nine-hour day. On May 8, 1878, twenty-five thousand marched through Fall River under the banners of the ILU.[26]

By 1882, after a series of lost strikes, the ILU faded away. The trial and jailing of J. P. McDonnell for libel had to be decisive for the fledgling ILU. Not only was McDonnell removed at a critical juncture but George McNeill was curtailed also, as he moved to Paterson to manage the *Labor Standard* and to assist the jailed McDonnell.[27] Further disruption resulted when the fatigued McNeill returned to a Boston sickbed until 1882. The loss of the two key organizers in this period may have sufficed to kill the International Labor Union. In this context, the formation of the Federation of Organized Trades and Labor Unions in 1882 removed the last vestiges of the ILU from the labor scene.

The importance of the ILU resides less in what it accomplished than in how it defined and addressed the central problem facing the labor movement. The ILU was a "proto-industrial" union, groping toward a form of national labor organization. It was no accident that George McNeill was chosen as its president. McNeill was acutely sensitive to the dangers and the possibilities represented by the growth of unskilled and semiskilled operatives. With its class-wide organizing strategy and eight-hour focus, McNeill's ILU broke with the prevailing artisanal posture of the trade unions. With his new understanding of the critical importance of centralized organization gained from the Marxists, McNeill was moving toward a conception of an industrial economic and political army.

Following the collapse of the ILU and the recovery from his illness, McNeill joined the growing Knights of Labor (K of L; the Knights) in 1883. By 1884 he was Treasurer of District Assembly #30, the largest in the Knights, with over thirty thousand members. McNeill's fervor for the K of L should not come as a surprise. As early as 1874 he had drafted the charter for a National Labor Congress, which was later adopted as the "Declaration of Principles of the Noble Order of the Knights of Labor."

The Knights articulated a class-wide approach to organizing that included unskilled and skilled, unionists and nonunionized, women and men, Black and white. They projected a credible semblance of centralized organization and possessed a political philosophy that blended native radicalism and cooperativist socialism.[28] At their apogee from 1884–1886, the Knights must have seemed to McNeill like the ILU "writ large."

Before concluding this sketch it is important to generalize the political outlook that drove this seemingly indefatigable organizer so that McNeill's rise and his premature eclipse may be understood. McNeill was driven by a view of the state rooted in three main traditions—Jeffersonian republicanism, New England Calvinism, and the triumphalism of radical abolitionism. McNeill's hybrid philosophy was implicit in his own political life. However, *The Labor Movement* contains sections that are quite explicit.[29] Within the last twenty years U.S. labor historians have rediscovered the importance of the New England eight-hour men. In *Beyond Equality*, David Montgomery argued that the demand of postbellum New England labor for eight hours posed an unanswerable challenge to the equalitarian rhetoric of the radical Republicans. But ensnared by republican political assumptions of their own, the eight-hour men pursued a self-defeating strategy of legislative reform.

Montgomery's version of the defeat of New England labor has been echoed by others. In *Boston's Workers*, James Green accuses McNeill of appealing to an illusory sense of community that "accurately reflected the immense faith labor reformers put in the democratic system."[30] Green bases his opinion on a quote from McNeill concerning the Paris Commune. When workers seized Paris and declared the Commune in 1871, the U.S. gentility reacted with more hysteria than their ancestors at the height of the revolutionary terror of 1794. McNeill reassured U.S. Americans that workers would not resort to arms because "No cry of 'commune' can frighten the descendants of the New England commune." Since New England was still a commonwealth, "its citizens would refuse to be ruled by class wealth," McNeill declared.[31]

McNeill's concept of the New England commune and commonwealth had nothing in common with the Madisonian notion of the republic as a political machine. Like his regional forbears John and Samuel Adams, McNeill refused to separate state and civil society. Like Samuel Adams, who when asked, "Is it a crime to be rich?" answered brusquely, "Yes, at the Publick Expense,"[32] McNeill believed in an activist state with a duty to ensure social equity and justice. This concept of an ends-oriented state was stoked by the activist moralism of abolitionism, and by the government itself during the Civil War. Yet McNeill saw the state in tension between its ideal form, as "God's terrible swift word" and its real form, as a reflection of the clash of class interests in civil society. When states resorted to increasing use of armed force against workers in the 1870s, McNeill declaimed:

The demand for stronger government is the demand of deadened consciences and enfeebled brains. Strength will not be found in a standing army; for, when our internal manufactures are protected by armed men, the Republic is dead. "Righteousness alone exalteth a nation."[33]

In 1872 the Boston Eight-Hour League issued a statement, later repeated in *The Labor Movement*, that displayed the labor reformers' view of radical Republicans who supported Reconstruction in the South but opposed the shorter-hours agitation in the North. The "lords of the loom" who enriched themselves upon wage slavery in their factories and justified it with "free labor" rhetoric, were no better than the "lords of the lash" who profited from chattel slavery. By 1886 McNeill could write:

there is an inevitable and irrepressible conflict between the wage-system of labor and the republican system of government—the wage-laborer attempting to save the government, and the capitalist class ignorantly attempting to subvert it.[34]

For McNeill, just as the republic could have been lost to the slave power, so also could it be lost to the power of capital.

McNeill viewed the state as an extension of the social relations pertaining at a given time (as current-day Marxists might say—a reflection of the relationship and balance of class forces at a specific conjuncture). As long as workers and farmers were increasing their level of consciousness and organization, they could press their demands within the legislative arena to gain concrete reforms, which spurred movement building in turn. By the mid-1880s, McNeill regarded the Knights of Labor as possessing all the prerequisites for pressing this struggle forward—organization, class-wide strategy, and a democratic program for achieving the "cooperative commonwealth" and ending wage slavery.

McNeill had concrete experience to support his view. If the strikes of 1866–1867 had not gained shorter hours, they had put the issue on the public agenda, and gained H. K. Oliver as Schooling Inspector, and eventually the Massachusetts Bureau of Labor Statistics. If Governor Washburn had purged the Oliver-McNeill Bureau in 1872, their Bureau had made its mark. If the Bureau had not realized its demand for factory inspectors by 1877, the demand was taken up by the WPUS as "state financed factory inspectors elected by the trades unions." McNeill was elected to the Cambridge, Massachusetts, school committee from 1872–1875, and succeeded in establishing free evening drawing schools for workers. In short, McNeill never ceded the state to the capitalists. If they succeeded in "expropriating" the state, it would only be over the dead body of the Republic.

CONCLUSION

Following his transitional experience with J. P. McDonnell and the Marxists, McNeill continued to play a key role in the labor movement of the 1880s. Once again McNeill was ubiquitous as Secretary of D.A. #30; United Labor Party candidate for Mayor of Boston in 1886; immersed in the eight-hour ferment of 1886; stump speaker throughout New England for the Knights in 1886–1887; publisher with Frank K. Foster of the Boston *Labor Leader* in 1886–1887; mediator between the newly formed AFL and the Knights; editor of *The Labor Movement: The Problem of Today* in 1887; and speaker at rallies around the country for the Haymarket defendants.

But by 1890, McNeill was only a figurehead in the U.S. labor movement. He turned the *Labor Leader* over to Foster in 1887.[35] Although a delegate to every AFL national convention from 1886–1898 and ceremonial orator, especially at Gompers's behest, George McNeill ceased to play an independent role. In the 1890s he became a warden of Reverend W.P.D. Bliss's Church of the Carpenter; composed an ode to Leo Tolstoy; hailed William Jennings Bryan as a savior; and agitated for Russian, Negro, Irish, women's, and Filipino freedoms. He was also a mover in the Anti-Imperialist League. In 1902, four years before his death, McNeill repeated the lines from O'Reilly's poem, "Submission is good, but will the hand of God light the torch of revolution."[36]

According to historian Arthur Mann, McNeill died thinking that soon "Christ's eternal reign will dawn . . . and we cleanse our hearts of Mammon's Lust."[37] An exponent of the Knights-AFL duality thesis, Mann attributed McNeill's passing as a labor leader to the ascendancy of the business unionism of the AFL. A close look at the actual period of his final transition suggests that the answer may be found in McNeill's turn to protestant millenialism.

As late as 1886–1887 McNeill was in the thick of the battle—running for Mayor, starting the *Labor Leader*, and leading a successful Knights legislative campaign culminating in a law establishing a state board of arbitration that gave impetus to eventual collective bargaining.[38]

After the eight-hour mobilization of 1886 the Knights began a precipitous collapse, which left D.A. #30 a ghost of itself by 1890. Owing chiefly to employer blacklisting campaigns that filled the pages of the *Labor Leader* after May 1886, Powderly's organizational sabotage, and the state of war between the Knights and the AFL between 1886 and 1890, McNeill saw his organization die. Just as significant may have been the execution of the Haymarket martyrs in November 1887. The executions, particularly of Albert Parsons, seemed to drain McNeill. His memorial speech for Parsons lacked the usual eloquent passion. The references to "John Brown's Body" were there, but a tone of religious resignation suffused his remarks.[39] This religious resignation became increasingly prevalent in his writings and speeches of the 1890s.

Albert Parsons had been McNeill's friend from the WPUS days. The Grand Eight-Hour Army of McNeill's dream had marched into battle in Chicago on May 1, 1886, to face an enemy, the likes of which it could not have imagined. McNeill's radicalism posited that the Republic could be killed if combined capital captured the state and used it as an organ of repression against the workers. Rather than simply the death of the Knights, or the deepening craft autonomism of the AFL, the most plausible explanation for McNeill's sudden eclipse was a personal despair that may have enabled him to foresee, as could few others, that Haymarket had killed the eight-hour movement for the next fifty years.

George McNeill and Samuel Gompers shared a platform at the Chicago International Labor Congress in 1893. McNeill's talk, "The Philosophy of the Labor Movement" was heavily religious and formal in composition. Gompers, on the other hand, concluded, "What Does Labor Want?" with an oratorical burst of uncharacteristic eloquence. One can only wonder what McNeill was thinking when Gompers said:

Save our children in their infancy from being forced into the maelstrom of wage slavery. See to it that they are not dwarfed in body and mind or brought to a premature death by early drudgery. Give them sunshine of the school and playground instead of the factory, the mine and the workshop. We want more school houses and less jails; more books and less arsenals; more learning and less vice; more constant work and less crime; more leisure and less greed; more justice and less revenge; in fact, more of the opportunities to cultivate our better natures; to make manhood more noble, womanhood more beautiful, and childhood more happy and bright.[40]

It is impossible to read these now-celebrated lines and not to hear the voice of George Edwin McNeill.

NOTES

1. George E. McNeill, *The Labor Movement: The Problem of Today* (Boston, MA, 1887), 120–121.

2. McNeill, 137.

3. Massachusetts Bureau of Statistics of Labor: *Report of the Bureau of Statistics of Labor*, 1870. *Report of the Bureau of Statistics of Labor*, 1871. *Third Annual Report of the Bureau of Statistics of Labor*, 1872. *Fourth Annual Report of the Bureau of Statistics of Labor*, 1873.

4. Daniel Horowitz, *The Morality of Spending: Attitudes toward the Consumer Society in America, 1875–1940* (Baltimore, MD, 1985), chapter 2, "How Workers Spent Their Money and Should Have Led Their Lives: Carroll D. Wright and Late-Nineteenth-Century Labor Statistics."

5. *Labor Standard* (New York), 7, 14, 21 April 1877.

6. Stuart B. Kaufman, ed., *The Samuel Gompers Papers* (Chicago, IL, 1986), 1:22.

7. Kaufman, Appendix.

8. "Marx to Bolte, 11/23/1871" in *Karl Marx to Frederick Engels, Letters to Americans, 1848–1895. A Selection*, trans., ed., Leonard E. Mins (New York, 1953), 93–94.

9. Kaufman, 23–44.

10. Philip S. Foner and Brewster Chamberlin, eds., *Friedrich A. Sorge. Labor Movement in the United States: A History of the American Working Class from Colonial Times to 1890* (Westport, CT, 1977), 33.

11. Foner and Chamberlin, *Sorge*, 139.

12. Kenneth A. Fones-Wolf, "Boston Eight Hour Men, New York Marxists, and the Emergence of the International Labor Union: Prelude to the AFL," *Historical Journal of Massachusetts* 9 (1981): 49.

13. Fones-Wolf, 49.

14. J. P. McDonnell, Papers of J. P. McDonnell, Massachusetts Bureau of Industrial Research, Reel #1.

15. Fones-Wolf, 50.

16. *Socialist*, (New York), 29 July 1876.

17. *Socialist*, (New York), 29 July 1876.

18. *Labor Standard* (New York), 12 August 1876.

19. David Roediger, "Ira Steward and the Anti-Slavery Origins of the American Eight-Hour Theory," *Labor History* (1985): 411–412.

20. *Labor Standard* (New York), 30 December 1876.

21. *Labor Standard* (New York), 2 September 1876.

22. *Labor Standard* (New York), 11 November 1877.

23. *Labor Standard* (New York), 11 November 1877.

24. *Labor Standard* (New York), 23 December 1877.

25. Foner and Chamberlin, *Sorge*, 166–167.

26. Philip S. Foner, *History of the Labor Movement in the United States* (New York, 1982), 1:503.

27. Papers of J. P. McDonnell, "Diary," Reel #1.

28. Bruce Laurie, *Artisans into Workers: Labor in Nineteenth Century America* (New York, 1989), "The Rise and Fall of the Knights of Labor," 141–175.

29. McNeill, 454–469.

30. David Montgomery, *Beyond Equality. Labor and Radical Republicans, 1862–1872* (New York, 1980); James Green and Hugh C. Donohue, *Boston's Workers: A Labor History* (Boston, MA, 1979), 31.

31. Green and Donohue, 31.

32. Gary B. Nash, *The Urban Crucible* (Cambridge, MA, 1986), 140.

33. McNeill, 461.

34. McNeill, 459.

35. *The Labor Leader*, Boston, MA, 8 January 1887.

36. Herbert C. Gutman, *Work, Culture, and Society in Industrializing America* (New York, 1977), 101.

37. Arthur Mann, *Yankee Reformers in the Urban Age* (Cambridge, MA, 1954), 184.

38. David Montgomery, *The Fall of the House of Labor* (Cambridge, MA, 1987), 166. In the following pages the author describes a host of legislative successes won by the Massachusetts Knights in this period.

39. *The Labor Enquirer*, Denver, CO, 11 November 1887.

40. Samuel Gompers, "What Does Labor Want?," *American Federation of Labor* (1893): 8 should be contrasted with McNeill's "The Philosophy of the Labor Movement" in the same publication.

2 "This Is a Crusade!": Socialist Party Amnesty Campaigns to Free Eugene V. Debs, 1919–1921

John Sherman

On a Monday evening in February 1919 a few U.S. citizens met at the national headquarters of the Socialist Party (SP or party) and pondered the Socialist Party National Executive Committee's mandate for an amnesty campaign to secure the release of political prisoners.[1] The call was timely: hundreds of U.S. Americans faced imprisonment for violation of the wartime Espionage Act, including socialism's magnific prophet, Eugene V. Debs.[2] Historians have neglected the amnesty campaigns, assuming them to be but the last gasps of a dying socialist movement decimated by the crises of World War I and the red scare.[3] However, the amnesty campaigns suggest that these crises did not paralyze the SP. Socialists, mobilizing their labor allies in the midst of red hysteria, engineered amnesty campaigns that may have influenced President Warren G. Harding in his decision to release Eugene V. Debs and others on Christmas Day 1921.

At the February 1919 meeting the participants responded to the party leadership's mandate by organizing the first socialist-oriented amnesty organization, the National League for the Release of Political Prisoners (NLRPP), and by appointing the Cigar Makers' Union's J. Mahlon Barnes as its director. The inchoate NLRPP sponsored the American Freedom Convention, held in the Machinists' Hall, Chicago, September 25–28, 1919. The vociferous Barnes reasoned that "a monster convention" constituted the best response "by the working people to the repressive measures now employed against them and their representatives."[4]

Among those "repressive measures" employed by the federal government were unreliable mail service and police harassment. During the spring and summer months of 1919 a red scare swept the country, led in part by Postmaster General Albert S. Burleson—to the continual vexation of Barnes, who was one of its first victims. "Some evil influence is working in the mails," concluded the indignant socialist, forcing Barnes to send out follow-up letters to a number of correspondents. Other, weightier consequences of the mail tampering followed. Organizers postponed the American Freedom Convention, originally scheduled for May 1, until July 4, and then rescheduled it again for late September. Time constraints caused the first delay; interference with the mails the second. Postal disruptions also slowed and limited organizational endorsements.[5]

More dramatic was the visit of a government agent to Barnes's downtown Chicago office on May 28. The investigator examined papers and sought to intimidate the director by asking about his employment, home address, and affiliations. Barnes protested the mail delays, and the agent advised him that such hold-ups were not permanent.

In addition to government interference, internal SP strife plagued convention organizers. Socialist feuding peaked in midsummer, when party leadership expelled foreign language federations and state and local bodies constituting the rebellious "left wing" of the party. The language federation secretaries retaliated with a resolution denouncing the amnesty convention for its cooperation with "non-socialist, petit-bourgeois elements." Some locals, critical of the purges and party use of funds, refused to support the amnesty drive and instead endorsed the left wing's call for an amnesty national strike, which never developed.[6]

Despite government harassment and internal opposition, three hundred delegates converged on Chicago for the American Freedom Convention. They created the American Freedom League, elected a national committee to steer it, and pledged to work "for the united action of all labor . . . to insure victory in the fight for freedom." At the convention's closing rally, William D. "Big Bill" Haywood of the Industrial Workers of the World and Chicago Congressman William Mason addressed an enthusiastic crowd of two thousand, and condemned government violations of basic civil liberties.[7]

The notion of labor as the instrument through which the fight for civil freedoms could be won reflects the importance socialist organizers placed on mobilization of their labor allies. The SP had a genuine working-class hero in Eugene V. Debs, who entered federal prison on April 13, 1919, after his Espionage Act prosecution for an antiwar speech delivered in Canton, Ohio, the previous summer. Barnes and his comrades pitched for working-class sympathy in the hundreds of appeal letters they sent to union locals. "We in America must stand by and see our best loved leaders sent to prison. . . . Arise, brothers of toil!" The working class responded. The four hundred organizations endorsing the American Freedom Convention's program included 357 local unions and six national labor bodies, prompting one journal to conclude that "the convention could not be dismissed as the manifestation of a mere radical point of view." Unions also played a key role in financing the project, as the NLRPP's finance committee concentrated on labor organizations in the solicitation of funds.[8]

The convention convened amid public hysteria. In late September red paranoia reached fever pitch with the nationwide steel strike led in part by William Z. Foster. On the day before the convention opened, the *Chicago Tribune* proclaimed in bold headlines, "Riots in East, Troops Act," and attributed tensions in nearby Gary, Indiana, to the reds. Even trivial events suggesting radical unrest aroused press and public ire. When the principal of Chicago's Hyde Park High School discovered the red flag flying above his campus on the morning of September 25, he launched an investigation and the *Tribune* reported the incident, noting "two students with bolshevistic tendencies are accused. . . . "[9] The *Tribune* did not see fit, however, to cover the convention at length. In a brief article the paper labeled member of Congress Mason a "Brutus," and dismissed the whole affair as "the free speech, free food, free shelter, free automobiles, free love, freedom from police restraint, freedom from work . . . convention."[10]

Although the Chicago convention constitutes one of the most noteworthy amnesty efforts of 1919, socialists and their labor allies pressed ahead in other forums. On May 1, the worldwide working-class holiday, various meetings and parades included pleas for Debs's release. A "May Day" march in Brooklyn, for example, featured banners urging freedom "for our comrade Eugene V. Debs" and all other "political prisoners." In Debs's hometown of Terre Haute, Indiana, five hundred socialists and sympathizers marched in protest on May 4 and heard pro-amnesty addresses in the courthouse square. Debs's old union, the Brotherhood of Locomotive Firemen and Engineers, adopted a resolution advocating his release.[11]

The SP inaugurated a month-long campaign in mid-November designed to arouse public support for amnesty. The effort collapsed in the hostile environment of late 1919. The experience of organizers in Reading, Pennsylvania, typified the difficulties: they canceled their rally plans after five thousand counterdemonstrators, led by the American Legion, met in the city square. In Elmira, New York, Legionnaires escorted the socialist orator to the railroad station and sent him on his way back to Chicago before a meeting could take place, while in New Jersey, Mayor Patrick Griffin of Hoboken refused to permit a rally and threatened police disruption should one be attempted.[12] Authorities arrested three men for distributing leaflets advertising an amnesty meeting in Syracuse, New York. The U.S. Supreme Court, in an unusual display of leniency, later overturned their conviction under the Espionage Act.[13]

When the SP National Executive Committee met in New York City in early December, the breakdown of its amnesty initiative overshadowed other topics of discussion. During the fall of 1919 its chances of drumming up popular support for amnesty appeared remote. Even forces deemed sympathetic to the drive had proven disappointing. Although a multitude of union district meetings—such as the Associated Teachers' Union of New York—passed amnesty resolutions, the American Federation of Labor's (AFL) national convention voted down a resolution supporting Debs's release.[14]

Official opinion reflected the public mood. Events in the 1919 Wisconsin Legislature manifested this and symbolized the disappointments experienced by amnesty agitators. In April State Senator Henry Huber, a former aide to Governor Robert LaFollette, introduced a resolution urging a general amnesty. At the time, J. Mahlon Barnes gave the measure "a fair chance of being adopted," and suggested like resolutions be presented to all state legislatures. By the end of May Huber had withdrawn his motion and the legislators in this hotbed of progressivism passed a countermeasure by a twenty-four to seven vote, which repudiated amnesty efforts "unless and until the boys who fought overseas, by plebiscite or referendum, ask for such legislation."[15]

In Washington, where official sentiment ultimately mattered, Congress took no action and President Woodrow Wilson grew intransigent. Before Debs went to prison on April 13, the President entertained the idea of granting clemency, conditioning such an action upon the favorable recommendations of Attorney General A. Mitchell Palmer and personal aide Joseph Tumulty. This liberal impulse, inspired by an appeal for leniency from Frank P. Walsh, Alan Benson, and Charles Edward Russell, died and never revived after Palmer and Tumulty counseled against clemency.[16] Incredibly, Palmer—a Quaker who crushed real and imaginary radicals in the heat of the 1919 summer—underwent a change of heart and, swayed by the compelling pleas of Clarence Darrow, advised the President that Debs's sentence was "too long and ought to be commuted." Wilson ignored this advice in July, and again in August and October when Palmer resubmitted it.[17]

If surveying the bureaucratic opposition and the ruins of the publicity campaign did not cast socialist amnesty crusaders into despair, an additional glance at the experiences of their amnesty allies should have. The Workers' Defense Union of New York City, an umbrella organization of radical and labor groups, staged amnesty rallies on November 5, Eugene Debs's birthday, that attracted little attention. When the National Civil Liberties Bureau began to set up local amnesty committees, criticism forced abandonment of the initiative.[18]

The hostility directed at New York's League for the Amnesty of Political Prisoners (LAPP) in its Christmas protest vividly elucidates the obstacles confronting amnesty activists. LAPP, also known as the People's Freedom Union, envisioned two thousand handcuffed persons marching single file up New York's Fifth Avenue to arouse support for amnesty among the city's Christmas morning churchgoers. When city officials refused to give LAPP a parade permit, the *New York Times* maliciously predicted:

If a group of men in misfit convict gray and wearing jingling manacles hike up Fifth Avenue at the church hour this morning . . . the police will add a theatrical sort of realism to the affair by putting the "convicts" in jail.[19]

LAPP, having mustered only two hundred protesters, sought to avoid the *Times*'s prophecy by marching participants six feet apart and without chains—technically evading the city's definition of a "parade." Onlookers, many of them members of the American Legion, booed and hissed as the silent marchers passed, led by a Methodist clergyman carrying a U.S. flag. When a squad of police charged the troupe the veterans joined in, tearing placards and threatening the minister when he accidentally dragged the flag in the snow. Afterward, New York newspapers absolved the police and condemned the protesters. The *Herald* concluded, "the behavior of the police was excellent under the most trying circumstances," while the *Times* reflected upon the "absurd" affair by asking what prompted people "to show their sympathy with Eugene V. Debs and other persons in jail for refusing to show their love for their country?" The editor of the *Times* decried the march as dangerous, since the "city swarms with revolutionaries and anarchists" awaiting revolutionary opportunities.[20]

After the winter of 1919–1920 there were fewer such "revolutionaries." The government deported three hundred radicals without trial in December, and in January Palmer conducted his most infamous raids, rounding up six thousand alleged conspirators with a harsh disregard for civil rights. In the public mind, terms like "red" and "radical" became synonymous with "socialist," contributing to the powder-keg atmosphere surrounding the amnesty activists. The SP was under siege. W. T. Fenton, a Chicago banker, denounced socialism as "the only real menace to the United States today."

Given the scope of the opposition, the willingness of the SP to pursue its amnesty campaigning is remarkable. With public opinion set against these libertarian sentiments, amnesty efforts hardly appeared politically prudent, yet the party pressed on. Socialists envisioned an "Amnesty Day" rally in Washington, D.C., on April 13, the first anniversary of Debs's imprisonment, only to discover coordination problems too great to overcome.[21]

The failure of the Amnesty Day rally marked a significant turning point in socialist amnesty campaigns. In view of the high-pitched opposition and apparent futility of attempting to shift the wide body of public opinion, the party National Executive Committee redirected its efforts toward government leaders and adopted strategies encompassing long-term projects. In May 1920 the party nominated Debs, the "Lincoln of the Wabash," for the presidency and the imprisoned leader's Chicago attorney, Seymour Stedman, as his running mate. The entire convention of two hundred delegates then descended on Washington and lobbied for amnesty. A committee headed by Stedman met with Palmer. The entire delegation visited the White House where Joseph Tumulty greeted them. Whatever hopes these visits may have raised, Wilson crushed them; he remained adamantly opposed to releasing Debs. Tumulty recollected the President as saying,

I will never consent to the pardon of this man. . . . While the flower of American youth was pouring out its blood to vindicate the cause of civilization, this man, Debs, stood behind the lines, sniping, attacking, and denouncing them.[22]

Recognizing Wilson's rigidity, socialists curtailed their amnesty activities until after the 1920 election.

The election itself was to some extent a referendum on Wilson's attack on civil liberties. Parley P. Christensen of the Farmer-Labor Party telegraphed his counterparts, Republican Warren G. Harding and Democrat James M. Cox, and suggested they jointly appeal to Wilson to release candidate Debs. Harding wired in reply that, while he believed in a "generous amnesty for political prisoners," he needed to review the Debs case before stating his opinion.[23]

The strength of the broader socialist movement carried the SP through the election. Handicapped by Debs's absence from the campaign trail, socialists relied on Seymour Stedman and novel publicity stunts to capture the electorate's attention. Stedman toured the country and reported his progress to Debs.

The meetings and the response was very much above our expectations. The attacks upon the party by the press and the American Legion and other thousand per cent patriots was vicious but it was astounding to the see the rebounding of the movement.[24]

Though unable to see him in person, newsreel footage of Debs accepting his party's nomination drew cheers from moviegoers—to the chagrin of the *New York Times*'s editor—while in Toledo, Ohio, socialists sparked public interest by dropping literature from four airplanes.[25]

Before and during the campaign public hostility did not quell criticism of Wilson and the Espionage Act. Liberal and radical publications condemned the repression and urged repeal of the wartime internal security laws. The *Nation*, for example, commended Debs as one who suffered jail for "the fundamental rights of man," while *Dial* argued for restoration of civil liberties as early as January 1919. The American Union Against Militarism issued a one-hundred-page pamphlet prepared especially for attorneys, entitled "Espionage Act Cases." Scott Nearing, an instructor at the socialist Rand School in New York, penned *The Debs Decision*, a small booklet that quoted Debs's Canton speech at length and glorified the leader as a libertarian martyr.[26]

One encouraging development in 1920 was the change of direction taken by Samuel Gompers and the AFL. Although the SP had turned its attention to the election campaign while awaiting an opportune time in which to resume public amnesty programs, the party welcomed the Federation's activities and joined the labor lobbyists. Gompers and the executive council had recommended an amnesty resolution to the AFL's Montreal convention, which passed unanimously after the International Ladies' Garment Workers' Union pushed the motion onto the floor. In August Gompers presented the resolution to Attorney General Palmer, who received a second delegation led by socialist member of Congress Meyer London.[27]

But questions regarding Gompers's sincerity tarnished his libertarian accomplishments. Before 1920 he created the Committee for Amnesty that seemed to persecute free radicals more than advance the cause of those in prison. The SP's executive secretary in 1920, Otto Branstetter, did not trust Gompers, but the labor leader absolved himself in his autobiography, proclaiming, "I assisted a movement to release him [Debs] and did everything within my power to accomplish that purpose."[28]

Before Wilson left office in March 1921, one final appeal from Palmer advising clemency for Debs reached his desk. The report, a product of a Justice Department study, suggested the socialist be freed on Lincoln's birthday. One last time Wilson declined. Debs responded in a widely circulated interview:

It is he, not I, who needs a pardon. If I had it in my power I would give him the pardon which would set him free. Woodrow Wilson is an exile from the hearts of his people. The betrayal of his ideals makes him the most pathetic figure in the world.[29]

Not everyone agreed with Debs. The *New York Times* lauded Wilson's decision as a "triumph of justice." Reflecting on Debs's wartime pacifism, the paper explained that "the worst felonies are venial compared with the crimes of which he was sentenced."[30] After Debs denounced the President in his interview, prison authorities held him incommunicado for nearly a month.

Shortly after Warren G. Harding entered office in March 1921, the SP National Executive Committee met in Boston and committed the party to an aggressive amnesty campaign. The SP also pressed forth with a membership drive, yet gave its amnesty work priority. Though red hysteria had subsided, popular opinion on the amnesty question remained cool, and many observers doubted that a conservative Republican president would pardon radicals.[31] The party leadership consulted with suffragist Harriot Stanton Blatch and persuaded her to head an amnesty lobby in Washington. Blatch accepted the task on the condition that the SP not use picketing to secure concessions (an action socialists had advocated in press releases and literature).

Harriot Stanton Blatch was no stranger to radical politics or grassroots agitation. Daughter of famed abolitionist and suffragist Elizabeth Cady Stanton, Blatch had organized the first suffrage parades in New York City around the turn of the century. In this, the most extensive socialist amnesty effort, her skills proved essential. The campaign featured a massive petition drive and Amnesty Day demonstrations in Washington on April 13, 1921, the second anniversary of Debs's imprisonment. Party officials named the project the Debs Amnesty Campaign, but they adopted the slogan "Let's Get Them All Out" to communicate a concern for all political prisoners. With the goal of one million signatures and ten thousand labor union endorsements, the party sent petition copies, union resolutions, and advertising leaflets to each socialist local. The national office urged "vigorous" use of petitions:

Local organizations should not depend upon the haphazard circulation of these petitions at meetings of the local, or at public propaganda meetings. . . . A systematic house to house canvas should be made with the petitions.[32]

If socialists perceived a change in public attitude sufficient to warrant attempting door-to-door solicitation, certainly events in Washington enhanced their heightened sense of expectation. President Harding ordered Attorney General Harry Daugherty to review Debs's case and subsequently Daugherty, with the President's permission, arranged for Debs to travel unescorted to the capital for a private conference. The event, shrouded in secrecy, took even Debs's Atlanta attorney Samuel Castleton by surprise.[33]

The activities of the Debs Amnesty Committee centered around the Washington office staffed by Harriot Stanton Blatch. Operating out of the Bellevue Hotel on McPherson Square near the White House, Blatch received petitions and registered Amnesty Day delegates. Both tasks presented difficulties. Some lean petitions arrived, such as one from New York accompanied by a note explaining "most of the people I have asked, refused point blank."[34] Travel costs discouraged would-be delegates and forced Blatch to recruit participants from the immediate area.

Amnesty Day featured several events. A delegation led by Morris Hillquit met with President Harding. Norman Thomas also participated, renewing his friendship with the President from his Marion, Ohio, days as one of Harding's newspaper employees; Thomas joked about Harding's dog, "Laddie Boy," which sat, distinguished, in a green armchair nearby.[35] Hillquit and Samuel Castleton were among a group of attorneys who visited Daugherty. Meanwhile, 215 delegates marched up Pennsylvania Avenue behind an automobile carrying the giant petition. Three hundred thousand signatures had been gathered, supported by seven hundred organizational endorsements representing nearly three million members. An Amnesty Day convention assembled at the Old Masonic Hall in the evening.

These activities produced mixed results. While the public demonstrations fostered no hostile opposition, private lobbying of official Washington seemingly did little good.[36] Delegates visiting Congressional offices reported a number of Senators and Representatives away—some reputedly "at the ball game." Representative Everett Sauders of Indiana, described by his lobbyist as indifferent, stated flatly that "his constituents . . . were not in favor of amnesty." A worker meeting with Senator Ovington Weller of Maryland pronounced him "badly afflicted with the malady called 'ignorant.' "[37] At the White House, Harding advised his delegation he would not grant a general amnesty for the time being and remained noncommittal about Debs.

Despite financial and logistical complications the SP maintained its Debs Amnesty Committee Office in Washington for the remainder of

1921. Mrs. Winnie Branstetter, wife of SP Executive Secretary Otto Branstetter, inherited Harriot Blatch's work until her own replacement by Miss Lillith Martin in early summer. Amnesty agitation emitted from party headquarters in Chicago, too, where grassroots efforts included mobilizing organized labor in Illinois. Every union local in the state received two posters, and nine hundred groups signed an organizational petition.[38]

Mid-summer 1921 brought with it the peaks and valleys veteran amnesty agitators had come to expect. Early July was gloomy. Although the Debs Amnesty Committee could boast impressive accomplishments—having collected $10,000, one thousand resolutions, and countless thousands of petition signatures—the prospect of Debs's release appeared as dim as in the dark months of late 1919. Amnesty resolutions stalled in Congress, public opinion remained cool, and mainline press ignored the amnesty question. Antagonists like the American Legion stood guard to act should positive signs emerge. On July 13 prison officials denied a SP representative access to Debs. From Washington, a disheartened Lillith Martin penned dour notes to party headquarters and sadly notified the editor of the *Nation* that lobbying continues "to no avail."[39]

Then, in late July, an upbeat audience with the President buoyed amnesty crusaders' hopes. Socialists dominated the delegation and engaged Harding in a frank discussion that left the participants "feeling very well satisfied." More encouraging news followed: Harding subsequently conferred with Attorney General Daugherty about Debs, and also received Oswald Garrison Villard, editor of the *Nation*, on Debs's behalf.[40]

The day after the socialists met with Harding, John G. Emery, National Commander of the American Legion, telegraphed the President asking assurance that "Debs and his kind" would remain in prison. The Legion, constant nemesis of the SP, acknowledged the amnesty efforts in a resolution passed by their 1921 national convention and sent to Harding:

Whereas, in numerous incidents influences have been brought to bear to secure the pardon of the criminals or to secure a general amnesty for all such so-called political convicts, now therefore, be it resolved, by the American Legion . . . that we oppose the pardon of Eugene V. Debs.[41]

Harding again counseled with Daugherty in August and announced he would not pardon Debs until securing official peace with Germany. By November, with the treaty signed, hopes of an executive pardon flourished. Early December saw socialists and their allies diligently lobby the President. Harding received letters and cables from prominent Austrian and French socialists, and from British Laborites. A delegation from the

Women's International League for Peace and Freedom called on the White House, as did former socialist member of Congress Victor Berger.[42]

Although liberals and other radicals agitated for amnesty in a flurry of fall activities, they did not always do so in cooperation with the socialists. When Roger Baldwin's Civil Liberties Union (CLU) embarked on an aggressive picketing campaign, the SP distanced itself. Picketing "will be promptly and ruthlessly suppressed," predicted Debs Amnesty Committee President Otto Wilson, who advised new Washington office coordinator Bertha Hale White to work with the CLU "without getting mixed up in their picketing crusade."[43] Central to the SP's resistance to the CLU'S demonstrations was its belief that Debs's release was imminent. Wanting to avoid any antagonistic gestures, the party showed its preoccupation with the Grand Old Socialist's release and its negligible interest in the cases of other Espionage Act prisoners. When the CLU adopted the position that Debs should not be released if others—such as Wobblies—remained imprisoned, the SP dissented. Otto Wilson bristled at the suggestion:

I have lost all faith in the Civil Liberties Union. . . . That bunch is trying to keep Debs in [prison] to continue the amnesty work for the sake of a few meal tickets.

When I get time I am going to write Baldwin a letter and it will smoke in every line.[44]

Though assisted by comrades abroad and some sympathizers at home, in the crucial days of December 1921 socialist amnesty activists created a master stroke themselves. Having collected twenty-one thousand signatures in Terre Haute in three weeks for the Amnesty Day petition drive, socialists returned to Debs's hometown for one final campaign. John Martin, a Chicago newspaper reporter, oversaw the project, which involved setting up a booth on Wabash Avenue to collect the signatures.[45] Thirty-eight hundred petitioners signed the first day. In the predawn hours of the second day vandals tied the booth to a street car that dragged it seven blocks, but socialists were able to fix the structure and gather thirty-two hundred more names by dusk of the second day. "Everyone signs without any trouble," reported pleased Debs Amnesty Committee Secretary Oliver Wilson. His prediction of twenty thousand signatures underestimated support; when the booth closed after a week twenty-nine thousand citizens had signed—a stunning success![46]

The Terre Haute petition marks the final effort by socialists to free their leader, Eugene Debs. Senator Thomas E. Watson of Georgia, the aged and feisty former Populist, arranged a presentation meeting with Harding, and on December 19, 1921, Mrs. Robert LaFollette and Bertha Hale White delivered the signatures to a cordial President.[47] Reporters flocked around the two women as they left the White House, one correspondent telling them Harding was glad to receive the petition, and others congratulating them for presenting it at a critical moment.

On December 24, 1921, Harding pardoned Debs and twenty-three other political prisoners.[48] Helen Keller, among others, commended the President, noting the pardons reflected "a Christmas candle in the dark window of the world." Many U.S. Americans, however, were not so pleased or so genteel. One Chicagoan wrote, "If a man can . . . poll a million votes, then he is above the operation of the United States laws. Is that the idea?"[49]

With the release of Eugene V. Debs the most substantial SP amnesty agitation came to an end. Many Espionage Act prisoners, the majority of them members of the IWW, remained imprisoned; the party continued some displays of concern, but for the socialists the focal point of amnesty work had always been Debs.

Debs returned home to Indiana via Washington, D.C., where he met the man who pardoned him. The irony of conservative Republican Harding freeing a socialist whom the idealistic, liberal Wilson imprisoned and neglected does not easily pass by unnoticed. The socialist press held that Debs's release was a product of personalities, not politics:

President Wilson is a hard, cold man with a passion for domination. And whoever stood in his way was accursed. Mr. Harding is an easy going gentleman, with no positiveness, with no well grounded ideas; and he will be the plaything of events.[50]

Such an explanation is too simplistic. Harding did, as Debs himself noted, possess "humane impulses." Yet pardoning the aged socialist was also in keeping with the Harding administration's goal of healing the nation's wartime wounds and restoring "normalcy." The President had little compassion for revolutionary Wobblies, but sympathized with those prisoners, like Debs, convicted in the unique atmosphere of Woodrow Wilson's war. That Debs had a substantial political following, too, weighed in his favor.[51] Debs's frailty may have helped inspire Harding's leniency, too. During the hot summer of 1921 Debs's weight dropped from 185 to 156 pounds, prompting concern among family that he might die in prison.[52]

The socialist amnesty campaigns spurred Harding to grant Debs clemency, and—if nothing else—freed the President's hand by providing a counterweight to the entrenched forces opposing pardon or commutation. Harding himself recognized in December 1921 both the highly visible socialist lobby and "the widespread hostility toward any grant of clemency." And even though red hysteria had subsided, in the closing days of 1921 this hostile element expressed dismay at Debs's release. "The majority of the American people will not approve this commutation," predicted the *New York Times*, adding that "a shallow, howling, whining minority has had its way."[53] Yet this minority "had its way" because of a determined effort by the SP. The perseverance of the party in its amnesty work, exercised in the face of broad opposition during and after the high tide of red paranoia, demonstrates its ability to mobilize working-class opinion and contribute to the political life of the country at the outset of the 1920s.

NOTES

The author thanks Professors Lorin Cary and Gerald Thompson, University of Toledo, for their help in revision, and Allen Ruff, for his useful conference commentary.

1. "Amnesty Work of the Socialist Party," *Socialist World* 3 (June 1922): 9. The article subtitle identifies it as a National Executive Committee report to the 1922 Socialist Party national convention; the *Socialist World* served as a semi-official party organ after its creation in 1920.

2. Debs delivered his famous antiwar speech in Canton, Ohio, on 16 June 1918. Authorities arrested him on 30 June and tried him in Federal District Court (Cleveland) under the Espionage Act. At the conclusion of a five-day trial, in which Debs offered little in the way of legal defense, the court sentenced him to a ten-year prison term. Debs entered prison on 13 April 1919 after losing an appeal to the U.S. Supreme Court.

3. James Weinstein refutes this traditional interpretation in the introduction to his *The Decline of Socialism in America, 1912–1925*, explaining that "after 1919, contrary to what little has been written . . . a general movement of a socialist character continued to exist, even, briefly, to flourish." He does not, however, use the amnesty campaigns to support his thesis. The biographers of Debs, including Ray Ginger and Nick Salvatore, refer to specific amnesty efforts without exploring them at length or in the context of the broader movement. No scholar has traced the early projects, such as the National League for the Release of Political Prisoners.

4. Minutes, Meeting of the NLRPP, 27 February 1919, Socialist Party Papers (SPP), Duke University, Durham, North Carolina; J. Mahlon Barnes to Sir and Brother, 8 September 1919, SPP. There is some confusion regarding the NLRPP name. The *Socialist World*, cited above, identifies this first organization as the American Freedom Foundation. The SPP and *Survey* specifically attribute that name to the permanent league created in September 1919.

J. Mahlon Barnes was well known in SP circles. A charter member of the party, he served it as national secretary until scandal drove him from office in 1911.

5. Barnes to unidentified union official, 26 July 1919, SPP; Barnes to Comrade Secretary, 17 May 1919, SPP; "Amnesty Work," *Socialist World*, 9; Barnes to Sir and Brother, 16 June 1919, SPP.

6. Barnes to Sir and Brother, 28 May 1919, SPP; untitled, undated report, SPP; Frank Senesy to Adolph Germer, 26 July 1919, SPP; " 'Left Wing' for Strike," *New York Times*, 26 June 1919; David A. Shannon, *The Socialist Party of America* (New York, 1955), 135. Shannon incorrectly states that the SP canceled the amnesty convention.

7. "Birth of the Freedom League," *Survey* 63 (22 November 1919): 136; "Haywood and Mason Seek to Free Objectors," *Chicago Tribune*, 29 September 1919.

8. C. B. Cline to the International Association of Machinists lodges, 28 July 1919, SPP; Unknown (probably Barnes) to Sir and Brother, 16 October 1919, SPP; "Birth of League," *Survey*, 135; meeting minutes, 27 February 1919, SPP.

9. "Riots in East, Troops Act," *Chicago Tribune*, 24 September 1919; "Hyde Park High School Seeks Raisers of Red Flag," *Chicago Tribune*, 27 September 1919.

10. "Haywood and Mason," *Chicago Tribune*, 29 September 1919.

11. "Soldiers and Sailors Break up Meeting," *New York Times*, 2 May 1919; "Socialist Parade Is Orderly Affair," *Terre Haute Tribune*, 5 May 1919. Reflective of the negative media attention socialists received is the May 5 *New York Times* article covering this event, entitled "Debs Demonstration a Failure."

12. "Reading Puts Ban on Debs Mass Meeting," and "Stop Socialist Meeting," *New York Times*, 24 November 1919; "Debs Meeting Forbidden," *New York Times*, 26 November 1919.

13. Untitled report, a list of Socialist Espionage Act cases, undated, Warren G. Harding Papers, Ohio Historical Society, Columbus, Ohio.

14. "Socialist Leaders Meet," *New York Times*, 7 December 1919; "Teachers Ask Inquiry," *New York Times*, 13 December 1919; "Debs Is Dead, Ill for Years," *Detroit News*, 21 October 1926.

15. Wisconsin, 1919 *Wisconsin Blue Book* (Madison, WI, 1919), 238; Barnes to SP State Secretaries, 9 April 1919; SPP; Wisconsin, *Index to the Journals of the Legislature* (1919).

16. Arthur S. Link et al., eds., *The Papers of Woodrow Wilson* 57 (Princeton, NJ, 1987), 282–283, 310, 618.

17. Stanley Cohen, *A. Mitchell Palmer: Politician* (New York, 1963), 202. In a cabinet meeting on 10 August four members advocated a pardon, but to no avail. See E. David Cronon, ed., *Josephus Daniels: The Cabinet Diaries of Josephus Daniels* (Lincoln, NE, 1963), 545–546.

18. Barnes to Sir and Brother, 31 October 1919, SPP; Cohen, 203.

19. "March in Manacles, Plan of Radicals," *New York Times*, 16 December 1919; "Police Will Stop Amnesty Parade," *New York Times*, 25 December 1919.

20. "Free Turkey Dinners Go Begging; Christmas Cheer Abounds in City; Amnesty Paraders Put to Rout," *New York Herald*, 26 December 1919; "The Amnesty Manifestants," *New York Times*, 27 December 1919.

21. Robert K. Murray, *The Red Scare* (Minneapolis, MN, 1955), 233–234; "Work Harder, Wrangle Less, Advice to Labor," *Chicago Tribune*, 1 October 1919; "Amnesty Work," *Socialist World*, 9.

22. Shannon, 158; Joseph Tumulty, *Woodrow Wilson as I Knew Him* (Garden City, NY, 1921), 505.

23. Shannon, 158; "Asks Nominees to Join in Plea to Free Debs," *New York Times*, 25 July 1920.

24. Stedman to Debs, 29 September 1920, Eugene V. Debs Papers, Indiana State University, Terre Haute, Indiana.

25. "The Debs Pictures," *New York Times*, 12 June 1920; "Use Airplanes for Debs," *New York Times*, 1 November 1920; "Socialists to Scatter Literature from Planes," *Toledo Blade*, 29 October 1920.

26. "The Higher Law," *Nation* 108 (19 April 1919): 596; "Release Political Prisoners," *Dial* 66 (11 January 1919): 5–6; advertising leaflet for booklet, undated, American Union Against Militarism Papers, Swarthmore College, Swarthmore, Pennsylvania; Scott Nearing, *The Debs Decision* (New York, 1919). In his Canton speech Debs lauded Nearing as "the greatest teacher in the United States." As a lecturer in economics at the University of Pennsylvania, Nearing came under fire for his principles and lost his job. Debs compared the incident to the persecution of Jesus Christ. See Jean Y. Tussey, ed., *Eugene Victor Debs Speaks* (New York, 1970), 255–256.

27. "Labor Makes Plea," *New York Times*, 16 June 1920; "Palmer Won't Free Political Prisoners," *New York Times*, 15 September 1920.

28. Nick Salvatore, *Eugene V. Debs: Citizen and Socialist* (Urbana, IL, 1982), 326; Samuel Gompers, *Seventy Years of Life and Labor*, 2 vols. (New York, 1925), 1:416.

29. "Ends Study of Debs Case," *New York Times*, 28 January 1921; "Anathematizes Woodrow Wilson from Prison Cell," *Atlanta Constitution*, 2 February 1921.

30. "Berger and Debs," *New York Times*, 2 February 1921; "A Soap-Box Jail," *New York Times*, 3 February 1921.

31. Ray Ginger, *Eugene V. Debs: A Biography* (New York, 1949), 406. The revocation of privileges prompted a terse SP protest. See "National Executive Committee Protest," *Socialist World* 2 (February 1921): 16. "Boston Meeting Asks for Debs's Release," *New York Times*, 7 March 1921.

32. Harriot Stanton Blatch to John E. Milholland, 18 March 1921, SPP. Debs also opposed picketing on his behalf. See "Debs Bars Picketing," *New York Times*, 19 March 1921. "Mrs. Blatch Dead, Famed Suffragist," *New York Times*, 21 November 1940; advertisement for the "Debs Amnesty Campaign" and "Let's Get Them All Out," both in *Socialist World* 2 (February 1921): 7, 9.

33. "Harding Directs Debs Case Review," *New York Times*, 18 March 1921; "Debs Goes to Washington and Talks to Daugherty; Makes Trip Alone," *Atlanta*

Constitution, 25 March 1921. Though evidence is lacking, one might speculate that the purpose of this trip was to test public reaction. A less likely but more colorful explanation would be that Harding and Daughterty hoped Debs might seize the opportunity to escape, as Haywood had done, and free them from the politically volatile decision of whether to pardon the socialist. Daugherty told reporters he "was not afraid Debs would try to escape," but it is difficult to explain why the prisoner traveled unguarded.

34. Blatch to Miss Helen Todd, 18 March 1921, SPP; unidentified to Blatch, 4 April 1921, SPP.

35. Blatch to Miss Elizabeth Gilman, 8 April 1921, SPP; "Harding Refuses Amnesty Grant Now," *New York Times* 14 April 1921; Robert K. Murray, *The Harding Era* (Minneapolis, MN, 1969), 166.

36. "Amnesty Day in Washington," *Socialist World* 2 (April 1921): 8; Blatch to Mr. A. Keep, 8 April 1921, SPP.

37. Reports of Amnesty Conference Delegates, 13 April 1921, SPP. There are twenty-seven unnumbered pages of reports. See in particular pages regarding Senators Penrose, Knox, Walsh, and Weller, and Representative Sauders.

38. "Harding Refuses," *New York Times*, 14 April 1921; William F. Kruse to Winnie E. Branstetter, 16 May 1921, SPP; Kruse to Lillith Martin, 8 July 1921, SPP; press release on meeting with Harding, 27 July 1921, SPP.

39. Kruse to Martin, 13 July 1921, SPP; Kruse to Martin, telegram, 13 July 1921, SPP; Martin to editor of the *Nation*, 19 July 1921, SPP.

40. Press release, 27 July 1921, SPP. This source notes that the committee gave Harding a copy of Debs's Canton speech. "President Hears Pleas for Amnesty," *New York Times*, 28 July 1921; Harold C. Hobart to Martin, 26 July 1921, SPP.

41. "Legion Warns Harding against Freeing Debs," *New York Times*, 30 July 1921; Summary of Proceedings, Third National Convention of the American Legion, 31 October, 1–2 November 1921, American Legion Papers, American Legion National Headquarters Library, Indianapolis, Indiana.

42. "No Debs Pardon till Peace Is Ratified," *New York Times*, 28 August 1921; "Amnesty Help by European Comrades," *Socialist World* 3 (January 1922): 3; "British Minority Laborites Ask Harding to Free Debs," *New York Times*, 13 December 1921; Paul Faure to Harding, 2 December 1921, SPP; "Asks Harding to Free 145," *New York Times*, 13 December 1921. WILPF President Jane Addams was not in the visitation committee and Harding did not personally receive the women. "Berger Calls on Harding," *New York Times*, 17 December 1921.

43. Otto Wilson to Comrade Baldwin, 15 November 1921, SPP; Wilson to Bertha Hale White, 13 November 1921, SPP.

44. Wilson to White, 13 November 1921, SPP; Wilson to White, 2 December 1921, SPP.

45. Reports of Delegates: Everett Sauders, 13 April 1921, SPP; "The Debs Petition," *Terre Haute Tribune*, 9 December 1921; "Urge Debs' Freedom," *Terre Haute Tribune*, 9 December 1921.

46. Oliver Wilson to Bertha Hale White, 12 December 1921, SPP; "Miscreants Mistreat Eugene Debs' Booth," *Terre Haute Tribune*, 10 December 1921; Wilson to White, 12 December 1921, SPP; "The Debs Party Leaves," *Terre Haute Tribune*, 15 December 1921.

47. White to Wilson, telegram, 17 December 1921, SPP; White to Wilson, 19 December 1921, SPP. Senator Watson actively supported amnesty efforts even to the point of introducing one of the resolutions in Congress. In his 1920 campaign he used the slogan "Debs in the White House and Wilson in the penitentiary," but was also staunchly anti-Semitic and anti-Catholic—promoting a bizarre mix of political viewpoints. See Watson to Harding, 17 December 1921, Harding Papers; Lillith Martin, "Side Lights on Amnesty Work in Washington," *Socialist World* 2 (August 1921): 7.

48. White to Wilson, telegram, 20 December 1921, SPP; White to Theodore Debs, 20 December 1921, SPP; "Debs Goes Free while Prisoners Cheer Departure," *Atlanta Constitution*, 26 December 1921.

49. Helen Keller to Harding, telegram, 25 December 1921, Harding Papers; Mr. J. J. Wait to George B. Christian, Jr., 29 December 1921, Harding Papers. Despite his pardon of Debs, Harding oversaw an administration with an uneven record regarding labor. The President frequently deferred to cabinet members on labor questions and these men lacked consensus. For the best explanation see Robert H. Zieger, *Republicans and Labor, 1919–1929* (Lexington, KY, 1969), 70–143.

50. "Debs Urges Support of the Amnesty Campaign to Free the I.W.W. Politicals," *Socialist World* 3 (January 1922): 5; "Debs Is Expected to Leave Capital for Home Tuesday," *Atlanta Constitution*, 27 December 1921; "Editorial," *Socialist World* 2 (15 February 1921): 5.

51. Ginger, 436; Murray, 169; Warren G. Harding to Charles L. Knight, 21 March 1922, Harding Papers; untitled, undated press release, Harding Papers.

52. Theodore Debs to My Very Dear Comrade, 2 December 1921, Henry and Elizabeth Vincent Papers, Labadie Collection, The University of Michigan, Ann Arbor.

53. Christian to Castleton, 6 December 1921, Harding Papers; "The Release of Debs," *New York Times*, 26 December 1921. For a like assessment of public sentiment in August, 1921, see Secretary to the President (probably George Christian, Jr.) to Mr. I. O. Barnhart, 17 August 1921, Harding Papers.

3   A Path Not Taken: The Proletarian Party and the Early History of Communism in the United States

Allen Ruff

Several different trends, each with various tactical and strategic outlooks, arose during the earliest days of the communist movement in the United States. Each of those groupings, in agreement over the inadequacies of the existing Socialist Party and encouraged by political developments at home and abroad, hoped to forge the new organization that would inspire and lead the working class in the elusive quest for socialism in the United States. Each trend also vied for recognition as the representative to the Communist or Third International at Moscow. Ultimately, the Communist Party won out as the recognized voice of communist politics in the United States. As such, it soon became the political home of numerous militants in that now so distant decade of the 1920s who viewed Lenin, the successes of the Bolshevik Party, and the first strides taken by the newly forged Soviet Union as beacons of hope in a hostile capitalist world.

Much of the subsequent written history of early U.S. communism, shaded by partisan views and agendas, has merely focused on the particular trajectory of the Communist Party. Partisan supporters and critics, communist and anticommunist alike, who wrote, rewrote, revised, and re-revised that history remained fixated on the Communist Party, either as the one truly representative vanguard voice of the working-class movement, or as a deformation of the ideal, and a conspiratorial agent of a foreign power. Such histories, often refracted through contemporary political and ideological exigencies and agendas, quickly disregarded or forgot members of the earlier movement not in the Communist Party, especially "outsiders" who helped shape the early political life of both U.S. communism and the broader workers' movement. Now, in this period of Cold War thaw and proclaimed "openness," historians in the former Soviet Union have begun to reopen and reexamine parts of a historical record long considered closed. At a time when historians long attacked and ostracized because of their politics are finally receiving some overdue recognition, it behooves those concerned with the history of the United States to look more closely at some of that history long neglected or glossed over.[1]

One such small but influential tendency, forgotten or given incredibly short shrift when mentioned at all, was the group that came to be known as the Proletarian Party, one of the earliest communist trends in the United States that developed out of the political chaos in U.S. socialism during the post–World War I era.

The leadership of what became the Proletarian Party, or "P.P.ers" in the alphabeical shorthand of the left, played a significant role in midwifing U.S. communism. The group also held the distinction of becoming the first organized faction to be banned by the very formation it had helped to sire. The particular political line it developed warrants some closer examination and raises several significant questions for historians and activists concerned with the history of the twentieth-century left. The Proletarian history is the story of a path not taken.[2]

That story very much paralleled the political biographies of its founders, most notably John Keracher. Born in Scotland in 1881, the self-taught shoemaker's son moved to Detroit in 1909, not long after his arrival in the United States. Already a committed socialist, he joined the Michigan Socialist Party in 1910 and soon began holding regular evening classes on Marx's *Capital* at the rear of his small downtown shoe store. He quickly forged a close working alliance with key figures within Detroit's socialist and labor circles. A second member of the "triumvirate" that came to forge a Socialist Party left wing in Michigan, Detroit-born Dennis Elihu Batt, tool and dye maker by trade, also served as a labor press editor and representative of the International Association of Machinists on the Motor City's labor council. His schooling as a Marxist began in the public library in Manila, the Philippines, where he served as a U.S. cavalryman during the Spanish-American War.[3] The third key figure was Al "Red Rover" Renner, the bespectacled accountant and socialist organizer who help found the party-owned socialist center, the "House of the Masses."[4]

Staunch partisans of a militant industrial socialism firmly based on a systematic understanding of Marxism that would combat the Michigan Socialist Party's reformist leadership and direction, the trio organized the Proletarian University, an alternative network of study classes and lectures, a kind of "socialist Chautauqua" for workers, centered at the "House of the Masses" and various other locations throughout the city and adjoining communities. Utilizing the "University" as an institutional organizing base, Keracher, Batt, and Renner successfully forged the left-wing pole that effectively challenged the conservatives for control of the Michigan Socialist Party.

Keracher, described as a "scholarly and reasoning man" and a "good lecturer" with "personal charm,"[5] won election as Secretary of the state organization in 1916. With Keracher at its head, the Michigan party grew into a significant organization, having some six thousand members by 1918. Late in the summer of 1917 Keracher also became editor of the party's monthly *Michigan Socialist*, but that paper was soon halted by the wartime Espionage Act restrictions. In its stead, the party left or "reds" launched the monthly *Proletarian* in May 1918, under control of the Proletarian University and owned by the Proletarian Publishing Company directed by Batt, rather than the Michigan state party.[6]

In control of the state apparatus in 1918 and determined in their desire to place the Michigan organization on a revolutionary course, the Detroit leftwingers proceeded to revise the state party's constitution and bylaws. They made any state socialist who advocated the "immediate" reform demands of the national platform liable to expulsion. The left-dominated 1917 state convention had already passed a resolution urging members to take a firm stance against religion "on the basis of the materialist conception of history." That motion placed the Michigan party in direct opposition to the long-standing national policy of neutrality on the "religious question." Their stance provided the eventual pretext for an assault on the Michigan leftwingers by the Socialist Party conservatives in control of the party's National Executive Committee (NEC), at that time still wedded to the reformism of the Second International.[7]

The broader Socialist Party had undergone sweeping changes during World War I. The experience of the war itself, at home and abroad, the collapse of the Second International, and the inspiration of the Bolshevik revolution in Russia radically altered the nature and composition of the U.S. movement. Weary of war, pressed by high prices, deteriorating labor and living conditions, and energized by events in Russia and Eastern Europe, countless recent arrivals flocked into the party's linguistically segregated foreign language federations. Largely unable to vote and therefore not overly taken with parliamentary reformism, their influx bolstered the already existing English-speaking industrial union left.

This "new left," broadly wedded to "mass action" and "revolutionary socialism," organized its own networks within the shell of the old party. Diverse in tactical outlook, political experience and training, various trends developed their own caucuses, membership rolls, systems of dues, propaganda organs, and theoretical journals in such centers as Boston,

New York, Chicago, Cleveland, and Seattle. The left wing, by April 1919, controlled locals in addition to Detroit at Akron; Buffalo; San Francisco; Seattle; Cleveland; Philadelphia; Newark; the Bronx, Queens, and Brooklyn in New York; and the Russian, Lithuanian, Latvian, South Slavic, Polish, Ukrainian, and Hungarian Language Federations.

Most significantly, the leftwingers, including the Michigan "reds," were determined to place the Socialist Party on a revolutionary course. Various left-wing caucuses repudiated all reformist planks wherever they held sway. Their strength showed itself in the national referendum election for seats on the party's NEC in March 1919. The rank-and-file gave twelve of fifteen seats on the national body to the left candidates and elected four of five international delegates. Those election results also exposed the true democratic nature of the reformists still at the helm. Refusing to abide by the outcome, the NEC at the end of May suspended the seven predominantly left-wing Eastern European Language Federations under a technical pretext concocted by New York's Morris Hillquit. Claiming irregularities, the NEC also voided the referendum results and called for new elections at a special Emergency National Convention to be held at Chicago on August 30, 1919.[8]

The NEC, determined in its attempt to discipline supporters of industrial unionism and revolutionary socialism, simultaneously seized upon the opportunity created by the Michigan left's stand against religion. It revoked the state party's charter in June 1919. The first of several state party organizations expelled by the national body, for a brief time the de facto leader of the left wing, the "Michigan group" cast about for allies. Meeting at a "State Emergency Convention" on June 19, the party issued a call for a national Convention to be held in Chicago on September 1 for the purpose of organizing a "socialist party" to be aligned with the Moscow-based "Communist" International, founded that March. Dennis Batt, acting as representative of the Proletarian Publishing Company, turned formal control of the *Proletarian* over to the State Executive Committee.[9]

Deciding "not to look back in the direction of the Socialist Party but to go forward to the organizing of a new party," a delegation of the Detroit "reds" including Keracher, Batt, Renner, printer John MacGregor, and teacher Oakley C. Johnson then attended the June 21 "National Left Wing Conference" organized by the Left Wing Section, New York.[10] That gathering of various dissident trends desiring a communist party soon fractured. One pole, mainly comprising English-speaking New Yorkers including John Reed, Benjamin Gitlow, and Bertram Wolfe, hoped to capture the Socialist Party's national apparatus at the party's upcoming convention.

The "Michigan group" and representatives of the foreign language federations, already expelled from that same body, pushed for the immediate organization of a Communist Party. They lost that key vote. Leaving the New York meeting, the aspiring communists selected a "National Organizing Committee" comprising of Keracher, Batt, and Oakley C. Johnson from Michigan and D. Elbaum, S. Kopnagel, I. Stilson, and Alexander Stoklitsky for the language federations. With Johnson as its Secretary, that interim National Organizing Committee, repeating the earlier call of the "Michigan group," issued a July call for a "National Convention for the Purpose of Organizing a Communist Party of America," set for Chicago on September 1.[11]

In anticipation of that gathering, the committee sent its representatives, including Dennis Batt, on speaking junkets throughout the Northeast and Midwest in an attempt to mobilize support. Batt temporarily became the coeditor of the trend's agitational organ, *The Communist*, launched in New York on July 19, 1919. He also sat on the committee alongside Louis Fraina, Nicholas Hourwich, Alexander Stoklitsky, and others who drafted the initial "Manifesto of the Communist Party."[12]

The "Michigan group," comprised not only delegates from that state, but also supporters from Buffalo, Rochester, Cleveland, Rockford, and Chicago, was well represented at what became that founding meeting of the Communist Party.[13] A considerable amount has been written about the events in Chicago at the beginning of September 1919. Most of the accounts have focused on the ejection of those hoping to "burrow from within" the Socialist Party, and the impromptu formation of the Communist Labor Party by those not recognized by or thrown out of the Socialist Party who shunned the founding meeting of the Communist Party. Refracted by later events, much of that writing hardly mentioned the role of Batt, Keracher, and company despite their central role in events. Batt with his deep bass voice, already well known in left circles as a "fiery orator," to some "the American Trotsky," gave the opening address to the convention and Al Renner was elected as chairman.[14] Despite their presence, however, the Michigan comrades already had political differences with the mood and political reading prevalent at that gathering.

The majority of leftwingers gathered at Chicago, predominantly immigrant members of the recently expelled Socialist Party language federations and recent movement arrivals encouraged by the pace of events in the United States and Europe, were propelled by a belief in the proximity of a revolutionary situation. After all, the range and scope of working-class militancy at home and abroad, accelerating that spring, from Seattle, Portland, and Butte, to Turin, Berlin, Vienna, and Budapest, suggested to many on the left that the long-anticipated "final contest" was inexorably near; that it was a short matter of time before the "world revolution" would successfully expand outward from its newly won base in the Soviet Union.[15] That reading of the situation, more a hope than a reality, was not shared by the Michigan representatives. Informed by their wartime experience in Detroit and other centers of the industrial heartland, the "Michigan group" differed with those gathered in Chicago primarily over the strategic reading on the nature of the capitalist state and the tactical debate over "political action."

The debate over what was to be done was strongly influenced by the Bolshevik party's success; as Keracher later described it, "The shadow of the Russian Revolution had fallen across America and the majority of the delegates had mistaken the shadow for the real revolutionary substance."[16] Most convention participants ambitiously adhered to the tactical line of "minority action," influenced by the Bolshevik record. Hoping to duplicate that experience by forging a small, disciplined organization in preparation for the seizure of state power, many of the leftwingers present eschewed parliamentary activity as a waste of time in a period rapidly approaching the "final contest."

The Detroit "reds," in opposition, insisted that conditions in the United States were qualitatively different from those in Russia. Supporters of a minority report within the "Committee on Manifesto and Program," dubbed the "Michigan Manifesto," they argued that "in highly developed capitalist countries such as the United States, the social revolution, whatever the circumstances, requires the aroused and intelligent interest of the great mass of the workers."[17] The Bolshevik opportunity and experience was historically specific, perhaps exceptional. Noting "a widespread misconception of the nature of world changes that have lately taken place," and "the recent growth of conflicting and anti-Marxian theories, in which every conceivable tactic, no matter how absurd, finds ample justification," the Michigan Manifesto advocated "revolutionary political action." Stressing the particularity of U.S. conditions, the minority report argued that such action should proceed through "parliamentary channels" and the "use of political democracy" as well as "mass action . . . inspired and guided by planful political action."

Observing that the U.S. working class was ill-prepared for its historic role, the program underlined "constant and intensive education" as "the first and most essential task" of the new party. Quoting Lenin, they emphasized "the necessity of patient, persistent educational work, of spreading understanding, adapted to the practical needs of the masses." The working class, as a class "in itself," would have to be prepared over a long period for that moment when it could enter the world stage as a class "for itself." The strategic response, for the Michigan comrades, lay not in a vanguard enamored with "minority action" and incapable of leading a reluctant mass, but in a long-term commitment to broad working-class political education, tactical parliamentary activity, when and where apropos, and work within the labor movement in order to win the "vast majority" of workers.

Opponents of the "Michigan group" charged that it held too narrow a conception of "political action," defined merely as parliamentary activity. Defining "political action" as the "organized might of the workers directed by industrial groups otherwise against the political supremacy of the capitalist class," the Michiganites argued, in defense, that parliamentary action was "but a phase of political action, but an important one in countries with a form of government like the U.S." Contending that the Communist Party should work "to arouse the workers to a conscious understanding of their class position and the use of revolutionary political action," they posited that the dominant elements at the convention had "reverted consciously or unconsciously to the syndicalist position."[18] The majority trend at the convention, labeling the minority "Michigan Mensheviki," went on to endorse "minority action." Largely noncitizens with a negative impatience for electoral activity and mainly comprising workers shut out by exclusivist craft unionism, the dominant faction also adopted a line antagonistic to the American Federation of Labor (AFL).[19]

In response, after declining nominations to the executive body of the new party, the "Michigan group" submitted a statement to the record of the convention that voiced concerns with the founding document adopted by the Communist Party of America:

We hereby publicly state our disapproval of the manifesto and program adopted by the convention and of the methods used in forcing its adoption. Therefore, we ask to be recorded in the minutes as not voting, either affirmatively or, on the adoption of said manifesto and program, and as not accepting nominations for, or voting on any party official elected by this convention.[20]

Keracher, dismayed by the direction of the convention, left before it ended. The rest of his comrades soon followed.[21] Returning home, the "Michigan group" nevertheless decided to remain within the Communist Party in order to struggle for the adoption of "sound communist program and policy." The October 1919 issue of the *Proletarian* carried a detailed report of the convention on its front page,[22] and Batt soon set off on a speaking tour in an attempt to mobilize support for the new party.[23]

Back in Detroit on October 6, the key figures of the "minority group" (as it now came to be known), in response to a request by the "Marxian Club" of San Francisco for a "statement concerning the formation of a party based upon Marxian principles," met "for the purpose of deciding upon the course to be pursued." They drafted a "tentative program," soliciting the opinions and suggestions of all those considered within their trend. Holding "that the time was not ripe for the launching of a new party," but confident that they would soon be joined by "elements within the ranks of the several parties . . . in existence," the minority trend decided to proceed with the task of "strengthening and unifying" their group and in "organizing and assisting new groups." Addressing the question of the appropriate time for the launching of a new party, they targeted May 1920, as "the ideal moment . . . immediately preceding the national convention of the present parties," as the most opportune date for the launching of a new organization. The Detroit-based group called upon its supporters for donations of time and money in order "to wage a vigorous campaign of agitation and education within the ranks of the existing parties."

Appended to the October document, a "Program of Action," submitted as a "basis for discussion," called for the "strengthening of existing Marxian groups . . . in accord with the position of the Minority Group . . . which favor[s] the formation of a party based upon the principles of scientific socialism" and the "formation of new groups in favorable localities" to be affiliated with the Proletarian University. With Detroit a "central point and clearing house for activities," and the *Proletarian* the official paper, the organization would initiate Proletarian Clubs, based on "common basis of action and uniform rules and regulations." Members would be assessed an initiation fee of $1 for a Proletarian University "Extension Fund." The plan called upon all adherents, in their activity within "existing working class organizations . . . , to criticize any reactionary tendencies of the officials or leaders, [while] endeavoring at all times to reach the membership directly."[24]

Concerned that their opponents might use the document as "a weapon with which to crush groups and classes now in the process of formation," the framers of the circular asked that its contents be kept "strictly confidential." The plan nevertheless apparently soon made its way into the hands of the Communist Party leadership. The newly formed "Central Executive Committee of the Communist Party," without giving any explanation for its actions, issued a directive in late November, reproduced in the Party press in December, instructing its members to disassociate from the Proletarian University, the *Proletarian* press, and the affiliated Proletarian Clubs in various cities. With room for organized factions within the party already constrained, the "Michigan group," ipso facto, thus became the first tendency to be purged from the foundling Communist Party.[25]

The opening rounds in the contest for leadership of U.S. communism had hardly been settled when the national round-up of left-wing militants, the infamous "Palmer Raids," struck. The arrest of some six-thousand radicals at the beginning of January 1920 forced the contentious Communist and Communist Labor Parties underground. A number of the people who would form the Proletarian Party the following June were also, in Keracher's words, "given a taste of American democracy in action." Keracher himself was arrested, held for deportation until early June, and finally released when he persuaded agents of the Labor Department, in charge of immigration and naturalization at the time, that he was not actually a member of the Communist Party and disagreed with its politics. Native born Al Renner was arrested along with eight hundred others when the Feds raided a social gathering at the "House of the Masses" on the night of January 2. He was handed over to state authorities for prosecution under Michigan state antisyndicalist laws. The Feds also raided the offices of the *Proletarian* and the Proletarian University where they seized mailing and membership lists, money, and virtually everything else that was not bolted to the floor. With so many of its members in jail, both the *Proletarian* and the Proletarian University briefly suspended operations.

Stifled by federal harassment and arrests and expelled from the Communist Party, the "minority" or "Michigan group" decided to move ahead. Looking back on that period, Keracher would recall it "was not the best time, nor presented the most favorable circumstances, for forming a new party." The repression, however, in Keracher's estimation, "had eliminated the timid ones who had been frightened away from the movement."[26] Following Keracher's release from jail in early June, the "Michigan group" decided to move forward with the formation of its own communist party. Meeting at Detroit on June 27–28, 1920, representatives of the trend adopted the "Manifesto and Program of the Proletarian Party."[27] That founding Proletarian document clearly demarcated a line. Arguing that "the way out of capitalism lies through revolutionary political action, and that there is no middle course possible in this struggle," the manifesto posited that no organization had appeared "to express the revolutionary requirements of the proletariat," in the United States:

Prior to the success of the working class of Russia, the dominant organization here expressed but the slightest kind of parliamentary opportunism, which found its equally reactionary complement in anti-political industrial unionism. This has recently been followed by a period of revolutionary impatience, marked by efforts to transport bodily the tactics applicable to the European situation into the essentially different conditions now prevailing here.

Due to this lack of understanding of, and indifference to American conditions, much confusion has resulted. Recently the movement has divided into factional warring camps, and is still far from having an understanding of the historical and economic background out of which American capitalism has developed, and consequently lacks a program adaptable thereto.[28]

Recognizing the "truth," observed by Marx and Engels, that "the class struggle takes in each country the form of a National struggle," the new party proclaimed its primary devotion to the class struggle "under the economic, social and political conditions" in the United States. Such conditions, they asserted, necessitated the utilization of "the regime of American political democracy for its organization against capitalism" by nominating candidates for office and by engaging in other forms of parliamentary activity "wherever and whenever" such activity might be used "as a means of reaching the workers with . . . revolutionary propaganda."

Political office would be used as a forum from which to "speak over the heads of the representatives of capitalism to the masses of the working people." Arguing that "the masses" were "still in the grip of ignorance and reaction," and that the "major portion of organized labor is dominated by the most narrow and conservative policies, . . . easily preyed upon by a hierarchy of reactionary leaders . . . openly allied with the corrupt representatives of the exploiting class," the Proletarian Party stated its goal "to cooperate where possible in the everyday struggles" of workers "in order to sharpen their understanding of the class struggle," and "to direct the workers toward the revolutionary act of abolishing the wage system." The Proletarian Party stood opposed to dual unionism.[29]

For a brief period of time the only "public" communist party, the Proletarian Party turned all its energies toward recruitment and political education. As Keracher later recalled, "From the outset, the Proletarian Party realized that it would take time to build a substantial Marxian party, and that it would have to recruit its ranks mainly from new people." For a time the only party carrying on street meetings due to the collapse of the Socialist Party and the clandestinity of the other communist formations, the young organization also circulated the *Proletarian*, conducted lectures and study classes, and worked to expand the Proletarian Clubs, now converted into locals of the Party in a number of cities such as Buffalo, Rochester, Chicago, and Los Angeles.[30]

Proclaiming in its initial "Manifesto and Program" that it had "no interest separate and apart from the proletariat as a whole," and stating that the interests of the U.S. workers were the same as the "entire world proletariat, regardless of sex, government, color, nationality, or country," the party voiced its desire "to establish and maintain relations with the revolutionary groups of all other nations and [to] ally itself directly with the Third International." In agreement with the principles and program of the Communist International and "endorsing unreservedly the conditions for admission to that body," the Proletarian Party sent Dennis Batt to the Third Congress of the Comintern at Moscow in June 1921. Dennis Batt, who had traveled to Moscow as the official envoy of Detroit's Federation of Labor to the "Red" Trade Union International, attended the Congress merely as an observer. The Comintern by that time had already recognized the Communist Party and the Proletarian Party's application as the U.S. affiliate was denied.

The outcast party soon described the Comintern's failure to recognize it as the result of "gross misrepresentations that have been made from time to time . . . by people suffering from such an acute form of 'infantile sickness of leftism' that a correct tactical position appeared to them to be centrist." Agreeing in principle that recognition by the International of but one party was "tactically correct," the Proletarian Party nevertheless resolved "to continue its work of organizing and teaching the principles of Communism." It vowed to "welcome the time when there will be but one revolutionary mass party in the United States."[31]

The Proletarian Party continued. Concerned with building a viable organization of informed cadre well versed in "scientific socialism," Keracher and his comrades, centered in Chicago after the early 1920s, soon became involved in the business of Charles H. Kerr & Company, the oldest ongoing radical publishing house in the United States. Major shareholders in the Kerr venture after 1924, the party with Keracher in the lead took up the reins of the book and pamphlet venture upon founder Kerr's retirement in 1928. The firm soon became a vital asset for the young party and a significant venue for pamphlets by Keracher and other Proletarian pamphleteers.[32]

Much of the latter history of the Proletarian Party awaits its historian. The party experienced a period of marked growth, as did other organizations of the left, in the 1930s. It eventually opened offices in an estimated thirty-eight cities from New York to San Francisco. Never having more than several thousand members, the party's organizers played a significant, though as of yet unheralded role in the sitdowns and early struggles of what became the Congress of Industrial Organizations (CIO) in Detroit and other cities. Considering its relative size, it provided the United Auto Workers a disproportionately large number of its ablest organizers—figures like Emil Mazey and Frank Marquart. A number of its onetime cadre went on to occupy significant leadership roles in several unions: Al Renner of the Restaurant Workers, Carl Berreiter of the International Typographical Union, Samuel Meyers of the Retail Clerks. The party, at various moments, experienced defections to the Communist Party. The largest opposition group to the Communist Party for some fifteen years, it also carried out its own occasional expulsions. Dennis Batt, for instance, after moving rightward in the mid-1920s, met that fate. Onetime member, Marxist theorist Paul Mattick, also was expelled. John Keracher remained at the helm of the organization until his retirement in 1953. He died in 1958. The Proletarian Party passed out of existence in 1971 when the last of its remaining members capable of running the Chicago office, activist Al Wysocki, died. Clearly, the history of this remarkable group—that which is known up to this time—suggests that there is a great deal more to be plumbed from the seemingly exhausted annals of communist historiography in the United States.[33]

NOTES

1. Most of the secondary sources consulted for this paper and for a broader extended study of the Left, while certainly informative, are tainted by the peculiarities of ideological and political agendas forged by later developments. All of the standard texts, while valuable, should be consulted with care. They include: Theodore Draper, *The Roots of American Communism* (New York, 1957/1966); Draper, *American Communism and Soviet Russia* (New York, 1960/1980); James Weinstein, *The Decline of Socialism in America 1912–1925* (New York, 1967); Philip S. Foner, *History of the Labor Movement in the United States*, vol. 8: *Postwar Struggles* (New York, 1988); David Shannon, *The Socialist Party of America, A History* (Chicago, IL, 1967); James P. Cannon, *The First Ten Years of American Communism* (New York, 1973).

2. All of the above standard texts mention the Proletarian Party or its forerunner, the left wing of the Michigan Socialist Party, commonly referred to as the "Michigan group." None of them gives any detailed or entirely accurate description of the formation's development and political perspective. More recently, the biographer of labor activist and lawyer for the United Auto Workers Maurice Sugar gave some attention to Proletarian activities in Detroit. See Christopher H. Johnson, *Maurice Sugar—Law, Labor and the Left in Detroit, 1912–1950* (Detroit, MI, 1988).

A number of other works dealing with the history of the U.S. left and the labor movement make some scant references to the Proletarians. See Ronald Edsforth, *Class Conflict and Cultural Consensus—The Making of a Mass Consumer*

Society in Flint, Michigan (New Brunswick, NJ, 1987), 146; Bert Cochran, *Labor and Communism: The Conflict that Shaped American Unions* (Princeton, NJ, 1977), 64, 119; Roger Keeran, *The Communist Party and the Auto Workers' Unions* (Bloomington, IN, 1980), 32, 90.

3. Oakley C. Johnson, "The Early Socialist Party of Michigan: An Assignment in Autobiography," *Centennial Review* 2 (1966): 147–162; "John Keracher," *Proletarian News* (March 1958). For Dennis Batt, see The National Archives, Washington, D.C., Record Group 65: Records of the Federal Bureau of Investigation, Investigative Case Files of the Bureau of Investigation, 1908–1922, (Henceforward, RG 65), Microfilm Reel 936, Item #202600-1362: "International Council of Trade and Labor Unions ("Red" Labor Union International) and Delegates to World Conference Moscow, Russia, May 1921"; and RG 65, Reel 940, Item #202600-1778–45x, dated 20 July 1921: "The Proletarian Party of America."

4. Oakley C. Johnson, 156.

5. Oakley C. Johnson, 156.

6. John Keracher, "Theory and Practice," *Proletarian* 11:5 (May 1928): 20; Keracher, "Ten Years of American Communism," *Proletarian* 12:9 (September 1929).

7. Oakley C. Johnson, 156; Shannon, 137–138.

8. The general narrative for events surrounding the in-house Socialist Party imbroglio and the subsequent fracturing of the Debsian party is drawn from readings of Draper, Foner, and Weinstein, as cited above. Informative as well is Robert A. Rosenstone, *Romantic Revolutionary—A Biography of John Reed* (New York, 1981).

9. *Proletarian* (July 1919): 14–15.

10. Keracher, "Ten Years of American Communism"; Oakley C. Johnson, 155; Foner; Draper, 165–167; Weinstein, 196–197. A similar call for a September 1 meeting had been issued on 31 May by the Left Wing Section, New York.

11. "Call for a National Convention for the Purpose of Organizing a Communist Party of America," in the National Archives, Washington, D.C., Record Group 28, Records of the Post Office Department, Documents Seized under Enforcement of the Espionage and Sedition Acts, 1917–1920 (henceforward RG 28) Box 14, Item #607; Oakley C. Johnson, 155; Foner, 243–245.

12. "The Proletarian Party of America" (typescript, dated 20 July 1921) in: *Military Intelligence Surveillance Collection* [microfilm: National Archives, Washington, D.C.] Reel 18, Items #620-532; "Call for a National Convention for the Purpose of Organizing a Communist Party of America."

13. "Communist Party Convention," *Proletarian* 2:6 (October 1919): 1.

14. "Communist Party Convention"; Oakley C. Johnson, 156–157.

15. Rosenstone, 341–343.

16. Keracher, "Ten Years . . . ," 4.

17. "Manifesto and Program—Minority Report of the Committee on Manifesto and Program at the Communist Party Convention," *Proletarian* 2:6 (October 1919): 13–16; Keracher, "Ten Years. . . ."

18. "Manifesto and Program"; *Proletarian* 2:6 (October 1919).

19. Dennis Batt, "Minority Action," *Proletarian* 2:7 (November 1919).

20. "Communist Party Convention"; Keracher, "Ten Years. . . ."

21. Dennis Batt remained behind, however. On the basis of notes taken by a federal agent, during his opening address to the convention, Batt was arrested September 3 by Illinois authorities and charged with violation of state sedition laws. Briefly held in Cook County Jail and subsequently released under a hefty bond, he was trailed by federal agents and informers well into 1920. See, for example, "Report of Agent E. J. Wheeler, 11/1/19, 'Meeting of Communist Party of America,' Erie, Penn'a, October 26, 1919," RG 65, Reel 832, Item #OG 379614.

22. *Proletarian* 2:6 (October 1919).

23. "International Mass Meeting: Newark, N.J., August 6, 1919." Report by Agent "K-40," RG 65, Item 253398; report of Agent A. H. Loula, dated 11 October 1919: "Weekly Review of Radical Activities" cited Batt as active organizing among "renegade Americans" in Chicago (RG 65, Reel 940, Item #202600-1778–x).

24. A copy of this communique was seized in a raid on the Buffalo Proletarian Club during the Palmer Raids. It later turned up in a report on the Proletarian Party from the Buffalo regional office of the Bureau of Investigation, dated 17 July 1920. RG 65, Reel 850, Item #OG 391626.

25. *The Communist* 1:11 (13 December 1919): 6.

26. Report of Agent Roy C. McHenry, dated 4 February 1920: "Proletarian University of America, 174 Michigan Ave., Detroit, Communist Activities," RG 65, Reel 386, Item #OG 38115; John Keracher, "Thirty-Five Years of the Proletarian Party," *Proletarian News* 24:7 (July 1955), in Box 36, the Charles Kerr Collection, Newberry Library, Chicago. For one account of the Palmer raid assault on the Proletarian Party, see: Dennis Batt, "A Year Gone By," *Proletarian* 2:9–10 (January–February 1920). For a general discussion of the Red Scare in Detroit, see: Christopher Johnson, *Maurice Sugar*, 92–94. Johnson, not necessarily sympathetic to the Detroit "reds," states that "The Proletarians suffered most severely from the Palmer raids."

27. "Manifesto and Program," *Proletarian* 3:1 (October 1920); " 'Communist Activities in the United States and Abroad.' Report of Agent J. S. Apelman, week ending October 2, 1920"; RG 65, Reel 661, Item # 248775.

28. "Manifesto and Program."

29. "Manifesto and Program."

30. Keracher, "Thirty-Five Years of the Proletarian Party"; Keracher, "Ten Years. . . ."

31. "Manifesto and Program of the Proletarian Party," *Proletarian* 3:11 (December 1921): 6; "International Council of Trade and Labor Unions ("Red" Labor Union International) and Delegates to World Conference Moscow, Russia, May 1921."

32. For the history of the Kerr publishing venture, see: Allen Ruff, "We Called Each Other Comrade!" Charles H. Kerr and the Charles H. Kerr &

Company, Radical Publishers, 1886–1928," Ph.D. diss., University of Wisconsin, 1987.

33. Al Wysocki, "John Keracher, His Life and Work," *Proletarian News* (March 1958); Committee on Un-American Activities, House of Representatives, Eighty-Fifth Congress, Second Session, August 1953, *Organized Communism in the United States* (Washington, D.C., 1953/rev.1958); Franklin Rosemont, "Proletarian Party," in Mari Jo Buhle, Paul Buhle, and Dan Georgakas, *The Encyclopedia of the American Left* (New York, 1990); "Rough Notes on Life and Funeral of Al Wysocki, August 19, 1971 by Virgil Vogel," typescript manuscript in possession of Franklin Rosemont.

Part 2   Women in Labor History

4   A "Society of Outsiders": Union W.A.G.E., Working-Class Feminism, and the Labor Movement

Rochelle Gatlin

"We can best help you," Virginia Woolf wrote in 1938, "not by repeating your words and following your methods but by finding new words and creating new methods. We can best help you . . . not by joining your society but by remaining outside your society but in cooperation with its aim. That aim is the same for us both." Although Woolf was not writing about working-class people or their struggles, her view that women should constitute themselves a "Society of Outsiders"[1] closely resembles the position taken by Union Women's Alliance to Gain Equality (Union W.A.G.E.), as it simultaneously attacked sexism in labor unions and workplaces and tried to make the concerns of working-class women more visible and central to the women's movement.

Founded in March 1971, Union W.A.G.E. was an organization of mainly white, working-class women headquartered in the San Francisco Bay Area. Until its demise in 1982, it made repeated efforts to become a national organization, but never grew beyond ten, generally short-lived, chapters. Dues-paying members numbered approximately 350 in late 1979, although the membership may have been as high as 900 a few years earlier. An additional 650–700 nonmembers, half of them outside California, subscribed to the organization's bimonthly newspaper, also called *Union W.A.G.E.*[2]

This chapter focuses on why the women of Union W.A.G.E. chose to be "outsiders" and how they defined this position in practice. Their achievements and limitations may suggest theoretical and organizational possibilities, as well as pitfalls, for working-class women inside and outside the labor movement.

As workers and women, Union W.A.G.E. members had to adopt a double identity and political perspective that addressed issues of their class as well as their gender. They could not embrace either "pure and simple" trade unionism or "pure and simple" feminism. The historic opposition between class and gender movements in this country, especially the subordinate and peripheral position of women workers in trade union organizations, has been well documented. Nancy Schrom Dye, for example, has traced the uneasy and ultimately unsuccessful relationship that existed between the Women's Trade Union League (WTUL) and the American Federation of Labor (AFL) during the first two decades of this century. More recently, Ruth Milkman has analyzed the difficulties women experienced within the more militant Congress of Industrial Organizations (CIO) during the Depression and World War II years. While the primary obstacle to class solidarity has been job segregation by sex, less permanent factors such as the exclusionary policies of AFL unions or the relative absence of feminist consciousness and organizations in the 1930s and 1940s have made it difficult for working-class women, in Dye's words, "to synthesize feminism with unionism."[3] In the early 1970s, working women, reflecting their growing numbers in the labor force and the re-birth of feminism, again tried to effect this synthesis. Their most enduring organizational accomplishments have been the Coalition of Labor Union Women (CLUW), founded in 1974, and 9 to 5, an organization of women clerical workers begun in 1973, which created an autonomous district within the Service Employees' International Union (SEIU) in 1981. Union W.A.G.E., on the other hand, did not survive the 1980s, in part because it took a more radical stance on gender and class issues.

Started by experienced trade union women with backgrounds in the "Old Left," Union W.A.G.E. developed into an imperfect partnership between older women who wanted to revitalize and democratize the labor movement, and radical, somewhat younger women, whose political consciousness had been formed mainly through their involvement in, or as an outgrowth of, the 1960s civil rights and women's movements. The founders had not only experienced sex discrimination in their trade unions, but also, as one of them put it, were "burnt out by male chauvinism in the socialist movement,"[4] especially elements of the Communist Party and the Socialist Workers' Party. Anne Draper, Jean Maddox, and Joyce Maupin, three of W.A.G.E.'s founders and early leaders, were all born before 1920. Maupin, the only one to remain alive and active in the organization during its entire eleven years, had spent two decades in the Socialist Workers' Party before resigning in 1962. She was extremely distrustful of leftist sectarianism, and in organizing women she criticized "the attitude that you have to convert them to a complete change, to world socialism, before you can organize a union. . . . The whole idea of Union

WAGE is to approach the job issues. These are the immediate issues that are affecting women in their daily lives."[5]

Although W.A.G.E. considered itself anticapitalist, it included women from a fairly wide political spectrum. Unlike socialist-feminist unions in the early and mid-1970s, W.A.G.E. did not try to build a bridge between the Left (whether "Old" or "New") and the women's movement.[6] Rather, it viewed itself as an organization that would infuse class consciousness into the women's movement and feminism into the labor movement, joining and radicalizing both of them.

In retrospect, W.A.G.E. appears to have acted more as a goad, or even a thorn, to both the labor and women's movements than as a bridge between them. According to Maupin, W.A.G.E.'s difficulties with trade unions and with CLUW were not caused by the organization's leftism:

I think the main reason was that they thought we were too critical of the labor bureaucracy. And that was very important. That was the reason we wanted to stay out—so that we could be critical. . . . We had an idea of being an upsetting organization and the feeling that that was necessary in order to get anything started.[7]

W.A.G.E. supported a wide range of women's issues and broadened its membership to include nonunionized and unpaid workers. Yet, its primary purpose was to improve job conditions for working-class women. The organization supported efforts to organize the unorganized and encouraged rank-and-file caucuses within existing unions. Maupin, along with Draper and Maddox, was steadfastly committed to the ideal of a revitalized and radicalized labor movement. "It's a matter of mutual need," Maupin wrote in 1979:

If the union movement is to survive and grow and again become a force for social change, it needs women. Women coming into the labor movement will do more than fight for their own rights. Together with minorities, they are two-thirds of the labor force. In alliance they can turn the unions around and build rank and file control.[8]

Whether working-class feminists should remain primarily committed to the labor movement became a central controversy within Union W.A.G.E. The discouragement of male participation, on the other hand, did not lead to any major organizational conflict. Men could join W.A.G.E. but only as "associate," non-voting members. Fewer than a dozen chose to do so. The reason for this two-tiered membership policy, Maupin explained, "was not so much being anti-male, but if you get men in a relatively small group like this, they have this tendency to dominate it."9

W.A.G.E.'s eleven-year history can be divided into three periods. Until 1974, it was mainly a women's organization with a trade unionist perspective, although it also devoted considerable energy on behalf of unorganized workers. The founding of CLUW in 1974 led to a split within W.A.G.E followed by a second period of growth and flexibility. W.A.G.E. incorporated new members and ideas from the women's movement and developed a greater interest in women's issues not directly related to the workplace or to paid work. However, one of the consequences of this broader focus and outreach was a devastating organizational conflict in 1979, during which Pam Allen, the newspaper editor, was fired, and a majority of the Executive Board decided that W.A.G.E. should again be primarily committed to working women, workplace issues, and democratic trade unionism, rather than to all issues affecting women.

In its early years, W.A.G.E. advocated what it called a "labor" Equal Rights Amendment (E.R.A.) in order to maintain and extend protective labor legislation. This put the organization at odds not only with the National Organization for Women (NOW), but also, to a lesser extent, with the United Auto Workers (UAW) and the AFL-CIO, which had endorsed the "pure" E.R.A. in 1970 and 1973 respectively. W.A.G.E.'s very first activity was to picket an Industrial Welfare Commission (IWC) hearing in San Francisco on March 30, 1971, and demand that California's protective legislation be extended to cover men and household workers. In late 1972, after the Bank of America took advantage of California's ratification of the E.R.A. to stop paying taxi fares for its women night employees, Union W.A.G.E. formed the Coalition for Equal Rights with Yellow Cab Drivers in Teamsters Local 265 and the Bank Employees Data Processing Association (BEDPA), an independent group organizing Bank of America workers. The Coalition, joined by women's groups and members of unions heavily represented in W.A.G.E., such as the Amalgamated Clothing Workers (ACW), Office and Professional Employees (OPEIU), and SEIU, held demonstrations in December 1972 and January 1973 in order to publicize the issue and pressure the Bank of America to restore the paid taxi service and extend it to male employees. W.A.G.E. also pursued a broader campaign to get state legislation passed that would allow the IWC to set health and safety standards for men as well as women. In 1976, California became the first industrial state to include both sexes under its minimum wage, overtime pay after eight hours, rest periods, and other protective legislation.

Although W.A.G.E. continued to lobby the IWC and monitor its activities, it also believed, especially in the early years, that unions offered workers the best protection. In its leaflet to the bank employees, W.A.G.E. stated:

The best way to safeguard these working conditions covered by protective laws is by having a union contract and seeing that it's enforced. Rather than relying simply on legislation, unorganized workers, such as the women at the Bank of America, should organize into Unions to gain some control over their working conditions.[10]

At the same time that W.A.G.E. was trying to increase union membership, it criticized middle-class organizations, especially NOW. "The middle class women's movement," wrote Maupin in 1974, "generally sees the problem of working women in terms of the advancement and promotion of individuals. . . . The goal of Union WAGE is to change the lives of all file clerks, factory workers, farm workers, and waitresses by improving wages and job conditions for all women."[11] This emphasis on collective, rather than individual, advancement remained Union W.A.G.E.'s basic and operational definition of working-class feminism.

Another example of class-conscious feminism was W.A.G.E.'s position on reproductive rights. After Maupin attended a conference of the Women's National Abortion Action Coalition in November 1971, she urged that in addition to repealing laws, "the demand for *free* abortion should be part of the public campaign of the abortion coalition."[12] W.A.G.E. officially added free abortion and contraceptives and no forced sterilization to its goals after a constitutional convention held in November 1974.

The revised constitution also allowed for local chapters, as W.A.G.E. dedicated itself "to building an organization which will properly represent working women on a national level."[13] It did not see the newly formed Coalition of Labor Union Women as capable of becoming that organization, because it excluded the majority of women workers.

The founding of CLUW in March 1974 marks the beginning of W.A.G.E.'s second stage, characterized by greater independence from and criticism of the trade union "establishment," including CLUW, as well as more interest in women's issues not directly related to the workplace.

Ironically, W.A.G.E. played an indirect role in the creation of CLUW by being largely responsible for a women's conference convened in May 1973 by the California State Federation of Labor. One of the resolutions adopted at that meeting called for a national trade union women's conference to be held the following year. As Philip Foner points out, by the spring of 1973, "the issue was not so much whether women workers would unite on a national scale . . . as who would take the initiative and assume the leadership of such an organization." As it turned out, CLUW's founding convention, held in Chicago on March 22–24, 1974, was planned by neither W.A.G.E. nor the California Federation of Labor, but rather by a group of top women officials from several AFL-CIO unions and the UAW, most notably Olga Madar.[14]

Eighteen W.A.G.E. members from northern California attended the Chicago meeting. Although initial W.A.G.E. reports were generally positive, both Maupin and Kay Eisenhower were critical of CLUW's exclusion of unorganized and unemployed women.[15] In her 1974 booklet, *Working Women and Their Organizations—150 Years of Struggle,* Maupin described CLUW as an "organization planned by bureaucrats" and "dominated by trade union leadership rather than the rank and file."[16] Five years later, W.A.G.E. President Jan Arnold claimed that W.A.G.E. members had a class-conscious perspective the mainstream labor movement lacked. "We are not loyal to union bureaucracy, but to the ideals of unionism, and only to those leaders who advance those ideals of struggle and solidarity." Unlike middle-class feminist groups or CLUW, W.A.G.E. has "spent very little energy trying to help a few women get promoted to interesting and well-paid managerial jobs."[17]

Although W.A.G.E. leaders had a tendency to exaggerate CLUW's emphasis on leadership training over its other, equally important goals— organizing unorganized women, affirmative action in the workplace, and political action and legislation—CLUW has been constrained by its decision to remain what Milkman calls "an insiders' organization," isolated from most of the nation's women workers. According to Milkman, the development of CLUW into "something more than a loyal opposition of women officials within organized labor" depends on the growth of rank-and-file activism and a revitalized labor movement.[18]

As an "outsiders' organization," W.A.G.E. attempted to revitalize the labor movement by supporting rank-and-file activities within existing unions and by encouraging unorganized women to form independent unions. Diane Balser, in *Sisterhood and Solidarity*, claims that W.A.G.E.'s "feminism became increasingly associated with independent organization."[19] Actually, W.A.G.E. never resolved the issue of favoring independent over established unions. Rather, in Maupin's words, "After years of debating and infighting, we decided you do the best you can with the situation that you're in."[20]

W.A.G.E.'s first commitment to an independent union resulted in a rather embarrassing situation for the organization, as well as considerable personal anguish for Maupin. During the spring and summer of 1975, *Union W.A.G.E.* had given front-page coverage to a struggle within SEIU, Local 400, involving two W.A.G.E. members, Maxine Jenkins and Louise Statzer. When Jenkins and Statzer formed an independent Union of City Employees (UCE), W.A.G.E. ardently supported them. However, after UCE quickly voted to affiliate with the Laborers' Union, the W.A.G.E. Executive Board issued a statement accusing Jenkins and Statzer of betraying women clerical workers and injuring the San Francisco women's movement. The Board's statement described the Laborers' Union as an organization with "a grim record of violence and corruption, male chauvinism and racism." By joining the Laborers, Jenkins and Statzer had "sold out not only the sisters who followed and aided them but any kind of principled position in either the labor movement or movement for women's liberation." The Board then admitted that it, too, was "due for some criticism" for its former support of Jenkins and Statzer. "We feel that some of us became enthusiastic without sufficient investigation of the facts of the struggle within the Local 400 caucus, and whether the new union was set up in the democratic fashion which its founders claimed."[21] Maupin had not only admired Jenkins's talents as an organizer, but also was "personally very fond of her." Nevertheless, she approved of the Board's action. "Union W.A.G.E.," she told me, "was a very principled group, no matter who it was."[22]

Other activities around the same time were less wrenching. Maupin, along with Maddox, Allen, and Eisenhower, wrote feature articles for the newspaper (later issued as a pamphlet) instructing clerical workers on how to organize a union and incorporate child care, maternity benefits, parental leaves, affirmative action, the elimination of forced overtime, and measures to combat sexual harassment into their union contracts.[23] W.A.G.E. joined with NOW, CLUW, and Black Women Organized for Action in the fall of 1974 to defeat Proposition L, an antiunion and antifeminist measure on the San Francisco city ballot. It also held a conference for clerical workers who were members of the American Federation of State, County, and Municipal Employees (AFSCME) locals in Alameda, Contra Costa, and Santa Clara counties, and considered "such inter-union meetings a valuable contribution toward reducing the fragmentation of the American labor movement."[24]

W.A.G.E.'s most successful activity in 1975 was the West Coast Conference for Working Women, cosponsored with the San Francisco and Berkeley-Oakland Women's Unions, two socialist-feminist organizations.

Maupin told the five hundred women attending the two-day meeting in November that their primary purpose was "to develop class-conscious trade unionism among women workers." Since the established union leadership had failed to do so, and was, moreover, racist and sexist, independent organizing should be given serious attention.[25]

W.A.G.E. subsequently became a major resource and support group for independent organizing, as well as rank-and-file activity. Although it continued to think of itself as a "liaison organization" between women and trade unions, W.A.G.E.'s criticism of "labor bureaucrats" kept it somewhat isolated from most of the existing unions and their leadership.

Its role in the 1980 San Francisco hotel workers' strike provides one of the clearest illustrations of W.A.G.E.'s "outsider" status. Prior to that strike, W.A.G.E. had entered its third and last phase as an organization. In late 1978, a serious conflict erupted between Allen, the newspaper editor, and the majority of the Executive Board. While it centered around the expanded coverage Allen had been giving to such issues as reproduction and women in prison, it actually involved much larger questions about the organization's purpose and direction, including the relationship of the newspaper to other W.A.G.E. activities.[26]

One of the central issues was "personal politics," or how much emphasis W.A.G.E. should give to women's sexuality and family relationships, compared to their economic and workplace struggles. In November 1979, the members voted against an antipornography proposal because many of them did not see a clear connection between pornography and the problems of working women. At the same time, they approved making "an end to sexual harassment in the workplace and in society" one of the organization's goals.[27]

Another, more important argument was over W.A.G.E.'s commitment to trade unionism. On this issue, Allen was somewhat insensitive, or as Diane Balser puts it, "Allen's arguments could have been interpreted as coinciding with the general anti-union sentiment held by some branches of feminism and by society as a whole."[28] For example, in late 1978, Allen stated that the only reason W.A.G.E. members "should try to work to change their unions" is because they "can learn from those struggles, not because I think the unions can be changed." Maupin felt it necessary to remind Allen that "workers don't get into union struggles for the experience but to win something."[29]

The controversy with and subsequent departure of Allen and her supporters left W.A.G.E. considerably smaller and weaker. The organization decided that its energies would be directed more toward workplace issues, and that one of its primary activities would be "encouraging the organization of working women into unions and caucuses."[30] In practice, however, this did not lead to closer or more harmonious relationships with trade unions. W.A.G.E. still preferred to work outside the union structure and did not hesitate to criticize labor leaders, including those heading San Francisco's largest union, Hotel and Restaurant Employees and Bartenders, Local 2.

W.A.G.E.'s interest in the city's hotel workers preceded the 1980 strike and centered around issues of workplace safety, especially sexual harassment and assault. A room-service waitress at the St. Francis Hotel was raped in October 1979. Because there had been previous assaults at the hotel, the women workers had already formed a safety committee. Along with representatives of Local 2, they filed a grievance charging that the hotel was negligent in providing safe working conditions. The waitress had also taken her case to several feminist groups, among them Union W.A.G.E. When the St. Francis management refused to respond to the grievance, W.A.G.E. sponsored a demonstration in which over twenty women's organizations picketed the downtown hotel in support of the workers' demands for two-way radios, self-defense classes, emergency phones in the employee locker rooms, and "the right of female employees to wear pants" instead of the required miniskirts.[31]

Although the hotel agreed to set up a joint health and safety committee, it did not consult with the workers on decisions regarding their safety. The management provided women employees with whistles, sponsored classes in self-defense, and installed alarms in their locker rooms, but claimed that it would be too expensive to equip individual workers with radio alarms.[32]

After a woman guest was raped in her room at the St. Francis on May 6, 1980, the resident manager told reporters that the assault was not important. The St. Francis safety committee responded by calling a press conference at which Local 2's president Charles Lamb appeared together with Union W.A.G.E., Women Organized for Employment, and San Francisco Women Against Rape. The workers, apparently with Lamb's support, submitted a strong health and safety proposal for the forthcoming hotel negotiations. Al Richmond notes that "the same proposals presented to the St. Francis management now became demands for incorporation in a contract to cover all the hotels."[33]

Although it appears that these safety demands were not fully met,[34] it is clear that they were initially raised and fully supported not by the union leadership, but by the rank-and-file with assistance from W.A.G.E. and other "outside" feminist groups.

By mid-July, over six thousand hotel employees at thirty-six hotels were on strike. Three-fourths of the workers were women and about two-thirds were from racial/ethnic groups, especially Asians, Latinos, and African Americans. It was a strike, in Richmond's words, "distinguished by an unusual degree of rank-and-file vitality and militancy."[35] W.A.G.E. member Karen Guma reported that demonstrators on July 22 included strikers and supporters who "showed up at the Hyatt with whistles, tin cans, two garbage cans to bang on, and a set of snare drums." The police "had to drag 46 people off to jail." A court injunction was then handed down "that all but made sneezing on the picket line illegal." It was violated by another march held a few days later.[36]

Guma's article applauded the activities of the rank-and-file, but criticized Lamb and the undemocratic manner in which the contract negotiations were conducted. Maupin also recalled how W.A.G.E. supported Local 2's rank-and-file, while eluding, even rebuffing, its leaders.

We ran a party to support the hotel workers' strike and it was very successful financially. And we called the union and invited everybody to come. And Lamb got very mad; he hadn't been invited. I said, "Brother Lamb, you're always welcome at our parties; you don't need an engraved invitation." And then he wanted to know why we hadn't turned the money over to the union. I said, "No, it wasn't for the union; it was a relief fund, and we had asked the picket captains on the lines who needed relief. Most of it went over to their choice." (For obvious reasons we didn't trust the union.) But he was mad; he was just furious. That's an example of our difficult relationships with unions.[37]

The majority of W.A.G.E. members, especially the "active core," were union members—Maupin estimates that thirty to forty different unions were represented in W.A.G.E.—and these women continually raised such issues as child care and parental leave within their locals.[38] But, unlike CLUW, W.A.G.E. neither sought nor obtained acceptance as a "legitimate" labor organization, nor did it receive financial support from AFL-CIO sources. The loss of members after the 1979 controversy intensified W.A.G.E.'s financial difficulties, and, combined with the inauspicious economic and political climate of the early 1980s, led to its demise in 1982.

As an organization, W.A.G.E. insisted right up to the end that working-class women needed to maintain a double perspective about the labor movement. On the one hand, they must continue to criticize labor unions for not addressing "feminist issues." "The concerns of women workers reach far beyond the workplace, and are not strictly limited to wages and hours. . . . Union officials will have to be more creative, and more committed to women workers." On the other hand, W.A.G.E. insisted that it "has neither lost its commitment to unionizing women workers, nor . . . decided that there are better ways for women to gain some control and dignity in the workplace."[39] While it chose to operate as an independent, community-based organization, W.A.G.E.'s commitment to union democracy and women's issues has been taken up, to some extent, by caucuses and organizations within the labor movement, most notably CLUW.

Although limited by its dependence on the AFL-CIO and restricted to union women, CLUW continues to play an important role in making women's issues part of the labor agenda. For example, its "Family Bill of Rights" passed at the 1988 Convention, calls for comprehensive health care, affordable housing, economic security, child and elder care, and the "right to equal pay for work of equal value." CLUW also opposes drug testing of employees and discrimination against people with AIDS.[40] Its positions on international issues have been more progressive than those of the AFL-CIO leadership. In 1984, CLUW supported disarmament and the nuclear freeze, called for the transfer of public funds from the military budget to social programs, and opposed U.S. intervention in Central America and military aid to El Salvador.[41] More recently, it has objected to the State Department's denial of visas to trade unionists on political grounds and resolved to support programs to deter plant closures and runaway shops.[42]

Unlike W.A.G.E., which never succeeded in becoming a multiracial organization, a sizeable proportion of CLUW members and leaders have always been women of color. According to Marjorie Stern, a founder with previous experience in the civil rights movement, CLUW may have "consciously fostered minority interests . . . because there are large contingents of women workers out there, both within and without the unions, who are not white, and the tendency is for minority groups to grow in size in the workplace." The result has been an organization in which Stern claims, "We all feel very comfortable—the whites and Blacks, the Chinese and the Hispanics—we are all really like sisters."[43]

The existence of this multiracial women's organization with close ties to the AFL-CIO has contributed to, as well as reflected, the increasing proportion of trade union members who are women. In 1956, women comprised only 18.6 percent of all union members; by 1978, they had risen to 24 percent, and in 1984 women were 33.7 percent of the union membership, the highest proportion ever. In fact, since the 1970s, women have been responsible for almost all the growth in labor organizations.[44]

Because the survival of the labor movement depends on its ability to organize white-collar and service workers, the majority of whom are women, it is not surprising that labor leaders no longer support the notion that women, especially married women, should be denied employment opportunities as long as men are unemployed. What Milkman calls the "feminization of the labor movement" at least guarantees "that the unions will defend women's rights to employment."[45] However, this acceptance of women as workers and union members, as well as increasing support for pay equity, parental leave, and child care, must be set against the overall decline in the strength of organized labor. In 1988, union membership had fallen to 16.8 percent of the nonagricultural workforce, down from 32.5 percent in 1953, and the lowest level since the 1930s.[46]

Since it is unlikely that the majority of working women and men are going to join trade unions in the near future, community-based organizations on the W.A.G.E. model, concerned with economic security, health, housing, reproductive rights, and environmental issues, may be more effective vehicles than labor unions alone for mobilizing working-class people.

One promising sign that U.S. unions, at least on the local level, are overcoming their isolation from the working-class majority is the recent growth of grassroots coalitions involving local union activists, community residents, and environmental, peace, and consumer groups. Also encouraging are new organizing strategies to reach the increasing number of workers who hold low-wage, less secure jobs in service industries. For example, 9 to 5 emphasizes that introducing women to the value of organizing, developing their will to organize, and providing them with an opportunity to become allied with the labor movement, even if there is no union at the workplace, must precede traditional union organizing methods. The goal of 9 to 5, according to field organizer Cindia Cameron, "is to build collective identity rather than collective bargaining units,"[47] and this author would agree that the need for a revitalized labor movement should take precedence over questions of organizational jurisdiction or even longevity. As Maupin put it in 1978, "What you want to do is build the struggle of working women and when you see the organization as a substitute for it, or as an equivalent, it's wrong."[48]

Women workers have already brought gender and family issues into their workplaces and unions; hopefully, they will also take the lead in extending the labor movement to working-class people "outside" the union halls.

NOTES

1. Virginia Woolf, *Three Guineas* (New York, 1938 and 1966), 143, 113.
2. These figures are based on the proposed 1980 budget submitted in October 1979. Labor Archives and Research Center, San Francisco State University, Union W.A.G.E. Collection (hereafter, LARC, SFSU-WAGE),

Financial reports, 1974–80, Box 12, Folder 12. In early 1979, there were 800 individual members and subscribers. "Readers Survey," *Union W.A.G.E.* 51 (January–February 1979): 15, LARC, SFSU-WAGE. Joyce Maupin recalled that the number of newspaper subscribers had been as high as 1700–1800. Executive Board Minutes, 19 July 1981, LARC, SFSU-WAGE, Box 2, Folder 3. I wish to thank Lynn Bonfield, director, and Leon Sompolinsky, Gordon Webb, and Suzanne Forsyth, present and former archival assistants, Labor Archives and Research Center, San Francisco State University, for their help and encouragement.

3. Nancy Schrom Dye, *As Equals and as Sisters: Feminism, the Labor Movement, and the Women's Trade Union League of New York* (Columbia, MO, and London, 1980), 4; Ruth Milkman, *Gender at Work: The Dynamics of Job Segregation by Sex during World War II* (Urbana and Chicago, IL, 1987).

4. Joan Jordan, handwritten notes, 24 October 1980, p. 2 of 2, LARC, SFSU-WAGE, Box 3, Folder 11.

5. Transcript of Oral History with Joyce Maupin, Union WAGE, by Patricia Yeghissian, The Twentieth Century Trade Union Woman: Vehicle for Social Change Oral History Project. Program on Women and Work, Institute of Labor and Industrial Relations (Ann Arbor, MI, 1980), 115, LARC SFSU-Maupin Joyce Papers, 1980, Access #1987/5. The oral history was conducted on 16 July 1978, and will hereafter be referred to as Maupin, Oral History, 16 July 1978.

6. See Karen V. Hansen, "The Women's Unions and the Search for a Political Identity," *Socialist Review* 16:2 (March–April 1986): 66–95.

7. Author's interview with Joyce Maupin, Oakland, California, 3 October 1988. On the other hand, Marjorie Stern, of the American Federation of Teachers, believes that W.A.G.E.'s leftism may have been responsible for its rejection by the San Francisco Labor Council. W.A.G.E. cofounder Anne Draper, who represented the Amalgamated Clothing Workers, tried without success in the early 1970s to secure W.A.G.E. a seat on the Council. "Anne was always considered a radical," recalled Stern, "and her union was far more to the left than the other unions." Author's interview with Marjorie Stern, San Francisco, California, 5 January 1989. Anne Draper died in March 1973, and by the following year, W.A.G.E. was no longer an organization mainly comprising women trade unionists. Without the time extended and information given by Joyce Maupin and Marjorie Stern, this paper could not have been written. My deepest thanks to both of them.

8. Joyce Maupin, Preface to *Talking Union: A Guide for Working Women*, comp. and ed., Joyce Maupin, Union W.A.G.E. (May 1979), 3, LARC, SFSU-WAGE.

9. Interview with Maupin, 3 October 1988.

10. Leaflet for 31 January 1973 demonstration, back side, LARC, SFSU-WAGE, Box 8, Folder 13.

11. Joyce Maupin, *Working Women and Their Organizations—150 Years of Struggle* (Berkeley, CA, 1974), 30, LARC, SFSU-WAGE.

12. Joyce Maupin, *Union W.A.G.E. Newsletter,* 1:7 (November 1971): 7, LARC, SFSU-WAGE. Emphasis in the original. The *Newsletter* became a newspaper in early 1972, running between eight and twelve pages until 1977, when it expanded to sixteen pages.

13. Constitution and By-Laws, approved 3 November 1974, Box 1, Folder 3; "Our Purpose and Goals," *Union W.A.G.E.* 26 (November–December 1974): 2, LARC, SFSU-WAGE.

14. Philip S. Foner, *Women and the Labor Movement: From World War I to the Present* (New York, 1980), 506, 505.

15. *Union W.A.G.E.* 23 (May–June 1974): 4, 5, 8, LARC, SFSU-WAGE. Continuing differences with regard to the ERA may have also divided the organizations. According to Maupin, Olga Madar "wanted us to be part of CLUW, but she wanted us to change our position on protective legislation." Interview with Maupin, 3 October 1988.

16. Maupin, *Working Women and Their Organizations*, 26. Maupin repeated this criticism in 1978; *Oral History* (16 July 1978): 118–119, LARC, SFSU.

17. Jan Arnold, "Why a *Union* Women's Alliance to Gain Equality?" *Union W.A.G.E.* 51 (January–February 1979): 3, LARC, SFSU-WAGE.

18. Ruth Milkman, "Women Workers, Feminism, and the Labor Movement Since the 1960s," in *Women, Work and Protest: A Century of US Women's Labor History*, ed. Ruth Milkman (Boston, MA, 1985), 314.

19. Diane Balser, *Sisterhood and Solidarity: Feminism and Labor in Modern Times* (Boston, MA, 1987), 140.

20. Interview with Maupin, 3 October 1988.

21. "Statement of the Union W.A.G.E. Executive Board," *Union W.A.G.E.* 31 (September–October 1975): 1, LARC, SFSU-WAGE.

22. Interview with Maupin, 3 October 1988.

23. See *Union W.A.G.E.* 25 (September–October 1974); 26 (November–December 1974); 27 (January–February 1975); 28 (March-April 1975); 29 (May–June 1975); and 30 (July–August 1975), LARC, SFSU-WAGE.

24. *Union W.A.G.E.* 27 (January–February 1975): 12, LARC, SFSU-WAGE.

25. "Organize" Conference (West Coast Working Women's Conference), 8–9 November 1975, LARC, SFSU-WAGE, audio cassette 6.

26. I wrote more extensively about this conflict in "Where It (Almost) All Came Together: Union W.A.G.E. and Working-Class Feminism in the 1970s," unpublished paper delivered at the Pacific Coast Branch Conference of the American Historical Association, San Francisco State University, August 1988.

27. Constitutional Referendum, November 1979, Box 1, Folder 4; *Union W.A.G.E.* 58 (March–April 1980): 15. Jan Arnold and Julee Heyer wrote articles on pornography for *Union W.A.G.E.* 53 (May–June 1979): 4, LARC, SFSU-WAGE.

28. Balser, 145.

29. Pam Allen, "Excerpt from an Answer," and Joyce Maupin, "Comment on Changing the Unions," *Inter-Chapter Newsletter* 6 (December 1978): 3, 5,

LARC, SFSU-WAGE, Box 14, Folder 4. Both articles were reprinted with slight changes in *Union W.A.G.E.* 51 (January–February 1979): 1–2.

30. At a members-only convention held in February 1979, President Jan Arnold proposed that W.A.G.E. state its main activities. These first appeared in *Union W.A.G.E.* 52 (March–April 1979): 13, LARC, SFSU-WAGE.

31. "Waitress Raped at St. Francis Hotel," *Union W.A.G.E.* 57 (January–February 1980): 1; Diane Sandrowski, "Hotel Stonewalls," *Union W.A.G.E.* 58 (March–April 1980): 16, LARC, SFSU-WAGE.

32. Al Richmond, "The San Francisco Hotel Strike," *Socialist Review* 57 (May–June 1981): 99. A copy of this article is deposited at LARC, SFSU, Lucy Kendall papers, Hotel and Restaurant Employees and Bartenders' Union, Local 2, San Francisco.

33. "Hotel Says Rape 'Not Important,' " *Union W.A.G.E.* 60 (July–August 1980): 4; Richmond, "The San Francisco Hotel Strike," 99, LARC, SFSU-WAGE, and Lucy Kendall papers.

34. This may have been the result of undemocratic contract negotiations. The rank-and-file negotiating committee was not even invited to secret sessions held in Los Angeles. The membership approved the contract, but only after an acrimonious meeting held on 12 August 1980. LARC, SFSU-Lucy Kendall papers, "Partial Transcript—Ratification Meeting," Kezar Pavilion, 12 August 1980, 19 pages.

35. Richmond, "The San Francisco Hotel Strike," 88 and 87, LARC, SFSU-Kendall papers.

36. Karen Guma, "6,000 Strike City Hotels," *Union W.A.G.E.* 61 (September–October 1980): 6, LARC, SFSU-WAGE.

37. Interview with Maupin, 3 October 1988.

38. Interview with Maupin, 3 October 1988. Also, Diane Sandrowski, "Women on the Move," KSFX FM Program, n.d. [late 1979], LARC, SFSU-WAGE, audio cassette; "Readers Survey," *Union W.A.G.E.* 51 (January–February 1979): 15.

39. "Don't Mourn, Organize," *Union W.A.G.E.* final newsletter, n.d. [1982]: 3, LARC, SFSU-WAGE.

40. "Family Bill of Rights," CLUW 1-1988; "National Health Care," CLUW 3-1988; "Employee Drug Testing," CLUW 9-1988; "AIDS," CLUW 11-1988, Coalition of Labor Union Women, Fifth Biennial Convention, Seattle, Washington, 17–20 November 1988. I wish to thank Marjorie Stern for letting me borrow her convention material.

41. Joan Walsh, "CLUW Moves out on Its Own Agenda," *In These Times* 8:18 (4–10 April 1984): 2.

42. "International Union Solidarity," CLUW 6-1988; "Plant Closures and Runaway Shops," CLUW 7-1988, CLUW Convention. See note 40 above.

43. Interview with Stern, January 5, 1989. Stern is a former president of the San Francisco chapter of CLUW.

44. Ruth Milkman, "Women Workers, Feminism, and the Labor Movement since the 1960s," 304; Larry T. Adams, "Changing Employment Patterns of Organized Workers," *Monthly Labor Review* 108 (February 1985): 29.

45. Ruth Milkman, "Women Workers and the Labor Movement in Hard Times: Comparing the 1930s with the 1980s," in *Women, Households, and the Economy*, ed. Lourdes Benería and Catharine R. Stimpson (New Brunswick, NJ, and London, 1987), 124–125.

46. Kim Moody, "Building a Labor Movement for the 1990s: Cooperation and Concessions or Confrontation and Coalition," in *Building Bridges: The Emerging Grassroots Coalition of Labor and Community*, ed. Jeremy Brecher and Tim Costello (New York, 1990), 216.

47. Cindia Cameron, "Noon at 9 to 5: Reflections on a Decade of Organizing," in Brecher and Costello, 182.

48. Maupin, Oral History, 16 July 1978.

5 Ellen Gates Starr: Hull House Labor Activist

Jennifer L. Bosch

One hundred years after the founding of the famous Chicago settlement Hull House, more is being discovered about the activities of this institution and its residents. One resident in particular was Ellen Gates Starr, the cofounder of Hull House and onetime partner of Jane Addams. Through her settlement work Starr created the Chicago Public School Art Society and became actively involved in Chicago's Arts and Crafts movement. Her most ardent participation, however, was in socialist politics and the city's labor movement. As Eleanor Grace Clark reminisced: "In her [Starr's] life-long labor for others, there is, perhaps, no more spectacular chapter than that which recounts her trade-union activities in Chicago. She was, in fact, one of the pioneers in the fostering of labor organization for women in this country." In this regard Starr left an indelible mark on Chicago and U.S. history.[1]

Ellen Gates Starr—a quiet, petite, frail woman of inner beauty who was not hesitant to stand firm against social injustices—was born March 19, 1859, in Laona, Illinois. Her father, Caleb, and her aunt, Eliza, were formative in her early political and social development. Her father's Grange activities taught Starr about democracy, equality of opportunity, and helping one's neighbor. Starr's aunt was instrumental in her formal education by ensuring Starr's placement in the Rockford Female Seminary. Here Starr learned of great ideas from authors like Charles Dickens, Thomas Carlyle, and John Ruskin. Her formal education ended after one year when Starr could not return to Rockford due to poor family finances. Starr studied on her own, however, while teaching in Chicago, never returning to college later, despite her plans. Instead, she and Jane Addams, whom she had met at Rockford, founded the settlement Hull House, opening its doors to Chicago on September 18, 1889.

Hull House was based on the premise of living among the poor to offer some means of alleviating class antagonisms and poverty. Many of the initial programs to meet these goals were educational. Starr taught classes in literature, art, English, and history. Eventually she, and other residents, branched out to teach other courses as well as vocational skills to their immigrant neighbors. But with time Starr realized that other avenues must be taken to help these people. Activism on the part of Hull House neighbors, especially in Chicago's labor movement, seemed essential to bettering their lot in life. Starr was quick to join the ranks of labor activists and is thus representative of labor participation by settlement workers of the Progressive Era.

Ellen Starr was drawn to Chicago's labor movement by her disgust over the poor conditions of the working-class neighborhood in which she lived and by her interest in the ideas of John Ruskin and William Morris. The opinions of these men, though enmeshed in discussions of art and handicraft, provided basic ideas about the situation of the laborer in a capitalistic society. Starr firmly grasped these notions, particularly the theories about industrialism, and applied them in her own life. She often lectured on Ruskin's "opinions and principles" to her various classes at Hull House and Rockford. Most notably, she recognized Ruskin's objection to competition in any shape or form. Starr understood his preference for "[socialized] labor as opposed to competitive struggle" and his assertion that "the fruits of labor should belong to the worker." Starr also drew upon Morris's important ideas in her writings and lectures. She discussed his belief that workers had a "double grievance" in a capitalistic society because as producers and as consumers they were "forced to make and to buy useless and ugly things."

More important was his belief that there should be beauty and joy in work for all laborers, not just for a select few. Summarizing his theories, Starr wrote, "life under competitive regime makes that [joy in one's work] impossible. Hence life must be revolutionized—competitive regime abolished." Competition was the by product of industrialism, which Morris and Starr understood led to the downfall of the worker and society as a whole. Only through socialized labor could the worker restore his or her rightful position in society, be joyful in work, and produce well-made and useful goods.[2]

Like Ruskin and Morris, Starr worried as well about the physical and mental conditions of the worker. According to Morris, only a free man could express himself in his work. If the worker "is doing slave's work under slavish conditions, it is doubtful whether he will ultimately have many thoughts worth the name." To be expressive and to enjoy one's work, one must have the right working conditions, not "slavish" circumstances. A worker must have physical and mental buoyancy as well as "wholesome and comely surroundings." Starr carried that thought further: "A healthy art cannot thrive on a depressed or morbid condition of mind or body. It cannot thrive on bad air or ugliness and squalor, domestic or civic." The improvement of the workers' living and working conditions would thus improve their demeanor for production. A healthier atmosphere bred a healthier worker, and thus better products. Yet Starr also pointed out that "to work joyfully, even to work tranquilly—the artist's [worker's] first requirement—he must be free from the pressure of immediate need." The artist or laborer, in producing goods for the rich and cultivated, should not have to pander to them for survival. Starr astutely summed up the ideal conditions for the laborer or artist as being "perfect freedom from pressure of personal necessity, combined with a wholesome degree of obligation to the service of others, beautiful surroundings, health and joy."[3]

Unfortunately, these conditions did not exist for Chicago's laborers. This was the primary reason why Starr became immersed in the city's labor movement. She believed that one of the purposes of the settlement was to insure the possibility of obtaining such ideal working conditions. To Starr, the settlement "must work with all energy and courage toward the rescue of those bound under the slavery of commerce and the wage-law; with all abstinence it must discountenance wasting human life in the making of valueless things." With these ideas and attitudes, Starr moved headlong into Chicago's labor activities.[4]

Hull House was centrally located in a working-class neighborhood that afforded its residents, especially Starr, a firsthand opportunity to examine the daily difficulties the immigrants faced at home and at work. One of the early purposes of Hull House was to assist the local immigrants in improving their daily existence. Many of the settlement workers who came to Hull House believed the only means of bettering the status of these workers was through the improvement of their working conditions. Jane Addams wrote that some of the early residents of Hull House "came to the district with the general belief that organization for working-people was a necessity." Early on, Hull House became identified as sympathetic to the unions, as it sponsored meetings for all types of workers. Several unions, both men's and women's, as well as strike committees, met or took refuge at the settlement. Because of its strategic location in the midst of Chicago's sweatshop district, which was dominated by the sewing trades, it seemed only natural for Hull House workers to take up the cause of the garment workers first. Hull House served as the meeting place for the shirtmakers, organized in 1891, and the cloakmakers, organized in 1892. Residents like

Florence Kelley, who later became Secretary of the National Consumers' League, were influential in helping pass labor legislation, such as Illinois' first Factory Inspection Act in July 1893, as well as child labor legislation.[5]

Participation in Chicago's labor movement was a natural outgrowth of Starr's developing social and political ideals. Her understanding of the plight of Chicago's laborers moved her to take direct action. While she was a petite and gentle woman with an introspective character, when it came to causes such as the betterment of working conditions of the laborer she would, without hesitation, overcome her contemplative, quiet side to join the picket lines to demonstrate her support. Starr believed in the need for labor organization and found the use of the strike to put forth the message of the worker. She saw strikes as battles between those with power and those without. She understood organized labor to be the solution to the problem of power.

Starr's first known participation in Chicago's labor movement came with the garment workers' strike of 1896. The clothing cutters and tailors protested against their low wages and poor working conditions. Starr and other Hull House residents took up collections to help feed the workers and their families during this "state of warfare." Starr wrote to Henry Demarest Lloyd, author and labor supporter, asking for his advice on this matter while also inquiring about how to raise money for the strikers. Later she wrote to tell him of her success of raising money. Through appeals to students and faculty, Starr managed to gather between $50 and $60 for the strikers. Though she did not like having to ask for money, she rationalized her actions by explaining, "The cause justifies it." Later, when the strike was not accomplishing its goals, part of the money she had raised was used to send the blacklisted leaders out of Chicago.[6]

Starr's interest in the labor movement became more intense with the push for the unionization of women. After 1896 she became more concerned with women workers. She picketed and gave speeches for them when necessary. To show her further interest and support for organizing women, in 1904 she became a charter member of Chicago's chapter of the Women's Trade Union League (WTUL). Starr's membership in the WTUL provided her with both professional and personal satisfaction. Professionally, it allowed her to put into action her ideas about workers and society. Personally, involvement in this organization allowed her to develop close bonds with women outside of the Hull House inner circle.

While the WTUL provided an avenue for friendship, it also served as an outlet for Starr to implement her Christian ideals of helping one's fellow human beings. Through various committees she helped the impoverished laborers during their strikes. Other settlement workers participated in labor activities, but not with Starr's fervor and determination. While Starr joined women strikers, people like Jane Addams often recoiled from public action. Starr accused Addams of "retreating to her study to write whenever a crisis occurred." Addams rarely joined picket lines, for she believed that she could be more helpful in other ways, such as by making speeches and writing prolabor articles. Other settlement workers like Alice Hamilton also recoiled. Hamilton admitted that she would "picket only in the evening, when she was least likely to be arrested." While women like Addams and Hamilton retrenched from aggressive public support of strikers, Starr joined the picket lines.[7]

Starr's actions greatly aided the cause of the workers in several strikes between 1910 and 1917. Her defiant defense of the workers won her the support of various labor leaders and organizations. "The Garment Workers Strike of 1910 was one of the greatest experiences of our early years at Hull House," stated Edith Abbott, a Hull House resident. The strike began on September 22, 1910, when Annie Shapiro, the daughter of a Russian immigrant, and sixteen other women walked out on their jobs at Hart, Schaffner and Marx, Chicago's largest manufacturer of men's clothing. The precipitant cause for the walkout was the lowering of wages from 4 to 3 ¾ cents, which amounted to a 6 percent reduction in yearly wages. This, coupled with the long hours and poor working conditions, prompted Shapiro and her followers to take to the streets launching a protest that would virtually shut down Chicago's clothing industry. Within weeks 10 percent of Chicago's working population had gone on strike in support of the striking women. The *Chicago Evening Post* reported on November 5 that since the initial walkout "garment workers in every part of the city, apparently without any relation to the action of any others in the same industry, have given up their work by the thousands until it was estimated today 40,000 men and women were on strike."[8]

The WTUL was quick to offer support and set up strike committees, which Starr joined. The committees were established to raise money and to solicit public support. On the picket committee, Starr became active in the strike through organizing various forms of relief, such as the milk fund for the hungry babies of striking families. In a letter to her close friend Charles Wager, Starr told of giving food to a poor family whose father was a striker with "one tuberculous child, & a baby whose mother has little for it because she hasn't enough to eat herself." Starr appealed for aid from local churches, with the *Chicago Record-Herald* reporting on November 28 of her appeal to the congregation of St. Martin's Episcopal Church.[9]

Ellen Starr, not the type of woman to sit back and offer only moral support and words of wisdom, could often be found near the picket lines, if not actually marching in them. She went to the lines to deliver food and comfort to the picketers. She also went to ensure the safety of the picketers, especially the young women, from police brutality. Upon her several visits to the picket lines, Starr witnessed such police violence. What she saw firsthand she reported to the Strike Committee, which then reported her sightings to local newspapers. Through the newspaper accounts, public sympathy for the strikers grew. Starr's reports concentrated upon the actions of the police. At first she was bemused by the twenty or so police officers huddling in the street near Price and Company. These officers were trying to contain a group of "three rather small women, who are never allowed to stand for an instant, but are ordered, usually roughly to 'move on.' "

Starr found the entire situation intolerable. She continued, "I addressed myself civilly to a police officer and asked him why those twenty-two men were allowed to stand on the pavement and I was not." The officer's response was that they were doing their jobs. He later added, "Don't ask me questions, Lady." From this response Starr bitingly observed that this "particular officer did not particularly like his job." She felt sorry for him in his situation but felt more sympathy for the subjected strikers. Soon after this encounter, an "insolent and brutal" superior officer arrived on the scene and began to ask Starr why she was walking back and forth in front of the factory. Starr reported, "After hearing that I was simply a citizen of the United States and a settlement worker here in the interest of justice and fair play, he informed me that if I passed by once more I would be sent to the station." Not really wanting to push the matter further with this particular officer, Starr crossed the street and watched the proceedings from a safe distance.[10]

Through the efforts of women like Starr, striking families were able to survive the four months of the 1910 strike. Starr's reports to the Strike Committee and their publication in local newspapers helped gain public support and so made the collection process for food, clothing, and money easier. Yet when the strike ended January 14, 1911, there were mixed results. An agreement on certain items was reached, but the garment workers would not get all of what they wanted. This left them with a sense of betrayal and led to their going on strike again in 1915. The primary reason why the strikers conceded was that they had been "starved into submission," as the Chicago newspapers claimed. Still, the one bright hope for these workers was the formation of a new union, the Amalgamated Clothing Workers of America established by Sidney Hillman, a man who would become a great supporter of Starr's later labor activities. While the garment strike of 1910 had come to an end, labor activity for Starr was now becoming a way of life.[11]

In February 1914, Starr became involved in the Henrici Restaurant Strike when the waitresses walked off the job. They demanded one day off, a raise in pay, and recognition of their union. This strike, unlike the one of 1910, saw Starr become more militantly active through her writing, picketing, and subsequent arrest. Starr's actions jeopardized contributions to Hull House from Chicago's upper echelon, who feared and resented her growing militancy. Alice Hamilton wrote to her sister, Agnes, "There is a big strike of waitresses in a downtown restaurant. . . . Miss Starr is picketing and passionately longing to be arrested. I do hope it will be over when I get there, Miss Starr is so difficult when she is striking." It is not too hard to understand why Starr would be difficult during times like this. She was never happy to see instances of brutality or injustice, and was probably unhappy about being arrested herself.[12]

As in previous strikes, Starr, representing the WTUL and the labor interests of Hull House, was present on the picket lines. Carrie Alexander, a Hull House acquaintance, reminisced to Starr, "I can see you now, walking up and down on picket duty you were such a fine picket, and the trile [*sic*] how they try to send you over the 'top.' " Yet, it was this "walking up and down" that got Starr arrested. Peaceful picketing was legal in the state of Illinois and the strikers were instructed not to touch anyone or to stand near or in front of the restaurant obstructing passage. Still arrests occurred. Obstruction of passage was caused by passersby, plainclothes policemen, and private detectives rather than the picketers, as Starr and others explained. The result was more than 125 arrests for conspiracy and/or disorderly conduct.[13]

Starr was among those 125 who were arrested for disorderly conduct. For four days, between February 22 and March 2, she visited the picket lines. The fourth time, March 2, she was arrested. As Starr proclaimed, "I went there for the purpose of getting first-hand knowledge of the situation, of preventing recurrence of brutality, if I could, by my presence, aid in doing so, and of protesting against illegal and unwarranted arrests." In protesting against illegal arrests she had a standard phrase for the arresting officer, in which she exclaimed that as a U.S. citizen she had to protest against the arrest of people who were not doing anything illegal. The third time she so spoke, Starr was arrested. As she noted, "I was booked at the police station on a charge of disorderly conduct, which was sworn to by the officer, and on my declining to send for bail I was placed in a cell but released shortly thereafter on the bond of a friend."

The friend who bailed Starr out was Mary Wilmarth. Wilmarth's son-in-law, Harold Ickes, served as Starr's attorney. The initial charge against Starr was later changed for no apparent reason from disorderly conduct to "interfering with an officer in the discharge of his duty." Starr could not comprehend why there was a change. In attempting to rationalize the shift, she stated that the charge was made for two reasons, "to avoid the incitement to mirth and consequent disadvantage to the prosecution of a middle-aged gentlewoman appearing on a charge of disorderly conduct" and "more important, that my case, pushed on to earlier trial, might not furnish a precedent for the many cases of waitresses arrested on the former charge."[14]

The trial thus began. Harold Ickes managed to get her case heard on March 18, after four continuences on the part of the prosecution. Starr claimed that the prosecution had four witnesses, "police officers who over-reached themselves and swore to statements nobody believed." An engaging account of the trial proceedings has been given by Starr's acquaintance, Eleanor Grace Clark. Clark explained:

Miss Starr was a very frail little woman, probably never weighing much over a hundred pounds; and her manners and speech were not only impeccable, but elegant, as indeed was everything else about her exquisite person. It was therefore a hilarious moment in the court-room when the officer who had arrested her declared that "she had attacked him with violence" and had "tried to frighten him" from the discharge of his duty by telling him to "leave them girls be!"

Needless to say Starr was acquitted.[15]

When the decision was announced, the courtroom filled with applause. Starr immediately stated that she hoped her case would establish a precedent for the right of free speech and show that there were too many needless arrests. She also hoped that her case would ensure that women who were arrested in the future would be given the benefit of a trial like hers. Agnes Nestor, president of the WTUL, stated her pleasure in this decision. Speaking of Starr, Nestor declared, "She is positively fearless. Whenever the cause of justice and the right of free speech and personal liberty is at stake, Miss Starr is always in the foreground of the battle."[16]

The Henrici strike was important to Starr for many reasons. First of all, it advanced the cause of the waitresses. As Clark wrote, "The trial of so prominent a civic and social worker [Starr], who had been known and admired in Chicago for her good works for more than twenty-five years, naturally created a great sensation, and hence much favorable publicity for the strikers." This incident also solidified Starr's relationship with labor activists. Starr was now more involved with the ranks of Chicago's labor activists than with the core of Jane Addams's settlement workers.[17]

The last strike in which Starr fully participated was the 1915 garment strike, the origins of which lay in the 1910 episode. The same grievances of 1910, multiplied with time, precipitated the 1915 walkout. This time, the strikers demanded a voice in determining their working conditions through obtaining the right to collective bargaining. While serving as chair of the Hull House Labor Committee, Starr once again set out to gain public sympathy for the strikers and to collect money for the needy. She served as the temporary treasurer of the Citizens Committee for Arbitration in the Clothing Industry until A. M. McCormick assumed the position. As she told a friend, Anita Blaine, "I have decided to act as a sort of temporary sub-treasurer & collect from people whom I know, handing the money over directly to the Clothing Workers."[18]

This strike, unlike the one of 1910, did not receive the support of the WTUL or the American Federation of Labor (AFL), which was under the direction of Samuel Gompers. Gompers urged his followers not to support the garment strikers led by Sidney Hillman's Amalgamated Clothing Workers of America because the ACWA had seceded from the United Garment Workers in 1914. Support of this group, Gompers believed, "would be to establish a standard that would endanger the existence of a united labor movement." Starr attributed the defeat of the strikers to this lack of support. She wrote in 1916, "The failure of support in the trade-union world has been the chief reason for defeat, if the end must be called defeat." As a result of Gompers's decision, Starr and the strikers had to depend upon support from different sources of Chicago society, such as the intellectual sector. Ministers and college professors took up the slack left by AFL and WTUL supporters. In the end, this was not enough. If there had been a united trade union front bringing the entire garment industry to a halt, as in years past, then perhaps the ACWA strikers would not have been defeated.[19]

During the course of the strike, from October to December, over seventeen hundred strikers were arrested and two were killed. Starr, determined not to let this strike end like the one of 1910 with strikers "starved into submission," became involved again. She defiantly wrote that "if one must starve, there are compensations in starving in a fight for freedom that are not to be found in starving for an employer." This philosophy served as a rallying point but still could not generate the union and public support that the strikers needed. In the end, nothing came of the strike. Neither side won a "decisive victory." The manufacturer's association signed no agreements nor submitted differences to arbitration.

Ultimately, Starr placed the fault of the loss on the "heavy hand of Mr. Gompers," winning his wrath.

Yet Starr won the heart and gratitude of Sidney Hillman. In commending her actions, Hillman wrote to Starr, "As a great deal of discomfort to yourself, you took your place on the firing line, and personally bore the insults of the police and private sluggers of the employers, so that by your presence and example you might be of assistance to others." As in the restaurant strike a year earlier, Starr was arrested several times for "inciting a riot." Once arrested, she and others insisted on a jury trial so that their friends had "a chance to find out from our evidence . . . the real state of things," as Starr explained. As a result of her work for the ACWA, Starr was made an honorary member of this union because, as Hillman described in his letter, she was "one of the best little soldiers in the fight."[20]

Ellen Starr's labor activism waned after 1916. Through her labor activities and the ideals she gained from Ruskin and Morris, Starr became involved in Chicago's Socialist Party. By 1916 she had set aside banners of protest to carry campaign posters in her bid as Alderman [*sic*] of the nineteenth ward. Starr's unsuccessful campaign took her attentions and energies away from union activity. In addition to her political interests, Starr's advancing age and declining health urged her off the picket lines. Her physical activism on the part of the worker became more passive as the years passed by, though she maintained her strong mental drive for justice.

Starr's last known support for laborers came in 1922. She supported striking coal miners who had walked out on their jobs in several states, including Illinois. The strikers demanded complete unionization of their industry, higher pay, a shorter workweek, and even distribution of work throughout the year. When several strikers came to Chicago to raise funds Starr housed many of them at her apartment. After this episode Starr's health took a precarious turn. By 1929 she returned to the hospital for surgery on a spinal abscess, an operation that left her paralyzed. This situation forced Starr to live her remaining years at the Convent of the Holy Child in Suffern, New York, where she could receive the medical, intellectual, and spiritual attention she needed. Here she would die in 1940.[21]

Ellen Starr's labor activism between 1895 and 1925 is representative of the fervor of settlement house participation of the Progressive years. Settlement workers realized that to help their neighbors they often had to step beyond the doors of their institutions. How these workers chose to help was dependent upon their character. Ellen Starr chose not to stay behind the scenes and only write about the injustices. Instead, she became a participant in strikes by raising money for strikers, becoming a union member, joining picket lines, and often being arrested in the process. In so doing Starr put her genteel high-society reputation on the line for the betterment of men and women around her.

Though Ellen Starr's name is not well known in historical analysis she contributed to the improvement of Chicago society. She left an indelible mark on history. Her place in the settlement movement is unquestionable. But her other interests and activities, especially her labor activism, are also important. Touched by her hand, garment unions, along with other Chicago progressive organizations, still protect workers' interests keeping Ellen Starr's memory alive.

NOTES

1. Eleanor Grace Clark, "Ellen Gates Starr, O.S.B. (1859–1940)," *Commonweal* 31 (15 March 1940): 446.

2. Ellen Gates Starr, "Notes on Ruskin" and "Art and Socialism of William Morris," Ellen Gates Starr Papers, The Sophia Smith Collection, Smith College, Northampton, Massachusetts (hereafter referred to as EGS Papers).

3. Ellen Gates Starr, "Art and Labor," *Hull House Maps and Papers* (New York, 1895), 167.

4. Ellen Gates Starr, "Art and Labor," 178, and "The Renaissance of Handicraft," *International Socialist Review* (February 1902): 571.

5. Jane Addams, "The Settlement as a Factor in the Labor Movement," *Hull House Maps and Papers* (New York, 1895), 184, 188–189; Jane Addams and Ellen Gates Starr, "Appendix," *Hull House Maps and Papers*, 214–215; Robert Woods, *The Settlement Horizon: A National Estimate* (New York, 1922), 179.

6. Allen F. Davis, *Spearheads for Reform: The Social Settlements and the Progressive Movement, 1890–1914* (New York, 1967), 106; *Hull House Bulletin* 1:4 (April 1896), Jane Addams Papers, Hull House Association Records, Swarthmore College Peace Collection, Swarthmore College, Swarthmore, Pennsylvania (hereafter referred to as JA Papers); Ellen Gates Starr to Henry Demarest Lloyd, 12 March 1896 and 17 April 1896, Henry Demarest Lloyd Collection, The State Historical Society of Wisconsin, Madison, Wisconsin.

7. Davis, 106; Allen F. Davis, *American Heroine: The Life and Legend of Jane Addams* (New York, 1973), 11, 115–116.

8. Edith Abbott, "Grace Abbott and Hull House, 1908–21, Part I," *Social Service Review* 24 (September 1950): 393; Elizabeth Anne Payne, *Reform, Labor, and Feminism: Margaret Dreier Robins and the Women's Trade Union League* (Chicago, IL, 1988), 86–91; *Chicago Evening Post*, 5 November 1910, JA Papers.

9. Ellen Gates Starr to Charles Wager, Holy Innocent's Day 1910, EGS Papers; *Chicago Record-Herald*, 28 November 1910, JA Papers.

10. "Official Report of Strike Committee Chicago Garment Workers Strike, October 29, 1910 to February 18, 1911," Papers of the National Women's Trade Union League, Arthur and Elizabeth Schlesinger Library on the History of Women in America, Radcliffe College, Cambridge, Massachusetts.

11. Payne, 91.

12. Ellen Gates Starr, "Efforts to Standardize Chicago Restaurants—the Henrici Strike," *Survey* (23 May 1914): 214–215; Alice Hamilton to Agnes Hamilton, 1 March 1914, in *Alice Hamilton: A Life in Letters*, ed., Barbara Sicherman (Cambridge, MA, 1984), 174.

13. Carrie Alexander to Ellen Gates Starr, 2 March 1939, EGS Papers; Starr, "Efforts," *Survey*, 214.

14. Starr, "Efforts," 215; Josephine Starr, "Notes," EGS Papers.

15. Starr, "Efforts," 215; Clark, "Ellen Gates Starr," *Commonweal*: 446.

16. "Miss Starr, Free; Differing Action; Congratulations," EGS Papers.

17. Clark, "Ellen Gates Starr," *Commonweal*, 446.

18. *Hull House Yearbook* (1 January 1916): 58, JA Papers; "Why Not Arbitrate?" Anita Blaine McCormick Papers, The State Historical Society of Wisconsin, Madison, Wisconsin; Ellen Gates Starr to Anita Blaine, 13 October 1915, Anita Blaine McCormick Papers. The State Historical Society of Wisconsin, Madison, Wisconsin.

19. Samuel Gompers to Ellen Gates Starr, 28 January 1916, American Federation of Labor Records: The Samuel Gompers Era, The State Historical Society of Wisconsin, Madison Wisconsin; Ellen Gates Starr, "Cheap Clothes and Nasty," *New Republic* 5 (1 January 1916): 218; Ellen Gates Starr, "The Chicago Clothing Strike," *New Review* 4 (March 1916): 63.

20. Starr, "Chicago Clothing Strike," 62; Starr, "Cheap Clothes," 218; Sidney Hillman to Ellen Gates Starr, 22 December 1915, EGS Papers; Mary Prentice Lillie Barrows, *Frances Crane Lillie: A Memoir 1869–1958*, unpublished biography, Ellen Gates Starr Papers, The Sophia Smith Collection, Smith College, Northampton, Massachusetts.

21. Ellen Gates Starr to Josephine Starr, 17 February 1925, EGS Papers.

Part 3   African American History

6 Black Labor Conventions during Reconstruction

Eric Foner

Between 1869 and 1872, statewide "labor conventions" were held in three southern states—Georgia, South Carolina, and Alabama. Initially inspired by the Colored National Labor Convention of 1869, these gatherings were organized by Black politicians rather than "men actually engaged in farming or in some mechanical occupation."[1] But they attracted a significant number of ordinary freedmen, especially artisans and agricultural laborers. Thanks to the diligent research of Philip S. Foner and Ronald L. Lewis in preparing their indispensable documentary series, *The Black Worker*, the proceedings of these conventions are now readily available.[2] Supplemented by contemporary newspaper accounts, private letters, and legislative debates on the conventions' proposals, these proceedings reveal Blacks' mounting frustration with the failure of Reconstruction governments adequately to protect the rights of plantation laborers or to promote their acquisition of land. And the reactions to the conventions of Republican leaders, Black and white, illustrate the ideological barriers that prevented a more radical approach to the economic plight of the former slaves.

The labor conventions of 1869–1872 took place against the backdrop of remarkable progress for Black southerners in the aftermath of emancipation.[3] In 1866, alarmed by the refusal of southern state governments established by President Andrew Johnson to recognize the basic rights of the former slaves, Congress enacted the Civil Rights Act and approved the Fourteenth Amendment to the Constitution. These for the first time established a national principle of equality before the law, to be enforced, if necessary, by the federal government. They also sought to guarantee Blacks' new status as free laborers in a competitive economy, securing their rights to sign contracts and sue in court to enforce payment of wages, while invalidating measures like the Black Codes of 1865, which had sought to reduce the former slaves to quasi-free plantation laborers.

In 1867 came the Reconstruction Acts, granting Black males in the South the right to vote, and setting in motion a process that brought to power, in every southern state except Virginia, Republican governments committed to equality of civil and political rights. The year 1867 also witnessed the widespread political mobilization of southern Blacks through the Union League and kindred organizations, which spread Reconstruction's principles throughout the plantation belt, and provided a vehicle through which a generation of local Black political leaders emerged to prominence.

These new governments moved aggressively to rebuild the South in the image of the free labor North. They established the first state-supported common school systems in southern history, democratized local government, expanded the social responsibilities of state authority, and in several states moved to prohibit racial discrimination in transportation and places of public accommodation. But their efforts to alleviate the economic condition of the former slaves proved less far-reaching. In the absence of a federal program of land distribution, as advocated by Radicals like Thaddeus Stevens and many former slaves, most freedmen found themselves compelled by necessity to labor on white-owned plantations as either wage-earners or sharecroppers. Equating emancipation with independence in both their private and working lives, former slaves viewed these arrangements as a mockery of freedom.

Three obstacles, however, stood in the way of effective prolabor action at the state level. One was the desire of the new governments, urged on by Republicans in Washington, to broaden their support among the southern whites, especially the progressive wing of the planter class. A second was that southern Republican leaders, especially carpetbaggers from the North, business-oriented southern whites, and former free Blacks, adhered to the party's dominant free labor ideology. This assumed that the interests of capital and labor were fundamentally harmonious, and that while the government should and could remove barriers to competition in the labor market, it should not intervene to favor one class over another. Finally, the new southern governments decided that the rebuilding and transformation of the regional economy required aggressive efforts to attract northern investment. They used their resources to assist railroad construction and other enterprises, in the hope that this would create a prosperity in which all classes would share. The labor conventions of 1869–1872 revealed the frustrations felt both by ordinary freedmen and the Black political leadership over the contrast between Blacks' quest for economic independence and the reality of the survival of a plantation-dominated economy. They also illuminated the difficulty Black leaders faced in attempting to devise a more far-reaching economic program than that implemented by the Reconstruction state governments.

The chief organizer and "ruling spirit" of the Georgia Colored Labor Convention, which met in Macon in October 1869, was Jefferson Long. Born into slavery in 1836, Long had opened a tailor shop in Macon at the end of the Civil War, and also became a leader in the Union League and was actively involved in Republican political organizing. Elected to serve in the short session (January to March 1871) of the Forty-First Congress, Long would become the first Black to speak in the House of Representatives.[4]

Over 200 delegates gathered at Macon. Among them were prominent leaders of Georgia's Reconstruction: Reverend Henry M. Turner, a former chaplain with a Black regiment and an active organizer of churches, schools, and the Republican party in Reconstruction Georgia; Tunis G. Campbell, who had taken an active role in the northern abolitionist movement, came to Georgia in 1865 to help organize Blacks on the Georgia sea islands, and as sheriff and justice of the peace became the political "boss" of the Darien area; and Philip Joiner, a political leader in Dougherty county.[5]

The proceedings addressed a broad range of issues. There was considerable discussion of "outrages" against Blacks—the violence that had spread through rural areas almost from the moment the Civil War ended, and reached a peak in 1868 and 1869 with the depredations of the Ku Klux Klan. Despite the installation of a Republican state administration based largely on Black votes, Black Georgians who took an active part in politics, sought to escape plantation labor, or challenged in other ways the traditions of white supremacy and plantation discipline, faced the real prospect of violent reprisal. A committee on education emphasized the need to establish schools throughout the state. Delegates also reported that employers frequently violated their contracts with freedmen, and that Blacks could not obtain justice in the local courts.

All southern Republicans could agree on the need for public education, protection against violence, the fair implementation of contracts, and justice in the courts. More problematical was the "labor question" that had inspired the gathering in the first place. Long, it appears, hoped the gathering could help organize Black agricultural workers to demand higher wages—$30 per month for male field hands and $15 for women were the figures mentioned in one newspaper. These goals were significantly higher than prevailing wages in 1869, since crop failures and collusion among planters for the previous two years had driven the wage rate down to no more than $10 per month in most counties.

But the sketchy reports that have survived from the convention indicate that a number of delegates went further. Some addressed the struggle for power on the plantations that was part and parcel of the sharecropping system as it developed after the war. Was the tenant a renter obligated to pay a share to the landowner at the end of the year, but otherwise free from outside supervision? Or was the tenant, as planters insisted, an employee, who received a share as a wage and thus could be directed to labor in whatever way the landowner desired? Not surprisingly, speakers at the convention opted for the former interpretation—not only should the tenant receive from half to three-quarters of the crop, but the tenant should remain "free from the superintendence, control or direction of proprietors or overseers." (Not until 1872, after Democrats regained control of Georgia's government, was this question settled, when the state Supreme Court ruled that legally, the sharecropper was a wage earner and not a renter.)[6]

Among its other resolutions, the convention recommended that Black women withdraw from field labor—a persistent aim of much of the Black community in the aftermath of slavery, and suggested that the freedmen form cooperative clubs to purchase land, and self-defense organizations to combat the spread of violence. Moreover, it offered "a hearty welcome" to immigrants who chose to enter Georgia, "and especially the Chinese." This was, to say the least, an unconventional position in post–Civil War America, where virtually every union excluded the Chinese from membership, and planters spoke openly of driving down Black wages by introducing imported "coolies." "Laboring men of whatever color, class or their previous condition may have been," said the convention's resolutions, "[should] unite for the elevation of labor," a statement that underscores the freedmen's strong conception of themselves as part of "the laboring class."

The greatest debate, it appears, took place over the desire of some delegates to "fix a price for the labor of plantation hands." It is not clear precisely what was proposed, but according to one newspaper, Long, Turner, and other leaders vigorously opposed this idea, and it was overwhelmingly defeated by the convention. It was one thing for laborers to cooperate in an effort to raise wages through negotiation, but quite another for either employees or the government to establish wage rates on their own. Georgia's Black leaders, most of whom had known slavery themselves, sympathized deeply with the plight of Black farm workers, yet they remained wedded as well to free labor ideas that contended that wage levels should be determined by supply and demand, and that the interests of employer and employee were, ultimately, identical. In the end, the convention voted to establish a Mechanics and Laborers Association, to "improve the condition of the colored people" (an organization that apparently held a few meetings but never really got off the ground) but made no specific recommendations either regarding wage rates or labor legislation.[7]

Even the establishment of a union provoked bitter opposition in white Republican circles, as can be gauged by the reaction of the local party newspaper, the Macon *American Union*, to the labor convention. J. Clark Swayze, the editor, was a northerner who had served with the Freedmen's Bureau in Georgia and had long displayed bitter hostility to unions. When he first conducted a newspaper, in Griffin, Georgia, he ran afoul of the local printers' union, which demanded that he meet their pay scale. "We want none of the Union printers," Swayze declared, "and will not employ one if we know it."

Moreover, Swayze was a political rival of Jefferson Long and John E. Bryant, a white Republican leader who encouraged the convention, and he had coveted a federal patronage appointment received by Henry M. Turner. Predictably, Swayze denounced the 1869 labor convention in harsh language:

These labor unions that are not so numerous in all branches of industry are offshoots from European tyranny, that are entirely antagonistic to everything Republican. . . . Our advice to the colored laboring people is to "let well enough alone." If you are industrious, and honest, you can thrive by buying land and working it. . . . Labor is labor, and cotton is cotton; both are marketable commodities. . . . Labor will regulate itself.

Swayze's personal resentments help account for the harshness of his language, but his basic argument reflected free-labor principles widely shared among Republican leaders both white and Black.[8]

Swayze's sentiments, however, were not necessarily those of Georgia's freedmen. To them, labor organization seemed a legitimate tool by which to combat the planter's overwhelming economic power. Indeed, the statewide convention catalyzed the creation of labor organizations at the local level. In Cass County, in the state's Upper Piedmont, a meeting of Black members of the local "Mechanic and Laboring Men Association" selected a local minister as president and decided to collect dues of $1 per month "until we can make some good amount to do some good with. We wants to buy land as soon as we can to give homes to our poor peoples."[9]

Given the fact that conservative white Republicans dominated Georgia's Reconstruction government (they had even colluded with Democrats in 1868 to expel Blacks from the state legislature), the Georgia convention did not waste its time making detailed proposals for prolabor legislation. This was not the case of the second convention, South Carolina's, the one that had the greatest impact on the Reconstruction statute book concerning labor relations. This gathering assembled in the state capital, Columbia, in November 1869, one day after the opening of the legislature. The convention took place at a time of heightened labor unrest throughout the state. Charleston that fall witnessed strikes by longshoremen, painters, and tailors. In the countryside, laborers' gatherings lamented the deplorable condition of sharecroppers and wage workers. One, in Chester County, complained that the freedmen "have worked hard all the year, and find themselves as destitute now as when they began. . . . [They] have been robbed and cheated of all surplus that might have given them some independence."

The key issue confronting the convention, declared the Charleston *Daily Republican* in the weeks before the delegates assembled, was to devise means of ensuring that plantation laborers were able to contract for fair wages, and that these were actually paid. The Union Leagues, it urged, should be reorganized as unions of farm laborers. The paper even suggested that the convention set an equitable scale of money wages and shares, and ask the legislature to enact laws fixing these as the basis for settlement in contract disputes. As it soon became clear, many Republican leaders were extremely uncomfortable with such a broad expansion of the state's powers over economic affairs, and the *Daily Republican* quickly retreated from its position.[10]

Over three hundred delegates assembled in Columbia, all but thirty of them Black, and largely composed of agricultural laborers and urban artisans. The white heads of Charleston's longshoremen's and painters' unions were among those present. As in Georgia, however, Black Republican politicians dominated the convention's leadership. Robert B. Elliott, who had come from Massachusetts after the war to become the state's most astute party organizer and was elected to the legislature in 1868, became the convention's president. Other officers included W. B. Nash (a former slave who after emancipation had acquired a considerable amount of property and won election to the state senate), Francis L. Cardozo (the free-born son of a leading Charleston merchant, organizer of schools for Blacks after the Civil War, and South Carolina's Secretary of State in 1869), Jonathan J. Wright (a Pennsylvania-born lawyer soon to become the only Black to serve on a state supreme court during Reconstruction), and Alonzo Ransier (a free Black of Charleston elected to the legislature in 1868 and who subsequently would serve as lieutenant governor and in Congress). Not all delegates seem to have approved the way political leaders took control of proceedings. The convention, Elliott later recalled, began in "turbulent and confused fashion." According to the *Daily Republican*, "there was manifest dissatisfaction" when the list of officers was first announced, "because the labor unions were not represented among the officials." Subsequently, some politicians withdrew as officials to make way for actual labor leaders.[11]

The proceedings underscored the hold of free labor precepts on the state's Black Republican leadership. Speaker after speaker called for better treatment of agricultural laborers, but also reiterated that capital and labor shared the same fundamental interests. The convention did not represent any particular "class or party," declared Wright, and Ransier added that an improvement in the condition of the laboring classes would in no way injure other South Carolinians. A few delegates, however, took a more militant stance. "A handful of Radical demagogues," reported the Charleston *Daily News*, a Democratic party organ, wanted the convention to insist upon higher wages for farm laborers, state regulation of the level of rents, "and generally to take a position directly and wilfully hostile to the whole employing class." Their motto, it claimed, probably in an imaginative flight of fancy, was "Higher Wages, or Strikes and Revolution."

The convention's actual demands, the *Daily News* had to admit, were relatively "moderate." In a state where Blacks comprised a majority of the legislature's lower house, and the party leadership was considerably more radical than in Georgia, the delegates made specific proposals for labor legislation. Laborers, they resolved, should possess a lien on their employers' crops superior to merchants' liens for supplies. The government should appoint in each county a "commissioner of contracts" to act as an "advisory counsel" to farm workers and prevent them from being defrauded. Laborers' suits for their wages should have precedence on court calendars, and local officials should ensure that in the makeup of juries, "the laboring classes" should have "a fair representation." When land was sold by the government, the resolutions went on, it should be divided into tracts of fifty acres or less. Nine hours should be declared a legal day's work in factories and craft shops, although not in the fields, and taxes on the sale of cotton and rice be repealed. Finally, the legislature should end the practice of granting aid to railroads, and use its funds to help laborers secure land of their own. (In March 1869, South Carolina had become the only southern state during Reconstruction to establish a land commission charged with purchasing land and selling it to residents on long-term credit.)[12]

These proposals were more far-reaching than anything put forward in other southern states. Rather than challenging frontally the existing plantation system, however, or calling on the state to intervene directly to establish wages, the resolutions in effect envisioned the passage of laws that would make the existing system work more equitably. The final resolution, however, envisioned a fundamental change in state economic policy, from a preoccupation with state-sponsored economic development and the attraction of outside capital to a policy of directly promoting a more equitable distribution of property. Although hardly as far-reaching as grass-roots activists would have liked, the proposals did envision a state role in labor-capital relations far more extensive than in other states, North or South.

No sooner had the labor convention's resolutions been presented to the legislature, than heated divisions among the Republican leadership became apparent. In accordance with the resolution concerning land sales, Ransier moved in the legislature that prospective purchasers at sheriff's sales be empowered to compel sellers to divide their land into fifty-acre plots. This, replied William J. Whipper, a Pennsylvania-born Black army veteran who had become a rice planter near Beaufort, "would be an unwarrantable invasion of private rights, as the parties owning the land should decide whether it should be divided." Then a bill came to the floor embodying the plan for the appointment of commissioners of contracts and the laborer's lien, and making ten hours a legal day's work in crafts and factories. In January, the measure was recommitted to the labor committee. The sentiment of the House, reported the *Daily Republican*, seemed to be against "any labor bill whatever."[13]

In February, yet another bill came before the House, this time one seeking to put teeth into a measure passed the previous spring penalizing those who defrauded workers of their wages. This new plan provided for the voiding of contracts when laborers did not receive the wages due them, awarded workers a first lien on the crop, and provided for the appointment of officials to record all agricultural contracts so as to prevent disagreements as to what obligations employers and employees had undertaken. In the previous bill, the government official would assist the laborer; here the official was simply an impartial observer, a "decided improvement" in the Charleston *Daily Republican*'s eyes. Nonetheless, the bill's preamble mentioned that laborers, as "wards of the public," needed governmental protection.

This strongly offended Whipper and white carpetbagger Reuben Tomlinson, both of whom insisted that laborers were perfectly capable of taking care of themselves. To them, the bill smacked of unwonted paternalism. Their assumption, as Thomas Holt has noted, seemed to be that laborers were independent contractors, dealing with their employers on a footing of equality. The state's only obligation was to make certain that all citizens, including laborers, enjoyed equality before the law. Another Republican legislator, John Ferriter, a southern-born white from the state's upcountry, condemned the bill for encouraging the freedmen to believe that they would soon receive higher wages. "The law of supply and demand," he insisted, "must regulate this matter. . . . It is wrong for the General Assembly to convey the idea that it is able to raise wages one cent."

Nonetheless, with freedmen providing far more support than white Republicans and free Blacks, northern and southern, the bill passed the house. It was watered down further in the state senate by the deletion of a clause for public funding of laborers' lawsuits. "If a plaintiff, however poor and humble," commented the *Daily Republican*, "has a good cause of action, he will have no difficulty in securing the assistance of an attorney to prosecute his case." Finally, early in March, it became law. In its final version, the measure required that labor contracts must be witnessed before one or more disinterested parties and, on request, be executed before a justice of the peace. In sharecropping arrangements, a third party or justice of the peace would supervise the crop division. Laborers were awarded a first lien on the crop, and in case of contract violations, the landowner would be fined from $50 to $500, while the laborer could be fined or imprisoned "according to the gravity of the offense."

Although it went further than Reconstruction legislation in other states in involving elected officials in supervising contracts, and in spelling out the penalties for fraud, the measure was hardly as powerful a remedy as the labor convention had envisioned. The same legislature provided that interest on the state debt be paid in gold, a highly expensive measure that indicated that the desire to attract outside capital to the state still governed South Carolina's economic policy.[14]

The following fall, the labor question again came before the legislature, when Aaron Logan, a farmer and former slave from Charleston, introduced a bill allowing laborers to set their own wages by ballot among themselves, with such elections to be conducted in each polling district. At the same time, another member proposed to allow the government to regulate the profits of retail merchants. "No person," Logan declared, "who is not acquainted with the glaring frauds which are now being practiced on the poverty-stricken laborers (and especially those of the rural parts) and who have not that ocular evidence falling daily under his personal observation, of the unequal contest between the unlettered laborers (generally) and their wily employer . . . can duly appreciate the object of the bill."

In effect, Logan asked the state to authorize an extension of Reconstruction's democratic revolution from politics to labor relations. Given prevailing free-labor attitudes, that the bill died in committee is not surprising. What is interesting however is the vehemence of the opposition. The Charleston *Daily Republican* condemned Logan's bill as "idiotic." "Crude and visionary" was how the South Carolina correspondent of the New York *World,* perhaps the nation's leading Democratic newspaper, described both bills—but in a sense they reflected how Reconstruction had, at least in the minds of some Republicans, opened new possibilities for the use of the democratic state to redress the pressing burden of economic inequality in a plantation society.[15]

Soon after the failure of these measures, in January 1871, Alabama's Labor Union Convention assembled in Montgomery. Unlike the Georgia and South Carolina gatherings, emigration from the state was high on the agenda of the organizers, who included James T. Rapier, perhaps the state's most powerful Black politician. From the Committee on Homesteads, George W. Cox, a former slave blacksmith who had recently served in Alabama's legislature, explained why the freedmen found it "impossible" to acquire land: private lands sold at exorbitant prices, and public lands available under the Southern Homestead Act were "unfit for cultivation."

His committee suggested that Alabama's Blacks emigrate to Kansas, "where the soil is virgin and where homes can be had by simply going to them, and where we will not be murdered and driven from our homes for exercising [the] inestimable rights of life and liberty." In Alabama, Cox continued, "I see nothing but misery in store for the masses." Moreover, in a stinging rebuke to his party's obsession with economic modernization as the key to improving the condition of the former slaves, Cox asked, "what reason have we to suppose that [new economic enterprises] would benefit us?" Capital, he observed, was unlikely to flow to the state so long as investment opportunities existed in the North and West. Moreover, given Alabama's history, it was reasonable to assume that if mines and factories did open, "they would employ all white help."

The following day, the convention heard a dire report from the Committee on the Condition of the Colored People of Alabama, headed by William V. Turner of Wetumpka. Born a slave in Virginia, Turner had emerged after 1865 as a teacher, Union League organizer, and legislator in Alabama. "From all over the state," his committee reported, "there rises a general cry from our oppressed people, of their grievances." Laborers were constantly defrauded of their earnings, schooling often unavailable, and violence a constant danger. The "panacea" for these conditions was emigration.

That Alabama's labor convention placed such emphasis on migration out of the state reflected the deepening frustration of the state's Black leaders over Reconstruction's inability substantially to improve the former slaves' living conditions. "We are today," said Cox, "where 1866 left us." Probably because Democrats had captured the governorship in 1870, the convention devoted little attention to possible legislative remedies. It did, however, establish a State Labor Union to mobilize agricultural workers. Its president was Jeremiah Haralson, a former slave who had recently been elected to the legislature from Dallas county, and would go on to serve a term in Congress.

The establishment of the Union suggested that Alabama's Black leaders took a more adversarial view of capital-labor relations than their counterparts in other states. Indeed, at the second state labor convention, held in January 1872, one speaker, enumerating Blacks' needs in Alabama, listed protection of political rights, aid in securing remuneration due them, and "protection of labor against the inroads and encroachments of capital." The convention again urged the freedmen to consider emigration to Kansas, and proposed that Congress incorporate a Freedmen's Homestead Company, to assist southern Blacks in acquiring land.[16]

The first statewide effort to organize southern agricultural workers into a union, the Alabama Labor Union, was an idea before its time. But the organization survived at least to 1874, when the Democrats regained full control of Alabama's government. Most of its organizers were Republican leaders who had been deeply involved in Union League activities—Cox, Turner, James K. Green, James H. Alston, and Lawrence Speed. All of these had served in the legislature, and all were former slaves.[17]

The full story of Black labor organization in Reconstruction remains to be written. The state labor conventions form only one part of the tale, which also includes unsuccessful efforts by Black legislators in several states to secure laws regulating hours and wages, the freedmen's persistent quest for land, occasional strikes by both urban and rural workers, and labor gatherings, such as one in Texas in 1871, whose proceedings have yet to be found.[18] But taken together, the record of statewide and local activity suggests both how Reconstruction opened the door to militant labor activity on the part of former slaves, and how powerful were the economic, political, and ideological obstacles that stood in the path of a dramatic improvement in the former slaves' economic conditions. They reveal how much was accomplished by Reconstruction, and how much remained to be done.

NOTES

1. Eric Foner, *Reconstruction: America's Unfinished Revolution, 1863–1877* (New York, 1988), 377.

2. Philip S. Foner and Ronald L. Lewis, eds., *The Black Worker: A Documentary History from Colonial Times to the Present*, 8 vols. (Philadelphia, PA, 1978–1984). The proceedings may be found in volume 2: *The Black Worker during the Era of the National Labor Union.*

3. The next three paragraphs are based on the account of the period in Foner, *Reconstruction.*

4. Foner and Lewis, *The Black Worker*, 2: 4–15; John M. Matthews, "Jefferson Franklin Long: The Public Career of Georgia's First Black Congressman," *Phylon* 42 (June 1981): 145–156.

5. Edwin S. Redkey, *Respect Black: The Writings and Speeches of Henry McNeal Turner* (New York, 1971); Russell Duncan, *Freedom's Shore: Tunis Campbell and the Georgia Freedmen* (Athens, GA, 1986); Susan E. O'Donovan, "Philip Joiner: Southwest Georgia Black Republican," *Journal of Southwest Georgia History* 4 (Fall 1986): 56–71.

6. Foner and Lewis, *The Black Worker*, 2:4–7; Foner, *Reconstruction*, 594.

7. Foner and Lewis, *The Black Worker*, 2:12–16; Macon *American Union*, 29 October 1869.

8. Griffin *American Union*, 16 August 1867; Macon *American Union*, 1, 15 October 1869.

9. Charles R. Edwards to John E. Bryant, 27 December 1869, John E. Bryant Papers, Perkins Library, Duke University.

10. William C. Hine, "Black Organized Labor in Reconstruction Charleston," *Labor History* 25 (Fall 1984): 511; Frank Carter to J. K. Jillson, 15 November 1869, Superintendent of Education Papers, South Carolina Archives, Columbia, S.C.; Charleston *Daily Republican* (15, 16 October 1869, 11, 13 November 1869).

11. Peggy Lamson, *The Glorious Failure: Black Congressman Robert Brown Elliott and the Reconstruction in South Carolina* (New York, 1973), 77; Carleston *Daily Republican* (26 November 1869). For biographical information on South Carolina's Black leadership, see Thomas Holt, *Black over White: Negro Political Leadership in South Carolina during Reconstruction* (Urbana, IL, 1977).

12. Foner and Lewis, *The Black Worker*, 2:22–27; Charleston *Daily News* (29 November 1869); Charleston *Daily Republican* (27, 30 November 1869).

13. Charleston *Daily Republican* (2, 3, 21 December 1869, 12 January 1870).

14. Charleston *Daily Republican* (17 January 1870, 2, 3, 8, 9, 25 February 1870, 2 March 1870); Holt, *Black Over White*, 154–162; *South Carolina Session Laws, 1868–69*, 227–229.

15. Charleston *Daily Republican* (17 December 1870); New York *World* (27 February 1871).

16. Foner and Lewis, *The Black Worker*, 2:120–136; Loren Schweninger, *James T. Rapier and Reconstruction* (Chicago, IL, 1978), 86–88. For biographical information about Alabama's Black leadership, see Richard Bailey, "Black Legislators during the Reconstruction of Alabama, 1867–1878," Ph.D. diss., Kansas State University, 1984.

17. *Congressional Record*, 43rd Congress, 1st Session, 431; Michael W. Fitzgerald, *The Union League Movement in the Deep South: Politics and Agricultural Change during Reconstruction* (Baton Rouge, LA, 1989), 168–169.

18. Charles Vincent, *Black Legislators in Louisiana during Reconstruction* (Baton Rouge, LA, 1976), 98–102; Peter J. Rachleff, *Black Labor in the South: Richmond, Virginia 1865–1890* (Philadelphia, PA, 1984), 56–61; Carl D. Moneyhon, *Republicanism in Reconstruction Texas* (Austin, TX, 1980), 159; Jerrell H. Shofner, "Militant Negro Laborers in Reconstruction Florida," *Journal of Southern History* 39 (August 1973): 402–408.

7 The History and Legacy of Mississippi Plantation Labor

Elizabeth Ann Sharpe

Long before Nathan Bedford Forrest's hooded Ku Klux Klansmen reigned terror on Black people throughout the South, the economic relations evolving on cotton plantations laid the groundwork for the counterrevolution that took away most of the freedom that had been won at such a great cost of blood and treasure during the Civil War. In the period between the advent of the Civil War (1861) and the Hayes-Tilden Compromise of 1877, there was an enormous struggle between southern Black people and the white elites of both the North and the South as to whose class interest would prevail. This struggle was resolved politically with the Hayes-Tilden Compromise, which permitted Rutherford B. Hayes, the Republican, to become President of the United States in exchange for a pledge to withdraw federal troops from the South, leaving the former slaves at the mercy of southern white rulers once again. But the Compromise would not have been possible had not the economic basis for it been established. At issue was control of southern agricultural production. Those who would control it would also enjoy the profits.[1]

The struggle was precipitated when southern Blacks seized the moment and began to walk off plantations seeking to join the Union forces, shortly after the war on the ground commenced. Slavery, the condition in which laborers are in total bondage, owning nothing, not even their own bodies, was abolished not because it was morally repugnant but because it was strategically necessary to win the war. Forced to defend the emancipation policy, President Lincoln stated:

My enemies pretend I am now carrying on the war for the sole purpose of abolition. So long as I am President, it shall be carried on for the sole purpose of restoring the Union. But no human power can subdue the rebellion without the use of the emancipation policy . . . to weaken the moral and physical forces of the rebellion.[2]

Effectively, the emancipation policy ended the grip of the southern planters on their labor force and soon on access to their land. Severing the slave/owner connection opened the door for ingenious, even revolutionary, relationships of producers to the land. On some plantations, such as those of Davis Bend, Mississippi, the newly freed laborers began to till the soil themselves as workers who also owned the land, in a collective scheme aimed at providing "increased economic cooperation through harmonious cooperation,"[3] as was further described in the *New York Times* on December 4, 1864:

The nest in which the rebellion was hatched is to be the Mecca of "The Freedmen." The home of Jefferson Davis, who represents the rebellion for slavery, is consecrated . . . as the home of the emancipated. . . . [This experiment] will strike an answering chord in all the loyal North, as it points out the fitness of the place for the humane and economic work of elevating thousands of an oppressed race, and of saving a vast and needless expense to the Government.

Word spread throughout the South that all freed people would receive "forty acres and a mule."[4] The pragmatic justice of this proposal, after centuries of free labor, caused an immediate sensation.[5] Production would be resumed but under conditions of dignity, with profits going directly to those whose life's energy went into working the land. From July 28, 1865, until September of that year it was the stated policy of the Freedmen's Bureau, an agency of the U.S. government, that a "region-wide redistribution of abandoned and confiscated lands in the South"[6] would take place. Some writers have pointed out that the policy was "understood (if not put into practice) by army officers in the South."[7]

The ultimate equity of land distribution to freedmen and women was of more than passing concern to U.S. industry. The possibility of land redistribution to the agricultural proletariat raised the question of the relationship of the industrial proletariat to the factory owners. If agricultural laborers actually owned their own land, how long would it be before the industrial proletariat also demanded ownership of the site and the machinery into which they too poured their life's energy. Northern elites, unwilling to support such a measure, began to shift their allegiance to southern elites.

Not willing to linger until they once again lost control of the South, northern industrialists pressed for the immediate resumption of southern production under a contract system analogous to the wage labor system operative in northern factories. In return for laboring on the plantation, workers would be paid partly in cash and partly in kind, a procedure to be implemented through the Freedmen's Bureau.[8]

Ownership of the land was restored to southern elites through the Amnesty Oath on May 29, 1865. Seeking another profitable system they settled upon the division of land into farms that could be cultivated by the families who lived on them. Dr. A. D. McCoy, supported by Jefferson Davis, urged persons

who have large tracts of land or landed estates, which they used to cultivate with a great number of slaves . . . [to] erect on them houses . . . and divide among them your stock and your farming utensils. See that each family is supplied with food sufficient to them. . . . Let your contracts be so made, that when exigencies arise . . . you may concentrate the labor on any portion of the estate. . . . Let half of these wages be paid at suitable intervals. . . . The other half retained, giving your obligation first, at the end of each year.[9]

McCoy thought that Black people could only work under conditions of bondage and suggested that the white sons and daughters of men who fought for the Confederacy but did not own any land would logically become the labor force. McCoy underestimated both the pressure northern industrialists were putting on the government to start southern production once again and the sheer size of the labor force that would have to be marshaled to accomplish such a feat. He suggested that "anti-slavery societies [would] . . . raise funds and provide for those [Blacks]."[10]

But essentially what McCoy and Davis were suggesting was the same physical configuration of land distribution that the premise of "forty acres" embodied. The difference between the two was in ownership. McCoy's plan would give the profits to the planter class while a distribution of land to the people who worked it would eliminate the planters as a class and spread profits to an entire new class of agricultural producers.

When Congress passed the legislation in the summer and fall of 1865 that created the contract system, the possibility of land ownership for freed people collapsed.[11] General Oliver Otis Howard, head of the Bureau and operating at the pleasure of the President, urged all his officials and agents to get the freedpeople to sign the contracts. Working for wages was supposed to be a measure of economic independence.[12] People who had been enslaved were now categorized as contract laborers. Planters were no longer slaveholders but employers. The economic basis for the Hayes-Tilden Compromise of 1877 was gradually taking shape on cotton plantations, the most important sectors of the southern economy as well as an important factor for northern industry.[13]

The success of the Davis Bend experiment in economic democracy paradoxically paralleled the disastrous labor contract system. Comparing the Rules and Regulations of the Freedmen's Bureau to the actual contracts reveals that the Bureau's primary aim was to begin production; the secondary purpose, which diminished over time, was to administer to Black workers. As the contracts reveal, once the working proletariat was again tied to the land, the planters began to implement what was to be another profitable system of labor extraction, sharecropping, as advocated by Dr. McCoy and Jefferson Davis.

Although the sharecrop economy developed over a period of years it is significant that the new labor system was described theoretically first, and was endorsed publicly by the one man who symbolized the old order more than any other. From this perspective, the labor contract system constituted an interregnum, a transition from slavery to peonage.

TWO LABOR SYSTEMS

When the Civil War commenced there were 4,441,830 people enslaved.[14] As laborers moved off the plantation, forever ending that form of bondage, various army units and volunteer agencies tried to take care of people's needs. But as the war pressed on matters became increasingly chaotic with services overlapping or contradicting one another. In 1863, the people providing the various services came together in a loosely knit coalition with Radical Republicans, politicians, and northern mill owners. They asked Congress to establish a national "bureau of emancipation"[15] to handle the needs of the freedmen. This request was bolstered by northern industrialists who were calling for the restoration of cotton production "to its pre-war level."[16] Before Congress addressed the issue, U.S. Adjutant General Lorenzo Thomas ordered that "the Bend with the exception of the Jefferson plantation will be leased to those who are willing and able to work lands upon their own accounts."[17]

General Thomas was referring to a ten-thousand acre peninsula jutting out into the Mississippi River where the plantations of Jefferson Davis and his brother Joseph were located. General Grant captured the "Bend" early in 1863 and planned to make it a "Negro paradise," a refuge for slaves who escaped from Davis's own Confederacy.[18] This military decision to lease the land to the producers launched an "experiment" in economic democracy. The entire peninsula was to be used by the freedmen and women. Federal authorities were to expand the program at Davis Bend in

November 1864 because the results thus far had been so promising. Although the original projection of fifteen hundred bales of cotton was reduced to 300 bales, the "experiment was a success"[19] because the producers realized a profit. After January 1, 1865, whites were not to be allowed on Davis Bend without express permission of the federal authorities. J. P. Bondmeyer, traveling through the deep South and sending reports to the American Missionary Association, noted in a letter in 1865 that the

bend is guarded by a regiment of colored soldiers stationed at the cut off and a gun boat at the west end. There are to be 5,000 freedmen now on the bend and government contemplates removing many more to this place. The design are [*sic*] to parcel out to them in such lots as they are able to cultivate.[20]

Finally, on March 3, 1865, the Congress assigned the Bureau of Refugees, Freedmen and Abandoned Lands responsibilities previously shared by military commanders and by agents of the Treasury Department. President Johnson appointed General Howard as Commissioner of the Bureau and in the same month granted amnesty "to person lately in rebellion, with restoration of all rights of property, except as slaves, and in cases where legal proceedings . . . for the confiscation of property (had) been instituted."[21] General Howard appointed Colonel Samuel Thomas as Assistant Commissioner for the state of Mississippi. Each state office was usually organized to include an Adjutant General, and Assistant Inspector General, a Surgeon-in-Chief, a Superintendent of Education, a Disbursing Officer, and a Chief Commissary of Subsistence. There was not widespread agreement as to the proper uses of the Freedmen's Bureau but everyone from local agents in the field to northern investors agreed that they "were all dependent on Negro labor." General Howard directed his commissioners to work with "certain capitalists of the North" to secure and organize labor for the cultivation of cotton.[22]

While Congress was creating the Freedmen's Bureau to administer to the new class of freed workers, the experiment in economic democracy revealed stunning results. Colonel Thomas reported to General Howard in 1865:

Colonies of freedmen working lands assigned them at Davis Bend, Camp Hawley near Natchez, are all doing well. Their crops are maturing fast. At least ten thousand bales of cotton will be raised by these people who are conducting cotton crops on their own accounts. Besides this cotton they have fine gardens and corn enough to furnish bread for their families and food for their stock till harvest time returns. . . . All passes and permits in use in these colonies have been abolished as it has been the constant aid of the Bureau to spare the colored people all annoyance possible from such causes. A more industrious, energetic body of citizens does not exist that can be seen in these colonies now.[23]

By November of 1865, the Boston Board of Trade, representing southern elite sentiments, called on the northern capitalists to "cooperate with southern landowners."[24] At the end of that year the *New York Times* said: "a workable adjustment of the realization of labor to capital was the most important work of the Freedmen's Bureau."[25]

Freedmen's Home Farms in each district served as centers for the registration and employment of freedmen "until engaged or hired by other employers." Homes were established for the "aged and infirm freedmen, and motherless children unable to perform labor." Planters, farmers, and other employers were to make application to the Superintendent of the Freedmen's Home Farms. If a person employed a father or a mother, the dependent children and/or near relatives with a "desire to go" were also sent to the plantation.[26]

Owners of plantations who swore they would obey the rules as prescribed by the Bureau were "officially" allowed to contract workers. They had to promise they would turn over one cent per pound on all cotton produced by freedworkers to the Bureau. This money was to support helpless and aged freedpeople and to promote education. Such conservative provisions aimed at eliminating widespread destitution did not challenge the structure of inequality. The transfers of money were horizontal in that they moved value from active members of the working class to inactive members of the same class. The transfers were all within the working class rather than between classes.[27]

All freed persons twelve years and older were expected to work. Laborers were classified by the Superintendent according to age. Number-one-hands were "sound" persons from twenty to forty years old receiving $25 per month if male and $18 per month if female. Persons twelve to fourteen and over fifty were considered number-three-hands and allowed to earn $15 per month if male, $10 per month if female. The Superintendent allowed one number-one-hand or the equivalent in other grades of hands to be employed for every twelve acres of tillable land.

If the employer preferred to pay "an interest in the profits . . . in lieu of the regular wages above specified" they could do so as long as the freedpersons agreed and it was approved by the Superintendent of the Freedmen's Home Farm as well as the Agent of the District. At the end of the contract period the "lessee" was to return the hands to the "Farm" from which they were taken. Full settlement was to be made and no cotton was to be "sold or shipped without previous written permit of the Special Agent of the District, or the certificate of the Superintendent of the Farm from which they were hired that wages have been fully paid."[28] The Bureau was to oversee the labor process and monitor workers and bosses who had a short time ago been slaves and owners.

Each lessee or land owner was to provide sufficient housing or "quarters" for each family. Everyone was to get "a sufficient supply of food; one acre of ground to each family of four or more persons, and also to others requiring it, same proportions." Workers were expected to labor in the owners' fields all day and then come home and work in their own small plots. If workers grew a proportion of their own food the pressure for supplying food would be eased. The above provisions are in Article XIII of the Rules and Regulations.[29] At this point it seems the lessee was to provide food at no cost to the laborers, but Article XIV stresses that the "lessee shall keep on hand a sufficient supply of wholesome food and suitable clothing which shall be sold to the laborers at the wholesale cost price, and fifteen per cent, thereon, keeping an account of the items with each laborer." Such transactions, of course, would come out of the money that was to go to the laborer at the end of the contract year.

People were to be paid for all labor performed unless they were sick, "or voluntarily neglect to work," conditions which the employer was to report to the Farm Superintendent in the first ten days after the end of the month. The Farm Superintendent would then check to see if the action should be endorsed and if so revise the contract accordingly. If a person "failed to labor," the Farm Superintendent would take the laborer back to the farm, canceling the contract when the employer paid what was due. If some quit "voluntarily" without the permission of the lessee and before the end of the term, all wages were forfeited and the employer would keep half and the government would get the other half. Greedy employers could run workers off to keep more of the profits. Colonel Thomas noted in his Annual Report to General Howard that they had to find workers at the beginning of each year to be placed on the plantations.[30]

If the lessee did not comply with the agreement through failure to furnish a proper supply of food and clothing, or otherwise was abusive, "the laborers could appeal to the Superintendent." The Superintendent could then forfeit the contract. If the employees were released the lessee would pay all wages due plus half wages until new employment was found. In practice, however, the army often refused to cooperate with the Bureau and enforce such provisions.[31]

Freedmen's Home Farms could employ: "all who were able to work, for which no wages shall be paid; food and clothing being considered an equivalent therefore; the labor performed being for the benefit of the occupations of Farm, and the general good."[32] Adult workers who resided together as man and wife were supposed to be married and assume a family name and register all births and deaths.

Plantation owners only had to pay half of the monthly wages, either in money, provisions, or clothing, until the crops were sold. Corporal punishment was strictly forbidden in Article XX: "The use of the lash, paddle, and all other cruel modes of punishment shall not be permitted or inflicted by lessees, or anyone in their employment, upon the persons of any one of the employees or their families."[33]

The Rules and Regulations concluded by instructing administrators to make provision for freedmen who wished to lease land for themselves. It is doubtful that many freedpeople knew this was possible. It is known, however, that the desire to acquire land was pervasive among the Black proletariat not only for livelihood, but also as a hedge against reenslavement.[34]

CONTRACTING IN PRACTICE

Just as slavery created the pernicious tradition that manual labor was the badge of the slave and the sphere of the Black person, the first historians of Reconstruction created the myth that freedmen refused to work, were "shiftless, lazy, and ran off to a life of hedonistic dissipation in the cities."[35] The fact is, many people were looking for family members who had been "sold off" during slavery in an effort to reunite. Further, in anticipation of receiving their own land, freedmen and women were hesitant to contract their labor. When the federal government failed to provide the land necessary to sustain a livelihood, people were forced to enter contractual agreements. People were told that if they signed contracts they and their families would become economically independent. In some regions people were required to work or were arrested for vagrancy if they refused to sign a contract.[36] In other areas General Howard had his commissioners break up the freedmen's camps and place their inhabitants where they could earn their living. Some Freedmen's Bureau commissioners thought that by reducing rations and coercing labor they were teaching former slaves not to confound freedom with idleness.[37] Others simply made the contract themselves on behalf of the workers.

Labor contracts were first made in Mississippi in the Vicksburg area in 1864. From 1865 through 1866, the year most of the contracts were written, the Freedmen's Bureau covered more and more of the state. In many areas, once the amnesty oath made restoration possible, many planters simply returned to their "landed estates" and recruited their own workers. By 1868 the accepted method of farming became sharecropping and planters simply ignored the Bureau, hiring and firing workers at will. Colonel Thomas complained bitterly that the army would refuse to take over the plantations of Confederates, leaving the door open for the return of the planters.

The contracts varied in terms of payment, expected behavior on the job, and conditions of work, despite the Rules and Regulations. Furthermore, the following provisions occurred:

— Children under twelve were contracted.
— People were expected to perform strenuous manual labor for ten hours a day, six and one-half days per week.
— People were forced to remain on plantations and could lose an entire year's wages if caught on public roads without the planter's permission.
— Workers were often expected to pay for or replace worn-out and broken equipment.
— Workers were not allowed visitors.
— Workers could be fired if their language was considered indecent.
— Many contracts failed to provide provision for the children's education, which was explicitly called for in the regulations.
— Workers were forbidden to grow their own cotton, even on their assigned garden plots.
— Employers were allowed to pay "an interest in the profits in lieu of the regulation wages" allowing them to declare there were no profits.[38]
— Workers were forced to assume responsibility for all livestock, even on Sundays.
— Police regulations were established at the discretion of the employer.
— Workers were "expected to serve their masters faithfully and respectfully."[39]
— Some workers were required to work all day and all night during the cotton harvest.
— Women were often expected to work not only in the fields, but also to perform such work as cooking, washing, ironing, and milking and "the little house-work" for the employers.

Mississippi planters colluded to keep wages depressed and at times insisted farmer "owners" give permission for a laborer to contract with another planter.[40]

Southern whites were slow to reject the ways of slavery, and the behavior of many whites often alarmed personnel of the Freedmen's

Bureau. General Howard reported that in Mississippi workers were often defrauded by whites who provoked quarrels and ran laborers off their places. In addition, after executing a fair contract, planters sometimes required workers to agree to adjustments that resulted in "unwitting consenting to the substitution of an unjust and deceptive agreement." Workers were so overcharged for "negligence or incidental expenses" that they were often poorer after a year's labor than they were at the beginning.[41]

When the federal government refused to distribute land and allowed the southern elite to reclaim the plantations, it abandoned the cause of freedwomen and freedmen. The Freedmen's Bureau propelled Black people into a variety of contractual arrangements, which were clearly exploitative, and designed primarily to produce cotton for northern mills.[42]

The failure of the labor contract system stands in sharp contrast to the triumphant success of what General Thomas characterized as the "Davis Bend experiment." During the height of activity on the Bend, 1,300 adults and 450 children comprising 181 companies or partnerships worked independently on 5,000 acres of land. People freely managed their own affairs and Bureau officials were not allowed to interfere in any way. Total profits for 1865 were $159,200. Once this was divided among the thirteen hundred adults, everyone "received an average of slightly more than $120 each for the year's work, a figure much better than that attained by freedmen who worked for white lessees in the area," reported General Thomas. He stated further:

The people have raised their own crops, made their own sales, and put the money in their pockets; none of it passed through the hands of white people or officers of the Government. The only opportunity there has been for cheating has been in the settlement made with white parties who furnish supplies.[43]

Despite the obvious success, the "experiment" in economic democracy was terminated in 1865 after four of the plantations were returned to their owners under the amnesty procedures. People were advised to seek employment elsewhere.

CONCLUSION

The labor system for Black people in the South evolved from slavery to wage labor, to peonage and sharecropping. The system operated to keep tenants poor and to make landowners rich, just as Dr. McCoy, who was supported by Jefferson Davis, had urged in 1865. The year after the fatal

Hayes-Tilden Compromise was reached (1877), the Mississippi Supreme Court restored Davis Bend to the Jefferson and Joseph Davis family. The freedom struggle was suppressed.

The rule of southern capital over the United States had ended when northern capital successfully destroyed the basis of southern wealth—slavery. In the process of capturing control of the South, the North had to abolish the slave labor system, creating a vacuum in authority that allowed many people to begin to till land in an independent manner as exemplified in Davis Bend. During this period white planters made every effort to exploit Black laborers who were contracted with them. They cheated. They lied and they stole from the workers. Eventually local power was restored and the southern elite, for the most part, was put back in place in the South, but now subordinate to the northern elite. The southern elite lost its grip over national politics, and economically the South became a virtual colony of the North. But the southern landed bourgeoisie were again allowed to plunder, exploit, and oppress Black people.[44]

Indeed, many narratives have been written about the various radical movements that flourished and realized political power during Reconstruction, but I am arguing that without a radical redistribution of the land, radical politics are ultimately doomed. And that is why Mississippi, and particularly Black Mississippi, suffers from dire poverty and economic retardation, so apparent since the Civil War. The failure to ground the civil rights revolution, dubbed by many the Second Reconstruction,[45] in fights for economic equality is historically parallel to the failure to redistribute land ten years prior to the end of Reconstruction.[46]

In the middle of this century continuing racial injustices spawned the civil rights movement. Some gains were made in educational and electoral arenas but the economic struggle was postponed until Dr. Martin Luther King, Jr., brought the two together by launching the Poor People's Campaign and by joining the Memphis sanitation workers' strike. It was at this point that Dr. King was assassinated.[47] The price today is a worsening of life for African Americans: "In 1984 the largest differential in wealth holdings occurred between white and Black householders. White householders had a median net worth of $39,140, while the figure for Black householders was $3,400."[48]

Today, the Mississippi Delta is one of the most fertile areas in the world and one of the most impoverished in the United States. In 1985, per capita income for the region averaged $7,001 compared to the nationwide figure of $12,464. As a 1989 development commission report found, "Tunica County, Mississippi is the poorest county in the country, with 52.8 percent of its population living in poverty."[49] In March 1984, regional unemployment averaged 11.12 percent compared to the U.S. average of 5.21 percent. The region's infant mortality in 1980–1984 was 23.7 deaths per 1000, compared to 10.7 nationwide.[50]

In the words of one resident, "the only jobs for Black people in the Delta are driving an iron horse, which is a tractor, working at a gin and compressing or harvesting catfish."[51] The world's largest catfish processing plant, part of a $650 million white-owned industry, is located in Indianola, where 90 percent of the heads of household are women under thirty. Wages in the Delta Pride plant are just slightly above welfare stipends, allowing women a little more cash but still forcing people to rely on food stamps to feed families.[52] Low wages, oppressive and dangerous plant conditions, and sexual harassment led twelve hundred workers at Delta Pride to strike on September 12, 1990. The entire South watched this battle, many progressives hoping it would renew the civil rights revolution—this time grounding itself in movements for economic equality.[53]

NOTES

1. W.E.B. Du Bois, *Black Reconstruction in America, 1860–1880* (1935; reprint, New York, 1983); Kenneth Stampp, "Triumph of the Conservatives," in *Reconstruction*, ed. Staughton Lynd (New York, 1967); Joel Williamson, *After Slavery* (New York, 1965).

2. T. Harry Williams, ed., *Abraham Lincoln: Selected Speeches* (New York, 1957), 211.

3. Janet Sharp Hermann, *Pursuit of a Dream* (New York, 1983), 61.

4. William S. McFeeley, *Yankee Stepfather: General O. O. Howard and the Freedmen* (New Haven, CT, 1968) 105; George R. Bentley, *A History of the Freedmen's Bureau* (Philadelphia, PA, 1955), 93.

5. McFeeley, 105.

6. Bentley, 89.

7. A. D. McCoy, "Labor in the South: Past, Present, and Future" (New Orleans, 1865), 30. Jefferson Davis, President of the Confederacy, was not allowed under the terms of the amnesty oath to agitate for the restoration of slavery, so Davis used McCoy's surname when addressing his constituency.

8. Bentley, 89.

9. McCoy, 30.

10. McCoy, 30.

11. John Eaton, *Grant, Lincoln and the Freedmen* (New York, 1907), 86.

12. *Rules and Regulations for the Government of Freedmen at Davis Bend, Mississippi*, Paragraph 1 (March 1864). National Archives, Washington, DC, Mississippi Volume 122.

13. C. Vann Woodward, *Reunion and Reaction* (New York, 1951).

14. Du Bois, 100.

15. Bentley, 30.

16. Bentley, 82.

17. McFeeley, 106.

18. James T. Currie, *Enclave: Vicksburg and Her Plantations, 1868–1870* (Jackson, MS, 1980), 75.

19. Col. S. Thomas, *Report to the Bureau for the Quarter Ending 31 December 1865*. National Archives, Washington, DC, Mississippi Volume 122.

20. Letter from J. P. Bondmeyer to the American Missionary Association, 1865.

21. Eric L. McKitrick, *Andrew Jackson and Reconstruction* (Chicago, 1960), 96.

22. Eaton, 150.

23. Col. S. Thomas, *Report to the Bureau for the Quarter Ending 31 December 1865*. National Archives, Washington, DC, Mississippi Volume 122.

24. Bentley, 84.

25. Eaton, 200.

26. *Rules and Regulations for the Government of Freedmen at Davis Bend, Mississippi* (March 1864). National Archives, Washington, DC, Mississippi Volume 122.

27. Edward Greenberg, *The American Political System*, 4th ed. (New York, 1986).

28. *Second Annual Report of the New England Freedmen's Society*, 21 April 1865.

29. *Rules and Regulations for the Government of Freedmen at Davis Bend, Mississippi* (March 1864). National Archives, Washington, DC, Mississippi Volume 122.

30. Col. S. Thomas, *Report to the Bureau for the Quarter Ending 31 December 1865*. National Archives, Washington, DC, Mississippi Volume 122.

31. Col. S. Thomas, *Report to the Bureau for the Quarter Ending 31 December 1865*. National Archives, Washington, DC, Mississippi Volume 122.

32. *Rules and Regulations for the Government of Freedmen at Davis Bend, Mississippi* (March 1864). National Archives, Washington DC, Mississippi Volume 122.

33. *Rules and Regulations for the Government of Freedmen at Davis Bend, Mississippi* (March 1864). National Archives, Washington, DC, Mississippi Volume 122.

34. *Rules and Regulations for the Government of Freedmen at Davis Bend, Mississippi* (March 1864). National Archives, Washington, DC, Mississippi Volume 122.

35. Eric Williams, *Capitalism and Slavery* (New York, 1961), 5.

36. Edward Magdol, *A Right to the Land: Essays on the Freedmen's Community* (London, 1977), 51.

37. Bentley, 84.

38. *Labor Contract Between Freedmen and Women and Ed Robinson.* The Mississippi Department of Archives and History.

39. *Labor Contract Between Twenty-four Workers and the Owners of the Deer Creek Plantation in Washington County.* The Mississippi Department of Archives and History.

40. Col. S. Thomas, *Report to the Bureau for the Quarter Ending 31 December 1865.* National Archives, Washington, DC, Mississippi Volume 122.

41. Col. S. Thomas, *Report to the Bureau for the Quarter Ending 31 December 1865.* National Archives, Washington DC, Mississippi Volume 122.

42. Eaton, 205; Bentley, 35.

43. Col. S. Thomas, *Report to the Bureau for the Quarter Ending 31 December 1865.* National Archives, Washington, DC, Mississippi Volume 122.

44. Du Bois, 3; C. Vann Woodward, 67; Louis Kushnick, "U.S.: The Revocation of Civil Rights," *Race and Class* 32:1 (July–September 1990): 51.

45. E. J. Dionne, Jr., "Politics: Civil Rights Ruling Have Many Asking, Is the Second Reconstruction Coming to an End," *New York Times* (13 July 1989): 12.

46. For an overview of the first Reconstruction, see Eric Foner, *Reconstruction: America's Unfinished Revolution, 1863–1877* (New York, 1988).

47. Taylor Branch, *Parting the Waters: America in the King Years, 1954–63* (New York, 1988), 922; Howell Raines, *My Soul Is Rested* (New York, 1978), 522.

48. "Household Wealth and Asset Ownership: 1984," *Survey of Income and Program Participation, Household Economic Studies*, Series P-70, No. 7, Bureau of the Census, 4. In 1984 the Census Bureau issued the first report indicating household differentials. The most recent 1988 report indicated that the median net worth of the African American household was $4,170 compared to $43,280 for white households. The estimates are not significantly different from the 1984 reports. According to the *Jackson Advocate* (21–27 February 1991): 3A,

The report defines net worth as the value of assets minus debts. Assets covered include interest-earning assets, stocks and mutual fund shares, real estate, own business or profession, mortgages held by sellers and motor vehicles. Liabilities covered include debts secured by any asset, plus credit card or store bills, bank loans and other unsecured debts.

49. "Body of the Nation," The Interim Report of the Lower Mississippi Delta Development Commission (16 October 1989), 41.

50. "Body of the Nation," xxix.

51. *The Delta 1990*, Special Publication of the Department of Mass Communications, Jackson State University, Jackson, Mississippi (Spring 1990).

52. *The Delta 1990*; "Coming of Age: the Mississippi Delta," *National Journal* 4 (6 October 1990): 2382–2389.

53. The workers voted to settle on 14 December 1990, ending the three-month strike. Among other things the workers gained slightly higher wages and an employee-management safety board. The compromise settlement reduced the

potential of this strike to serve as a spark for labor insurgency. Per capita income in Mississippi in 1992 was $9,700, while the national average was $14,420. In the past ten years the number of people living below the poverty level in Mississippi jumped from 18.7 percent to 22 percent.

Part 4 Culture, Education, and the Working Class

8 Legitimizing the Mass Media Structure: The Socialists and American Broadcasting, 1926–1932

Nathan Godfried

Conventional wisdom holds that the U.S. mass media, operating in a private enterprise structure, allow relatively open access to all interested parties and grant success to those participants who best respond to market forces. Supporters of this system "celebrate the media status quo" with praise for the media's freedom, objectivity, diversity, public access, and social responsibility.[1] Such a perspective, however, ignores fundamental contradictions of the mass media in the United States, among them that certain privileged classes or ruling elites own, operate, or otherwise dominate the nation's means of mass communication. Throughout the twentieth century, these groups have monopolized the media in order to maximize their profits. At the same time, they have used the media to "inculcate and defend" their socioeconomic and political agenda and to regulate and often repress the expression of ideas they deem dangerous to the established order.[2]

The U.S. media's concentrated nature and problematic rhetoric have been well documented.[3] Several scholars of U.S. labor, radicalism, race, and ethnicity have noted the significance of the media—especially the print media—for their subjects. Philip S. Foner's extensive writings, for example, have included helpful analyses of leading radical and labor periodicals and editors.[4] Less apparent in the histories of radicals, labor, or the media are systematic analyses of the dialectical relationship between the dominant media structure and its challengers.[5] This study explores the interaction between one "dissident" group, the Socialist Party, and the nascent medium of radio broadcasting in the United States during the 1920s and the early 1930s.

THE DOMINANT BROADCASTING STRUCTURE

Radio broadcasting burst onto the U.S. scene during the 1920s. The Commerce Department issued only twenty-eight broadcasting licenses in 1921, but it recorded 571 stations operating in the United States in 1925. That same year, Commerce Secretary Herbert Hoover declared that the ether had reached a "saturation point"; that there were too many radio stations operating; and that no further licenses would be issued. Over the previous years, Hoover had established an informal radio regulatory structure based on a series of national radio conferences—dominated by corporate interests. A U.S. District Court ruling in April 1926 and a similar decision by the Justice Department in July, however, forced Hoover to abandon both his ban on the issuing of radio licenses and his extralegal regulatory apparatus.[6]

The absence of a state regulatory system exacerbated an increasingly chaotic radio field in 1926. All the broadcasting participants, from corporate giants to amateurs, demanded some kind of federal supervision. Congress passed a compromise radio bill in early 1927. The Radio Act of 1927 created a temporary (later made permanent) Federal Radio Commission (FRC) and authorized it to regulate the medium. In particular, Congress gave the FRC the power to grant licenses, classify stations, assign wavelengths, and provide an equitable distribution of facilities. The 1927 law also designated the electromagnetic spectrum as a valuable but limited national natural resource. Broadcasting became a privilege rather than a right. Private licensees could not own but merely use the public airwaves for a limited period (a maximum of three years). The FRC would grant, renew, and transfer licenses on the basis of the "public interest, convenience and necessity."[7]

During 1927 and 1928, the commissioners and staff of the FRC struggled with creating a radio system based on the vague public interest test. A distinct pattern gradually emerged as the FRC approved licenses and assigned and reassigned wave lengths. Commissioner Orestes H. Caldwell later explained that the FRC favored "good-behavior" stations, which consistently put "out programs in the public service." The Commission reasoned that the public interest required the most economical, efficient, and full use of the limited available frequencies. The public interest also demanded that radio serve the general public rather than special interests. Adequately financed broadcasting stations, endowed with the most advanced technology and the skilled staff to use it, could provide continuous service and thus pass the public interest test. FRC logic deduced that these same stations, owned and operated by large business organs and seeking to sell air time, developed programming aimed at the largest possible audience. Religious organizations, educators, civic groups, and organized labor on the other hand, constituted special interests. According to the FRC, radio stations under the direction of these special interests served small, select audiences and suffered from underfinanced and poorly equipped facilities and unskilled personnel. Thus the FRC concluded that large commercial stations best served the general public. In a series of frequency allocation decisions during 1928, the FRC enhanced these stations' already privileged position by bestowing upon them exclusive wavelengths, unlimited time, and huge power allocations.[8]

The U.S. radio industry had developed, by 1929, the framework that would define it for the next quarter century. Private commercial radio broadcasters devoted themselves to maximizing profits and to protecting licenses as permanent private property rights. They talked about serving the public welfare, but defined the concept in self-serving terms. They had little interest or desire to insure equality of access of radio facilities to varying views.[9] Workers, trade unionists, farmers, peace advocates, and other social activists enjoyed few alternatives to the corporate radio monopoly. Powerful independent stations such as the *Chicago Tribune*'s WGN differed only minimally from stations controlled by the network giants—the National Broadcasting Company (NBC) and the Columbia Broadcasting System (CBS).

Corporate control over the resources and institutions of broadcasting (radio's "means of production") was neither inevitable nor complete. As historian George Lipsitz has explained,

dominant groups must not only win the war of maneuver . . . , but they must win the war of position as well; they must make their triumph appear legitimate in the eyes of the vanquished. That legitimation is hard work. It requires concessions to aggrieved antagonistic groups, and it always runs the risk of unraveling when lived experiences conflict with legitimizing ideologies.[10]

Thus corporate radio broadcasters fought off their numerous critics by demonstrating that the dominant system was the best of all possible worlds; that it served the interests of all groups and classes in society. To some extent they succeeded in this effort.

As radio broadcasting's commercial and regulatory structures developed during the 1920s, leaders of industry, the federal government, and conservative labor unions hailed the emerging system as beneficial to all groups in society. *Radio Broadcast*, a mouthpiece for the industry, proclaimed in 1929 that "there is no instrumentality which serves the public without discrimination on a broader scale than radio broadcasting." William Green, president of the American Federation of Labor (AFL), bought into the dominant ideology. He argued that organized labor needed to work with the commercial broadcasting system, not against it. If business firms advertised and sponsored programs on commercial radio, organized labor could do likewise. As Green often noted, "ownership of a station is not necessary in order to have time allocated for discussion of the problems of workers."[11] Social activists in various parts of the nation nevertheless worried that the immense power and influence of the mass media, which resided in the hands of the capital sector, threatened progressive interests.

When confronted with the dominant institutions of the broadcast media during the late 1920s and early 1930s, progressives and radicals responded in one of two ways.[12] Some worked through the legislative and judicial branches to alter the existing system. This meant seeking antitrust action against radio manufacturers and broadcast networks or legislation mandating clear channels for educators, farmers, trade unions, and civic organizations. Other groups challenged the private corporate radio structure by attempting to construct their own alternative broadcast outlets. The Socialist Party of America chose this latter option in 1926 when it decided to erect a broadcasting station. At the same time that the socialists attempted to create an *alternative to* the dominant media, however, they worked *with* dominant radio institutions—in particular NBC—to get their message to the public. The Socialist Party's dual radio strategy revealed a contradictory relationship between the party and its radio station on the one hand, and the corporate radio structure and the state regulatory apparatus on the other. This relationship reveals much about the process of legitimizing the dominant mass media structure in the United States.

WEVD, 1926–1928

The Socialist Party of the 1920s and 1930s was a mere shadow of its former self. The upheavals of World War I irrevocably split the party. When the "Old Guard" purged the organization's left wing in 1919, it lost perhaps as much as two-thirds of the party membership to newly formed communist organs. Morris Hillquit, Adolph Germer, and other "conservative" veterans retained control over the party name and machinery, but little else. A decimated Socialist Party suffered from a lack of leadership, growing factionalism, weak local and regional organization, and financial crises through most of the 1920s. The party reached a low point in the 1928 presidential election when it received less than 1 percent of the total vote cast and recorded fewer than eight thousand members.[13]

Although humiliated by his showing in 1928, the party's new leader, Norman Thomas, displayed enormous energy and commitment. He directed a brief revival of the party between 1928 and 1932, helping to double the party's membership rolls by 1932 and to secure some nine-hundred thousand votes in that year's presidential election. Thomas's "perpetual speaking" to strikers, civil libertarians, students, and others stimulated much interest in, if not support for, the Socialist Party.[14] Searching for vehicles to spread the socialist message directly to the people, party officials quickly realized the educational, informational, and propaganda value of radio.

Personal experience with the corporate radio systems taught the socialists that "reactionary interests" and especially the hated "radio trust" threatened to dominate this vehicle of potential change.[15] AT&T's station WEAF in New York, for example, refused to broadcast a Norman Thomas speech in April 1926. WEAF managers found the talk on the role of the schools in achieving peace "full of controversial topics." Thomas denounced the decision as a "virtual censorship of ideas." He warned that broadcasting would become a "social curse" so long as corporate radio "arbitrarily" exercised its immense influence to obscure social questions.[16]

Many socialists held out little hope for popular control of broadcasting. Editors of the Socialist Party newspaper, the *New Leader*, explained that the expense of constructing and maintaining a radio station involved large sums of capital investment and that this "automatically" made radio "an instrument of the capital owning class." Capitalists obviously viewed radio as their property and sought to use it to maximize their profits, not to engage in the free discussion or dissemination of ideas. As the radio industry became more and more concentrated, broadcast programs became "as standardized as the products of a Ford factory." All these bleak observations notwithstanding, the *New Leader* urged "more diversity of views" in the ether and alternatives to the dominant system.[17]

At its December 1926 meeting, the Socialist Party's National Executive Committee decided to erect a radio broadcasting station as a living memorial to Eugene V. Debs, the great socialist leader who had died a few months earlier. The proposed station, WDEBS, would "champion the cause of liberty and social justice in the broad and liberal spirit" of Debs, while entertaining its listeners.[18] Socialist Party officials Norman Thomas, Morris Hillquit, and G. August Gerber became chair, treasurer, and secretary, respectively, of the Board of Trustees of the Debs Memorial Radio Fund. Seeking to create a nonsectarian station, the fund's officers selected trustees from across the liberal-radical-labor continuum. Included were such progressive luminaries as Harry F. Ward (theologian and social activist), A. Philip Randolph (president of the Brotherhood of Sleeping Car Porters), Upton Sinclair (radical writer), Abraham Cahan (editor of the *Jewish Daily Forward*), Roger Baldwin (civil libertarian), and Harriot Stanton Blatch (feminist leader).[19]

At a meeting of the trustees of the Debs Memorial Radio Fund in March 1927, Gerber reported on organizational plans and unresolved problems. A mailing of 15,000 letters soliciting support for the station produced some $2,656 of contributions from labor organizations, the *Jewish Daily Forward*, and individuals. The trustees recognized the need to continue fund-raising efforts among these and other sympathetic sources. Prospective contributors, explained Gerber, feared that the FRC would not license a Socialist Party radio station. The trustees selected a "delegation" to plead WDEBS's case before the FRC in April 1927 and discussed "launching a freedom of the radio fight" if "Debs radio" failed to secure a license.[20]

On the mundane matters of station location, construction, maintenance, and operation, Gerber referred to the experience of Chicago station WCFL. Created by the Chicago Federation of Labor in 1926, WCFL dedicated itself to serving the U.S. working class.[21] Gerber noted the possibility of linking WCFL with WDEBS and "creating a chain . . . of progressive, liberal, labor and radical stations." WCFL engineer Larry J. Lesh helped Gerber estimate the annual expenditures for WDEBS. Gerber hoped that by raising $250,000, the Debs Fund could pay the initial cost of the plant—approximately $100,000—and use the income from the invested surplus to meet maintenance and operating costs. The trustees concluded by reaffirming their commitment to creating a "forum for liberal, progressive, labor and radical purposes, and not merely and solely as a Socialist Party enterprise."[22]

Gerber and other officers of "Debs radio" spent the spring and summer of 1927 raising money, negotiating the purchase of a broadcasting station, and securing a license from the FRC. Debs radio received the bulk of its contributions from trade unions closely associated with the Socialist Party (unions centered in the garment trades), local and state branches of the party, and organizations linked to the socialists (e.g., the League for Industrial Democracy).[23] As financing proceeded, radio fund trustees received assurances from FRC members that the commission would grant a license the moment the fund purchased a station. WCFL's Larry Lesh visited New York in early June to help Gerber inspect the equipment of station WSOM. The Debs fund bought the Long Island station in early August. It received a license from the FRC shortly thereafter. Since only aircraft could use five-letter call names such as WDEBS, Debs radio became WEVD. It broadcast over the frequency of 1220 kc, but shared its wavelength and hence broadcast time with small stations in Long Island and New Jersey.[24]

As WEVD prepared for operation, August Gerber promised that the station would not merely report events and provide music and entertainment, but would become "a fighting, militant champion of the rights of the oppressed" and all those who produced the country's wealth. Gerber stressed another basic premise of the station: WEVD "will guarantee to minority opinion in America, its right to be heard without censorship."[25] Various speakers echoed these sentiments at the station's dedication ceremony on October 20, 1927—the first anniversary of Eugene V. Debs's death. Norman Thomas, among others, pledged the station to serve the causes represented by Debs, but not to make WEVD into strictly a Socialist Party voice. Like a daily newspaper, WEVD would supply the radio audience with firsthand news of events of interest to workers, while offering "distinctly different" entertainment programs. Thomas urged supporters of the station to give "a multitude of small monthly gifts."[26]

Financial problems plagued WEVD's first years of operation. The station received support from New York area trade unions. The International Ladies' Garment Workers' Union gave WEVD free use of the entire sixth floor of its building in New York City. The station converted the floor into studios and reception rooms. Morris Sigman, ILGWU president, acknowledged the importance of radio "in the lives of the masses of American workers and accordingly in the lives of our own members." At a meeting organized by the ILGWU in December 1927, eighty representatives from various trade unions and fraternal orders discussed how to provide WEVD with "year-round" assistance and how to make increasing use of the station.[27]

Seeking wider support from the New York progressive community, WEVD's Board of Trustees negotiated with the American Civil Liberties Union and the American Fund for Public Service. In return for periodic payments from the ACLU, WEVD promised not to censor speeches or to discriminate against representatives of any social group. The radio station once again pledged to give preference to "authorized representatives of minority movements who are not given equal opportunity on other stations."[28] Thomas praised such efforts by Gerber to keep WEVD alive, but he wrote to Gerber in early January 1928 that "we can't go on living like this."[29]

On May 25, 1928, the FRC asked 164 stations, including WEVD, to show cause why their licenses should not be revoked. This was one of many decisions by the commission to rationalize and stabilize the chaotic radio field by eliminating small, weak special interest stations. Gerber responded to FRC General Order No. 32 by calling on the labor and progressive community to circulate petitions and write letters supporting WEVD. Station officials also urgently requested money to cover the expense of defending the station against the FRC and to make needed improvements. Failure to defend WEVD, Gerber told New York labor leader Harry Wander, would leave radio in the hands of "reactionaries, labor haters, . . . ministers of religion, . . . and other propagandists." Liberal politicians from New York, civic organizations in New York, Pennsylvania, California, and elsewhere, religious groups, and labor unions and trade union councils sent protest letters and petitions to the FRC. They insisted that only WEVD was dedicated to minority opinion, peace, and the labor movement. Although the FRC refused to consider such examples of public sentiment, Gerber contended that this mass outpouring of support for WEVD proved that the station fulfilled an important public service.[30]

WEVD and the Socialist Party questioned the FRC ruling by focusing on the issues of free speech and minority rights. Why, wondered the Socialist Party, did the broadcasting of labor, progressive, socialist, and peace speakers fail to constitute a public service? Why condemn WEVD as one of those "small and comparatively weak stations that cumber the air," when it was the FRC that had assigned the station to the radio "graveyard"? Why consider a station that emphasized education, minority viewpoints, and free speech "superfluous" and order its elimination? Answers to these questions inevitably led some socialists to conclude that collusion between the radio trust and the state regulatory agency produced the class-biased General Order No. 32. Denying a license to WEVD amounted to suppressing minority opinions. Gerber demanded that the FRC not only renew WEVD's license, but also increase its power and grant it an exclusive wavelength.[31]

WEVD accompanied 109 other threatened stations to the Interior Department building in Washington, D.C., where the FRC held hearings for two weeks in July 1928. There Gerber and Norman Thomas "argued the right of dissident minorities to free speech over the radio." They contended that WEVD represented the only broadcast outlet in the East controlled by and "devoted to working class and liberal causes." By linking "dissident minorities" with the working class, Thomas and Gerber reinforced, rather than challenged, the view of the radio trust and FRC that workers constituted a special interest group. This flawed strategy revealed a fundamental weakness in the Socialist Party's understanding of the nature of the corporate mass media and the state. WEVD officials, on the other hand, clearly stated the station's political perspective: WEVD was "not interested in the latest quotations on the stock market but in giving information on the administration's war in Nicaragua, the use of gunboats in China, and all other fundamental matters of politics and of social and industrial struggle." Thomas insisted that WEVD stood with community-based stations "against the big chain system which 'tends to standardize—to make robots and Babbitts of the American people.'"[32]

Gerber and Thomas attempted to shift the burden of proof from WEVD to the FRC. They explained that criticisms of WEVD's audience size really reflected the FRC's failure to provide Debs radio with adequate power, time, and frequency. WEVD's noncommercial, listener-supported structure, personnel, audience, programs, and clear popular support demonstrated, by definition, public service. The FRC handed corporate interests the best frequencies, maximum power, and full time "on a silver platter." WEVD sought only a fair chance. Closing WEVD, asserted Thomas and Gerber, "will be correctly construed by the public as extreme intolerance and complete censorship of the air."[33]

The FRC approved the renewal of WEVD's license one month following the hearings. The commission dismissed the complaints against the station—problems of interference and character of programming—as unjustified. "The evidence shows," reported the FRC, "that the station has pursued a very satisfactory policy." So long as a station complied with the requirements of the law and respected the opinions of others, the FRC refused to abolish "any station doing an altruistic work, or which is the mouthpiece of a substantial political or religious minority."[34]

The members of the commission obviously objected to the doctrines broadcast over WEVD, but they recognized that the weakened Socialist Party represented only a minor irritant to corporate and state elite by the late 1920s. The FRC clearly embraced the argument of Gerber and Thomas that WEVD catered to a variety of "minority" opinions. "To eliminate a station because of its political views," commented *New York Times* editors immediately following the WEVD decision, "would be both unjust and stupid."[35] Federal commissioners viewed this case as the perfect opportunity to demonstrate the openness and fairness of the state regulatory system and private corporate broadcast structure. Scholars of U.S. broadcasting such as Ruth Brindze, Fred W. Friendly, and Erik Barnouw have all commented on how the WEVD case served, in Brindze's words, as "a useful and convenient" defense against criticism that the FRC favored "the air monopolists over the 'little fellow.' "[36] By allowing the weak and apparently ineffective WEVD to continue its operations, the FRC "proved" the diversity and democracy of the U.S. broadcasting system.

Having survived their first battle with the FRC, WEVD officials turned to improving station programming. Some observers already considered

WEVD a "militant" supporter of trade unions in New York City by 1928. WEVD's news commentary shows also won praise for their thoughtful analyses. The diversity of political, social, and economic issues discussed over WEVD matched, if not surpassed, that of any other broadcast outlet in the metropolitan area. During its first year of operation, WEVD presented debates on U.S. foreign policy in Nicaragua, talks on general labor conditions, an eyewitness account of the industrial conflict raging between coal operators and miners in Colorado, and, of course, extensive lectures on socialism. "Debs radio" was the only New York station to broadcast music, poetry, and speeches celebrating May Day. In general, the classical and dance music over WEVD was, as one newspaper columnist wrote, "well selected and soundly performed."[37]

WEVD presented shows for New York's diverse population. These included a "Jewish Hour" and a "Negro Art Group" program. During one week in February 1928, WEVD produced and broadcast three shows (total time ninety minutes) on African American literature, music, and history. The Brotherhood of Sleeping Car Porters sponsored a weekly "Pullman Porters Hour" consisting of "Negro singers and musicians, together with talks" on the union's "fight for a living wage" and its general goals and services. WEVD was one of the few stations with a regular woman announcer. Debs radio listeners shared the sentiments of a *New York Sun* columnist: "WEVD has a definite place to fill, and it is filling that place effectively."[38]

WEVD's educational director, Paul Blanshard, implemented an extensive program for workers' education following the renewal of WEVD's license in August 1928. A. J. Muste of the Brookwood Labor College conducted a series of evening educational courses on economic problems. A Sunday afternoon forum series, inaugurated in September 1928, included such speakers as Walter Lippmann, Rabbi Stephen S. Wise, Oswald Garrison Villard, and Roger Baldwin. The Rand School—an adult education institution founded by the Socialist Party in 1906—also produced a weekly program for WEVD during 1929–1930. The Federated Press, the independent radical labor news service, organized a news show each Thursday evening during 1929. WEVD, of course, aired the campaign speeches of Socialist Party candidates, covered the party's 1928 national convention, and carried local labor announcements and talks. To facilitate this expanded educational and political programming fare, WEVD management requested more evening airtime and greater power from the FRC.[39] But Norman Thomas understood the limitations of the station and took other steps to guarantee the party's access to the air waves.

THE SOCIALIST PARTY AND NBC

Writing in January 1929, Thomas noted that the experiences of the last campaign reinforced "the great value of radio" to the Socialist Party. While hoping that the Debs Radio Fund could adequately build up WEVD, neither Thomas nor other party officials were willing to wait the indeterminable period necessary for WEVD to realize its potential. Even when the station did fully develop, it would not reach either a regional or national audience. Since the socialists retained dreams of operating in the national arena, they would need access to radio on a national level. Thomas concluded that the party had to expand its efforts to secure free time over commercial stations.[40] Socialist Party efforts to gain access to the corporate broadcasters coincided with the conception of WEVD and the emergence of the National Broadcasting Company.

The Radio Corporation of America created NBC on September 9, 1926. Two New York stations, WEAF (which had refused to broadcast the Norman Thomas speech in April 1926) and WJZ became "flagships" of NBC's Red and Blue networks, respectively. A child of RCA—the heart of the radio trust—NBC sought to dispel rumors of a radio broadcast monopoly by proclaiming its intention to broadcast all shades of political opinion. The Socialist Party inadvertently tested this claim in December 1926 when the New York branch of the party asked WJZ about the possibility of broadcasting a speech by Thomas on the subject, "An American Labor Party." NBC President Merlin H. Aylesworth answered the inquiry by explaining that NBC now managed WJZ. While he remained uncertain as to how many listeners would be interested in Thomas's topic, Aylesworth nevertheless "decided to resolve this doubt in favor of the speaker and the subject." NBC scheduled Thomas to speak over WJZ on January 10, 1927 from 8:15 to 8:30 P.M..[41]

This decision and subsequent ones revealed Aylesworth's understanding of the need to "legitimize" the new network structure. As managing director of the National Electric Light Association for many years prior to coming to NBC, Aylesworth supervised a massive propaganda campaign aimed at schools and colleges to legitimize private corporate control over power projects and to prevent government interference and public programs.[42] To head off any "public" effort to control corporate network radio, Aylesworth jumped at the chance to demonstrate the openness and fairness of NBC to "dissident" political opinions.

When the WJZ station manager sent Aylesworth a copy of Thomas's talk two days before the broadcast, the NBC president immediately returned it. The network wished to avoid all appearances of censorship. "I have not read the speech," Aylesworth wrote to the WJZ manager, "preferring to hear it over the radio. Certainly I do not care to censor it." Upon reading this, Thomas commented that "it was the first time in his radio experience that an official did not wish to censor his copy."[43]

Aylesworth's action also impressed WJZ listeners who commended the network policy of broadcasting "well-balanced programs" of public importance. Every subject, from music to politics to religion to education, contended the NBC president, "is more or less controversial. . . . My only interest is to produce that which the listening public will appreciate."[44] Not everyone, however, embraced NBC's tolerance. Ralph M. Easley, chair of the executive council of the National Civic Federation, lambasted Aylesworth for helping to promote "irrelevant" socialist propaganda. According to Easley, communists and "free speech fakers" would now demand equal rights with socialists over NBC. Easley recommended that Aylesworth prepare his "stuffed club."[45]

NBC never needed to use a "stuffed club" with Norman Thomas and the Socialist Party. The powerful broadcast network and the weak political organ developed a fairly close working relationship—best exemplified by the growing professional friendship between Thomas and Aylesworth. When Thomas sought national radio coverage of the Socialist Party convention in April 1928, he wrote directly to Aylesworth. Thomas admitted that WEVD was in poor shape and might not be able to broadcast even to the New York City area. The two men worked out a deal whereby WEAF and its Red network broadcasted a twenty-minute summary of each day's convention proceedings at 11:00 P.M. Aylesworth also assured Thomas that during the upcoming presidential campaign, NBC would provide "equal treatment" to candidates of the three parties.[46]

The Socialist Party's commitment to WEVD must be viewed within the context of the party's symbiotic relationship with NBC. Aylesworth provided Thomas and his party with valuable, albeit restricted, national exposure, while the socialists helped NBC to legitimize the existing corporate radio structure. Party leaders tried not to ignore "Debs radio" while seeking access to the corporate networks. Gerber and Thomas continually urged the party faithful and progressive civic and labor groups to use WEVD's facilities and to support the station financially. The response, however, was disappointing. Despite its important programs, WEVD continued to suffer from poor frequency, an erratic schedule, financial problems, and the divided attention of Socialist Party officials.[47]

LOSING THE "WAR OF POSITION"

The Debs Memorial Radio Fund secured a new frequency (1300 kc) from the FRC in the late winter of 1929. Still forced to share time with three other stations, officials fixed the broadcast schedule at fifty hours per week (varying from a high of eighteen hours on Wednesday to a low of two on Friday). WEVD managers launched a massive campaign to solicit contributions. They proclaimed WEVD "Your Broadcasting Station" and "The National Free Speech Forum," and listed the organizations (from ACLU to Workmen's Circle) and the 108 individuals (including Roger Baldwin, Fiorella LaGuardia, and W.E.B. Du Bois) who had used WEVD's facilities "free and uncensored." The station's value to the labor and progressive communities certainly would increase as broadcasting became "the established and favorite medium of publicity." Increased power meant heavier operating expenses, hence WEVD needed more assistance from its listening audience. "Send us money and send it today."[48]

Although fund-raising efforts continued throughout 1929, by the spring of 1930, WEVD officials conceded that "the Labor and Liberal movements have not shown the interest in the enterprise which its possibilities merit"; nor did the station have "the means or facilities to make the necessary mechanical improvements." Although the Socialist Party, the garment trades unions, the *Jewish Daily Forward*, and others attempted to build up the station, WEVD was caught in a vicious circle. Its poor frequency, weak power, and limited time made it difficult to build substantial community support. The divided interests of the Socialist Party leaders and the general intellectual bankruptcy of the party probably contributed to the indifference of workers to WEVD. The Great Depression's increasing devastation of the financial resources of prospective contributors undermined efforts to improve equipment and expand community outreach programs.[49] Equipment and staff problems soon brought WEVD into another confrontation with the state.

The FRC had accumulated a number of complaints against WEVD that threatened the station's future. At hearings in mid-October 1930, FRC Examiner Elmer W. Pratt declared WEVD guilty of repeated violations of the 1927 Radio Act, including failure to announce its call letters every fifteen minutes, to announce beforehand that it was playing music from a phonograph record, and to stay on its assigned wavelength. The quantity and duration of these violations indicated "such carelessness and negligence as to prove," at least to Pratt, that the station deliberately disregarded the law and FRC regulations. Pratt recommended denying WEVD's application for renewal of license.[50]

Gerber, who attended the hearings, immediately challenged Pratt's assessment. WEVD's managing director did not deny the charges, but argued instead that the station's "crimes" arose because WEVD lacked sufficient funds to employ the best personnel, purchase the best equipment, or increase its power. The "competition of the lavishly-financed programs of the (high power) radio trust stations" virtually drowned out WEVD. Norman Thomas later described WEVD's dilemma: an unsatisfactory wavelength and power made it difficult to increase funding for the station; and without stronger financial support, the station could not ask for a better wavelength and more power! The Federated Press astutely noted that the FRC action threatened to punish WEVD "for its sins of poverty."[51]

Thomas, Gerber, and Hillquit again tried to mobilize public support to save WEVD. They reiterated the right of "political and industrial minority groups . . . to broadcast their views in competition with an overwhelming volume of reactionary opinions." Thomas, shocked at the FRC decision, raised the issue of "freedom of the air in broadcasting minority opinion." The ACLU promised to help the station make the case a national fight for radio civil rights. The New Leader voiced no surprise in the revocation of WEVD's license: "All the trends in radio broadcasting are in the direction of uniformity of thought in support of the capitalist system." Both WEVD and the Chicago Federation of Labor's WCFL, according to the New Leader, sought to follow their own independent paths in broadcasting; thus the capitalist broadcasting system subjected them "to all sorts of petty annoyances" and threatened them with "summary execution."[52]

FRC Examiner Pratt formally submitted his "execution" report on December 11, 1930. Seven days later, the FRC officially notified WEVD of the examiner's non-renewal decision. Mobilized since mid-October, labor unions, civic and peace organizations, and liberal newspapers campaigned to raise sufficient funds to enable the proper operation of WEVD. WEVD officials completed and submitted, in early January 1931, a seventeen-page report showing that the examiner's recommendation was "palpably improper." Considering this information, the radio commissioners upheld WEVD's claims and granted a license renewal on January 13. But just three days later, the FRC reversed itself because the Paramount Broadcasting Company of Brooklyn, owners of WFOX, had applied for WEVD's wavelength and operating time. Debs radio station officials denounced the FRC policy as "wanton and reckless."[53]

The FRC held another round of hearings in March and then May of 1931. Examiner Pratt continued to argue that WEVD lacked the necessary finances to meet the FRC's legal and engineering requirements. In addition, Pratt contended that WEVD provided no special service to its listening area because the "speeches or other program matter broadcast by this station" could have been broadcast by other area stations.[54] Paramount's WFOX concluded that its "superior fitness to serve the 'public convenience, necessity and welfare' " gave it the right to take WEVD's wave length. WEVD, represented by Gerber and Louis G. Caldwell, the well-known corporate radio attorney and former counsel to the FRC, contested Pratt's analysis and ridiculed WFOX's spurious request. Gerber argued that the "hot" debate over WEVD's future and the possibility of handing over WEVD's wavelength to a commercial station had already intensified the public's "cynical suspicion" of the corporate-state relationship.[55]

WEVD's "public" certainly grew suspicious of the dominant media structure as they rallied once again to support their radio station. Over three hundred labor and civic organizations sent five hundred delegates to a mass meeting in New York City in early March 1931. The assembled trade unionists and community organizers adopted resolutions urging the FRC to renew WEVD's license and praising WEVD's educational programming and its open-door policy to all viewpoints.[56]

Public accolades notwithstanding, WEVD's latest difficulties with Washington forced the station's closest advisers and supporters to confront the serious problems of a lack of funds, inadequate equipment, unsatisfactory location—hence poor reception—a lack of cooperation from other organizations, and insufficient income from advertising. Morris Hillquit confessed to Gerber in late March that if the station somehow secured its license, "we shall have to get together and undertake a radical reorganization of the enterprise." Even before the FRC decided the fate of WEVD, however, a committee to reorganize the station formed in the spring of 1931. Thomas, Hillquit, Mary Fox (executive secretary of the League for Industrial Democracy), and other committee members considered four basic, interrelated issues: equipment and station location, adequate funding, the formation of a support network to plan policies and programs for the station, and "the development of a genuine educational program which will establish WEVD as a radical university of the air." Failure to resolve these problems and to save WEVD's license would be, as Mary Fox told Benjamin Schlesinger of the ILGWU, "disastrous to our labor movement and all minority movements."[57]

The reorganization committee made recommendations in each of the four problem areas. Relocating the station would improve reception over most of the city and "within a radius of 100 miles." New equipment would guarantee full use of the available five hundred watts of power and the sought-after one thousand watts. Raising $50,000, by selling stock in WEVD, would fund these changes, pay off outstanding obligations, and still leave a few thousand dollars for the inauguration of a new educational policy. Hillquit planned to modify the capital structure of "Debs radio" and form a stock-granting corporation and a membership association. Common-stock holders would elect the majority of members of the Board of Directors who would manage the affairs of the corporation. Among other functions, the board would supervise station operations, select the station general manager, and determine station policies.[58]

All of these structural changes meant little if WEVD failed to make a distinctive mark for itself in radio programming. The reorganizers decided to transform WEVD into "a university of the air for Public Education by [the] Progressive Movement." This required careful planning and direction of educational policies and daily programs. A special working committee would supervise the educational programs and, during its first six months, veto any commercial programs that might detract from the value of the station's educational work. WEVD's weekly allotment of air time included forty-four hours of "very desirable" time. Planners determined that at least half of these hours "could be devoted to straight educational work" and the other twenty-two hours could be sold to "bring in enough revenue to carry the cost of operating the station." The reorganization committee hoped that the commercial hours might "actually be educational in character" and thus fit into the larger educational program.[59]

The reorganization committee also recommended the establishment of a "newspaper of the air" with editorials, news, literature, dramatic criticisms, and special features. They proposed an editorial staff consisting of Thomas, Hillquit, Heywood Broun, B. Charney Vladeck, and others. Each editor would take a fifteen-minute period at frequent intervals "to editorialize on the news from a radical point of view." Different organizations might sponsor educational courses involving a series of fifteen-minute lectures several days a week for one or two months. While welcoming sustaining features, the reorganizers suggested that, wherever possible, such programs might have "a unique educational value." In any event, the program committee would have carefully to supervise all advertising material for sponsored programs.[60]

Adhering to the recommendations contained in the June 1931 report, WEVD underwent significant modifications during the summer and fall of 1931. One important change was the new dominant financial role played by the *Jewish Daily Forward*. The *Forward*, the world's largest Yiddish newspaper, and its editor and publisher, Abraham Cahan, had supported many Socialist Party activities. But Cahan's socialism became "steadily more diluted until by 1932 it was hardly distinguishable from conservative trade unionism." Cahan nevertheless believed in the importance of a broadcasting outlet for the cause of liberal politics in the United States. In preparation for another set of hearings before the FRC in the fall, the *Forward* deposited $70,000 in a New York bank for the purpose of improving WEVD once it secured its license. By the end of 1931, the *Forward*'s total investment in WEVD amounted to some $200,000. With the firm backing of the *Forward*, WEVD representatives prepared for the next round of battle with the FRC.[61]

Accompanied by their lawyer, Louis Caldwell, WEVD officials appeared before the commission in late September. Contending that Examiner Pratt "misunderstood the nature" of WEVD's service, Thomas and Caldwell defended the station as an open public forum available to "all schools of thought," especially "when other avenues are closed." Caldwell explained that the station was undergoing significant changes and that $70,000 had been deposited in a New York bank for improvements if the FRC renewed the station's license.[62]

The FRC's decision to approve a license renewal for WEVD, filed on October 30, 1931, was not unanimous. Two commissioners, FRC Chair Charles McK. Saltzman and Commissioner William D. L. Starbuck, a retired major general and patent attorney respectively, dissented. They rejected the argument that WEVD's role as "the voice of a minority" excused it from violating government regulations. The majority of radio commissioners, however, accepted WEVD's assurances that the station would rectify its past abuses and continue to serve those groups ignored by the powerful corporate commercial broadcasters. In addition, the majority of the FRC continued to recognize the importance of WEVD as a token demonstration of the diversity and fairness of the U.S. broadcasting system.[63]

With the financial backing of the *Forward*, WEVD moved out of the ILGWU building into its own studios and constructed a new transmitter on Long Island by the fall of 1932. The *Nation* magazine thanked the "public spirit and generosity" of the *Forward*. Acknowledging WEVD's acceptance of the basic "law" of the private corporate U.S. broadcasting system—that is, each radio station "must of course eventually pay for itself"—The *Nation* still found the station superior to other commercial stations because it would air free thought and free speech.[64]

In a tribute to Eugene Debs on September 28, 1932, WEVD celebrated the opening of its new studios. A completely reorganized executive staff, led by Program Director George Maynard—formerly of NBC—brought

John Dewey, Morris Hillquit, Oswald Garrison Villard, Abraham Cahan, and Heywood Broun to speak at the opening ceremonies. The new business department announced its goal of promoting "interesting innovations in sponsored programs."[65] Within months, WEVD officials accelerated plans for the "university of the air." A meeting of 200 writers, educators, and others at the Algonquin Hotel discussed plans for the new program. Heywood Broun, one of the founders of the new WEVD "Air College," saw "no reason why showmanship and entertainment might not be mixed with Kant, Karl Marx, Beethoven and Herbert Spencer."[66]

These changes guaranteed the survival of WEVD, but not of a socialist or radical radio station; they maintained the form, but not the substance of alternative radio. WEVD's new managers emphasized elitist "educational" fare and the expansion of sponsored (advertised) programming. Such programming eventually overwhelmed WEVD's "radical" editorials and service to working-class movements. The *Forward*'s immense financial stake in "Debs radio" (approximately $250,000) soon gave it corresponding decision-making power. As the decade progressed, WEVD became less and less committed to socialist causes. Julius Gerber, a Socialist Party official, complained on numerous occasions that the *Forward* officials in charge of WEVD spent too much time catering to U.S. liberals such as Villard (editor of the *Nation*) and too little time to the real needs of Socialist Party candidates and ideas. Station officials admitted in 1937 that "we are more conservative than we should be." Labor unions increasingly had to buy time on the station. Even when they acquired free access to WEVD's facilities, socialists and workers were subject to abrupt cancellations if sponsored programs became available. The growing importance of securing advertisers gradually pushed "the minority views" off prime-time schedules. WEVD began to define itself as an "educational" force rather than a vehicle for dissident ideas.[67] As early as 1933, WEVD turned down an offer from NBC to pick up a WJZ broadcast of a Norman Thomas speech commemorating Eugene Debs. WEVD's station manger, Morris S. Novik, thanked NBC for the offer, but noted that "unfortunately our schedule doesn't permit us to pick up this program."[68]

The vacillating fortunes of WEVD never affected the second component of the socialists' radio strategy—that is, their "special" relationship with NBC. When Norman Thomas requested air time to give a socialist response to the encyclical of Pope Pius XI in May 1931, Merlin Aylesworth complied. After the usual exchange of friendly correspondence, Thomas secured Aylesworth's agreement to provide an entire hour of coverage— via WJZ and the Blue Network—of the May 1932 Socialist Party convention. The Columbia Broadcasting System, in an effort to demonstrate its openness to dissident views, also broadcast portions of the socialist convention.[69] As the 1932 campaign proceeded, Thomas sought more air time. In a special plea to Aylesworth in August, he wrote that while he was grateful for the time NBC already had given him, he would be even more grateful for more time. "But my gratitude won't be too humble for I think it is due us in sound public policy!" Somewhat embarrassed by Thomas's supplication, Aylesworth assured Thomas that "it is not necessary for you to beg" for airtime, "we will make satisfactory arrangements with you personally."[70] When Socialist Party Executive Secretary Clarence Senior assessed the party's use of radio during 1932, he praised the nationwide hookups via NBC and CBS, but barely mentioned the role of WEVD.[71]

CONCLUSION

The Socialist Party hoped that its own radio station would disseminate socialist, progressive, pacifist, and trade union ideas. Financial problems, a poor frequency, limited time and power, and a weak Socialist Party hindered station operations from the very beginning. Increased competition from expensive network programming and technology, combined with the Great Depression, exacerbated the financial situation of WEVD. Federal radio regulators further punished WEVD for the "sin of poverty" by forcing it to justify—at tremendous cost in time, money, and energy—its very existence in 1928 and 1930–1931.

The station's supporters defended WEVD as a free speech forum for minority political and economic views. This argument—which constituted WEVD's challenge to the corporate capitalist radio structure—was fundamentally flawed. It assumed that the groups WEVD purported to serve (workers, peace advocates, immigrants, African Americans, and social activists) comprised "minorities" or "special interest" groups. Yet together, these groups, at least in the New York area, accounted for the majority. WEVD failed to articulate a challenge to the real special interests—the powerful capitalist class and its state collaborators. Socialist Party officials occasionally raised fundamental questions regarding corporate radio. While fighting for WEVD's license in 1931, for example, the *New Leader* asserted that "the advances made in corporate control of the air within the past fifteen years show the folly of permitting capitalism to dominate the radio." Yet in the same editorial, the socialist editors failed to name corporate lawyer Louis Caldwell as the leading opponent of the Chicago labor station WCFL, because he represented WEVD in its license battle![72] Radical rhetoric notwithstanding, the Socialist Party of the 1930s did not embrace a class orientation, and this weakened its attack on the capitalist-dominated media structure. WEVD failed to fulfill its potential as a counter-hegemonic institution—as an alternative to the dominant media.

By working with the corporate radio system, the Socialist Party helped the capitalist owners of radio to legitimize their power. Norman Thomas told Merlin Aylesworth, in October 1931, that he understood the role he played for NBC. Noting how some people called him Aylesworth's "pet radical," Thomas agreed that he had been "valuable" to NBC "as proof of [its] liberalism." At the same time, however, Thomas appreciated that NBC gave the Socialist Party air time and supported the continued existence of WEVD.[73] Thomas never fundamentally questioned the legitimacy of NBC to wield the influence and power it did.

NBC and CBS displayed their openness and fairness selectively. When educators, clergy, trade union officials, and politicians criticized the commercial radio networks for their worthless programming or excessive advertising and profits *and* when community leaders and groups demanded congressional action to reverse the growing power of the radio trust during the 1928–1932 period, then the networks and powerful independents moved to circumvent criticism, to undermine their opponents, and to protect the U.S. broadcasting system. They raced to serve non-threatening "dissidents" such as Norman Thomas and the Socialist Party.[74] But when the pressure lessened or when profits threatened to decline, the diversity and openness of the radio system became an illusion. Thus, in the spring of 1933, after receiving complaints from corporate enterprises regarding NBC's broadcasting of a series of talks by the League of Industrial Democracy, NBC officials decided to "discontinue" the programs.[75]

The success of alternative broadcasting rests in its responsiveness, its links, and its commitment to its immediate community. "Participation," argued Herbert I. Schiller, "may be the only means of developing and maintaining individual and group consciousness and thus keeping alive the dynamic of change and renewal."[76] WEVD held the potential for becoming a radical alternative to the dominant mass media structure. Its early programming and service to labor offered information, education, and entertainment rarely heard over commercial radio. Socialist Party officials sapped WEVD's radical potential, however, by losing sight of its immediate community and by pursuing a contradictory radio strategy of developing WEVD *and* working through the dominant mass media structure. The Great Depression and the commercial requirements of radio— the "natural laws" of radio advertising—sealed the fate of the Socialist Party's alternative to the dominant media. Norman Thomas's effort to make the best possible use of the dominant corporate radio system—to broadcast the socialist message to the nation-at-large—proved woefully inadequate. The dual radio strategy ultimately failed. In the end, WEVD and the Socialist Party did more to legitimize the dominant mass media structure than they did to challenge or alter it.

NOTES

A summer research grant from Hiram College funded a portion of the research for this article. Professor Beth McKillen provided helpful comments on an earlier draft of this article. I also wish to acknowledge the thoughtful questions raised by the students, especially Ruth Fairbanks, in my Hiram College WEC class on U.S. broadcasting.

1. John Downing, *Radical Media: The Political Experience of Alternative Communication* (Boston, MA, 1984), 3.

2. Gregory T. Wuliger, "The Fairness Doctrine in its Historical Context," Ph.D. diss., University of Illinois at Urbana-Champaign, 1987, 689; Noam Chomsky and Edward Herman, *Manufacturing Consent: The Political Economy of the Mass Media* (New York, 1988), 298.

3. See, for example, such excellent studies as, Morris L. Ernst, *The First Freedom* (New York, 1946); Ben H. Bagdikian, *The Media Monopoly* (Boston, MA, 1983); Wuliger; Chomsky and Herman; and Noam Chomsky, *Necessary Illusions: Thought Control in Democratic Societies* (Boston, MA, 1989).

4. A few of the many important works by Foner that incorporate examinations of the media include, Philip S. Foner, "A Labor Voice for Black Equality: The *Boston Daily Evening Voice*, 1864–1867," in Foner, *Essays in Afro-American History* (Philadelphia, PA, 1978), 112–133; Foner, *The Workingmen's Party of the United States: A History of the First Marxist Party in the Americas* (Minneapolis, MN, 1984); and Foner's multivolume *The History of the Labor Movement in the United States* (New York, 1948–).

5. Several studies have begun to assess radical and labor challenges to the dominant media. See, for example, Sara U. Douglas, *Labor's New Voice: Unions and the Mass Media* (Norwood, NJ, 1986); Elliott Shore, *Talkin' Socialism: J. A. Wayland and the Role of the Press in American Radicalism, 1890–1912* (Lawrence, KS, 1988); Jessie Lloyd O'Connor, Harvey O'Connor, and Susan M. Bowler, *Harvey and Jessie: A Couple of Radicals* (Philadelphia, PA, 1988); Nathan Godfried, "The Origins of Labor Radio: WCFL, the 'Voice of Labor,' 1925–1928," *Historical Journal of Film, Radio and Television* 7:2 (1987): 143–159; Stephen J. Haessler, "Carl Haessler and the Federated Press: Essays on the History of American Labor Journalism," M.A. thesis, University of Wisconsin, Madison, 1977; Steven J. Ross, "Struggles for the Screen: Workers, Radicals, and the Political Uses of Silent Film," *American Historical Review* 96:2 (1991): 333–367; and Robert W. McChesney, "An Almost Incredible Absurdity for a Democracy," *Journal of Communication Inquiry* 15:1 (1991): 89–114.

6. Erik Barnouw, *A Tower in Babel: A History of Broadcasting in the United States, Vol. 1,—to 1933* (New York, 1966), 91, 94–96, 121–122, 174–175, 177–180, 189–190; Christopher Sterling and John Kitross, *Stay Tuned: A Concise History of American Broadcasting* (Belmont, CA, 1978), 510, Table 1; Philip T. Rosen, *The Modern Stentors: Radio Broadcasting and the Federal Government, 1920–1934* (Westport, CT, 1980), 47–76, 93–94, 101–102; Federal Radio Commission, *First Annual Report: 1927* (Washington, DC, 1927), 10–11.

7. Barnouw, 195–199, 201; Rosen, 11, 104–106. Legislators specifically denied the commission "the power of censorship" over radio stations and prohibited all interference with "the right of free speech by means of radio communications."

8. *The Reminiscences of Orestes H. Caldwell* (1951), Oral History Collection, Columbia University, New York, New York, 10–12; Rosen, 12–13, 124, 133–134.

9. Susan Douglas has argued that the critical precedents of radio broadcasting were set by 1922. See her insightful *Inventing American Broadcasting, 1899–1922* (Baltimore, MD, 1987).

10. George Lipsitz, "The Struggle for Hegemony," *Journal of American History* 75:1 (June 1988): 147. See also Lipsitz, "This Ain't No Sideshow: Historians and Media Studies," *Critical Studies in Mass Communications* 5 (1988): 147–161.

11. *Radio Broadcast* 15 (September 1929): 273; *American Federationist* 35 (December 1928): 1426–1427.

12. The analysis below is adapted from Colin Sparks, "The Working-Class Press: Radical and Revolutionary Alternatives," *Media, Culture and Society* 7:2 (April 1985): 133–146.

13. Philip S. Foner, *History of the Labor Movement in the United States, Vol. 8: Postwar Struggles, 1918–1920* (New York, 1988), 237–249; James Weinstein, *The Decline of Socialism in America, 1912–1925* (New York, 1967), 177–233, 326–332, 336–339; David Shannon, *The Socialist Party of America: A History* (New York, 1955), 126–203.

14. Shannon, 204–226; Harry Fleischman, *Norman Thomas: A Biography, 1884–1968* (New York, 1969), 111–137; Irving Howe, *Socialism and America* (New York, 1985), 49–52; Paul Buhle, "Socialist Party," in *Encyclopedia of the American Left*, ed. Mari Jo Buhle, Paul Buhle, and Dan Georgakas (New York, 1990), 720.

15. The trust consisted of the electrical equipment manufacturers and dealers (the Radio Corporation of America, Westinghouse Electric Company, United Fruit Company, American Telephone and Telegraph, and General Electric Company) and the broadcast networks (the National Broadcasting Company and the Columbia Broadcasting System).

16. Memorandum, WEAF assistant vice-president to Edgar S. Bloom, 20 April 1926; Letter, G. F. McClelland, WEAF manager, to Norman Thomas, 23 April 1926; Letter, Norman Thomas to George F. McClelland, 21 April 1926,

Box 5, folder 49, National Broadcasting Company Records, State Historical Society of Wisconsin, Madison, Wisconsin (SHSW); *New Leader*, 24 April 1926: 2.

17. *New Leader*, 24 April 1926: 10; 20 November 1926: 10.

18. Letters, William H. Henry, Executive Secretary of Socialist Party, to Morris Hillquit, 11 November 1926 and Hillquit to Henry, 16 November 1926, Box 3, folder "1926 Mar.–1926 Dec.," Correspondence, Morris Hillquit Papers, SHSW; *New Leader*, 23 December 1926: 1–2; *New York Times*, 22 December 1926: 16.

19. *New York Times*, 28 February 1927: 5; 15 May 1927: II, 1.

20. Meeting of the Trustees of the Debs Memorial Radio Fund, 25 March 1927, Miscellaneous Documents, Records of the Amalgamated Clothing Workers of America, 5619, Box 215, folder 4, Labor-Management Documentation Center, M. P. Catherwood Library, Cornell University, Ithaca, New York.

21. For a brief history of WCFL, see Godfried.

22. Meeting of Trustees Radio Fund, 25 March 1927, Miscellaneous Documents, Records of Amalgamated Clothing Workers of America, 5619, Box 215, folder 4.

23. *New Leader*, 12 March 1927: 1, 3; 26 March 1927: 2; 2 April 1927: 1–2; 30 April 1927: 2; 4 June 1927: 1; and 25 June 1927: 2.

24. *New York Times*, 15 May 1927: II, 1; 6 June 1927: 26; 5 August 1927: 14; 22 August 1927: 20; 8 September 1927: 22; *New Leader*, 2 July 1927: 3; 6 August 1927: 3; 27 August 1927: 1, 3.

25. *New York Times*, 5 August 1927: 14; *New Leader*, 6 August 1927: 3.

26. Letter, G. August Gerber to ILGWU, 19 October 1927, Box 6, folder 10, Morris Sigman Correspondence, Collection 6, ILGWU Records #5780; *New York Times*, 20 October 1927: 26; 21 October 1927: 28.

27. Meeting 21 September 1927, Minutes of General Executive Board of International Ladies' Garment Workers' Union, Collection 16, ILGWU Records, 5780, Labor-Management Documentation Center, Martin P. Catherwood Library, Cornell University, Ithaca, NY; *New York Times*, 30 September 1927: 22; *New Leader*, 10 December 1927: 2; Letter, G. August Gerber to Morris Sigman, 26 January 1928, Box 6, folder 10, Sigman Correspondence, ILGWU Records.

28. The ACLU had developed a strong interest in the issues of free speech in radio and public access to the air waves. The American Fund for Public Service, established in 1922 by Charles Garland, sought to finance progressive and radical causes. American Civil Liberties Union, *Annual Reports 5 (1925), 6 (1926), 7 (1927), 8 (1928–29), 9 (1929–30)* (New York: 1926, 1927, 1929, 1930); ACLU, *Radio is Censored! A Study of Cases Prepared to Show the Need for Federal Legislation for Freedom of the Air*, collected by Minna F. Kassner (New York: November 1936); Morris L. Ernst, *The Best Is Yet . . .* (New York, 1945); Shannon, 186; Gloria Garrett Samson, "Toward A New Social Order: The American Fund for Public Service—Clearing House for Radicalism in the 1920s," Ph.D. diss., University of Rochester, 1987. It is unclear whether the

directors of the Garland Fund ever advanced any money to support WEVD. They seriously doubted the station's commitment to absolute free speech for all "minority" groups. Letters, Robert W. Dunn to Forrest Bailey, 20 November 1927; G. August Gerber and Morris Hillquit to the American Fund, 21 November 1927; Robert Dunn to Debs Memorial Radio Fund, 29 November 1927; and Forest Bailey to American Fund, 13 December 1927, folder 14, Box 52, Reel 33, American Fund for Public Service Records, 1922–1941, Rare Books and Manuscripts Division, New York Public Library, New York, NY.

29. Minutes of Meeting, ACLU Executive Committee, 5 December and 12 December 1927, Vol. 320, ACLU Archives, 1912–50, microfilm, reel 51, New York Public Library, New York, NY; Letter, Norman Thomas to G. August Gerber, 4 January 1928, Series I, General Correspondence, Oct. 1905–Oct. 1933, Reel 1, Norman Thomas Papers 1904–1967, microfilm edition, Manuscript Division, New York Public Library.

30. Barnouw, 215; Letter, G. August Gerber to Harry Wander, 7 June 1928, Box 6, folder 10, Sigman Correspondence; Meeting 25 June 1928, General Executive Board Minutes, ILGWU, Collection 16, ILGWU Records; *New Leader*, 9 June 1928: 1, 8; *New York Times*, 11 June 1928: 26; 13 June 1928: 15; 22 June 1928: 20; 28 June 1928: 18; 1 July 1928: II, 4; Letter, Abe Baroff to Rubin, 2 July 1928, and letter, A. Baroff to FRC, 2 July 1928, Box 6, folder 10, Sigman Correspondence; *New Leader*, 16 June 1928: 1, 7; 23 June 1928: 7; 7 July 1928: 1.

31. *New Leader*, 2 June 1928: 1–2; 9 June 1928: 8; 23 June 1928: 3; 30 June 1928: 6.

32. Barnouw, 215–216; *The Federated Press Labor Letter* 15:14 (12 July 1928): 3; *New Leader*, 14 July 1928: 1, 3; Ruth Brindze, *Not to Be Broadcast: The Truth about the Radio* (New York, 1974 [1937]), 152.

33. *New Leader*, 14 July 1928: 1, 3.

34. U.S. Federal Radio Commission, *Annual Report to Congress, 1928* (Washington, D.C., 1928), 154–155.

35. *New York Times*, 23 August 1928: 20.

36. Brindze, 154. Also see Barnouw, 216–217; Fred W. Friendly, *The Good Guys, the Bad Guys and the First Amendment: Free Speech vs. Fairness in Broadcasting* (New York, 1975), 18.

37. *Federation News* 18 (24 December 1927): 10; *New Leader*, 15 September 1928: 6; 4 February 1928: 3; 18 February 1928: 6; 3 December 1927: 3; 3 March 1928: 6; 24 March 1928: 6; 28 April 1928: 1.

38. *New Leader*, 11 February 1928: 6; 1 September 1928: 6; and the *Sun* columnist quoted in *New Leader*, 15 September 1928: 6.

39. "WEVD to Be Radio Labor College This Winter," no. 3389, Eastern Bureau, 17 September 1928, folder: Press Releases September 1928, Federated Press Papers, microfilm Reel 9154, Rare Book and Manuscript Library, Columbia University Libraries, New York, NY; *New York Times*, 14 September 1928: 32; *Labor's News [The Federated Press Labor Letter]* 17:10 (22 June 1929): 3; 17:11 (29 June 1929): 7; *New Leader*, 14 December 1929: 8; 1 February 1930:

4; 5 October 1929: 2; 4 October 1930: 3; 22 October 1927: 2; 14 April 1928: 1, 3.

40. Letter, Norman Thomas to National Executive Committee, 30 January 1929, Series II. Organizational Files, Subseries A. Socialist Party, 1. Correspondence, Reel 54, Norman Thomas Papers, microfilm edition, NYPL.

41. Barnouw, 186–191; Letters, Herbert M. Merrill to Director, Station WJZ, 9 December 1926, M. H. Aylesworth to Merrill, 20 December 1926, and Aylesworth to Merrill, 31 December 1926, Box 5, folder 28, NBC Records, SHSW.

42. Barnouw, 188, 263; Ernest Gruening, *The Public Pays: A Study of Power Propaganda* (New York, 1931), 28, 222–224; M.L. Ramsay, *Pyramids of Power: The Story of Roosevelt, Insull and the Utility Wars* (Indianapolis, IN, 1937), 264.

43. Memorandum, Bertha Brainard, WJZ Manager, to Aylesworth, 8 January 1927; Letter, Aylesworth to Brainard, 8 January 1927; and Letter, Brainard to Aylesworth, 11 January 1927, Box 5, folder 28, NBC Records.

44. Letter, M. H. Aylesworth to Sidney Hertzberg, 12 January 1927, Box 5, folder 28, NBC Records.

45. Letters, Ralph M. Easley to M. H. Aylesworth, 8 and 11 January 1927, Box 5, folder 28, NBC Records.

46. Letters, Norman Thomas to M. H. Aylesworth, 12 March 1928, and Thomas to G. F. McClelland, 9 April 1928, Box 5, folder 28, NBC Records; *New Leader*, 14 April 1928: 1, 3.

47. *New Leader*, 9 February 1929: 10. For evidence of WEVD's erratic program schedule and broadcasting hours, see listings for WEVD in the *New Leader* from November 1928 through February 1929.

48. *New Leader*, 2 March 1929: 5; 9 March 1929: 5; 16 March 1929: 5; 23 March 1929: 5; Letter, G. August Gerber to "Friends," 28 June 1929; and Circular Letter, Chicago Branch of Socialist Party to Members, 17 August 1929, Reel 12, Series I. National Office Papers, A. Correspondence, Socialist Party of America Papers, Duke University, microfilm.

49. *New Leader*, 8 March 1930: 3; 15 March 1930: 1, 3; 22 March 1930: 2; Letter, Morris Hillquit to J. Spielman, 9 May 1930, Box 1, folder 16, Dressmakers' Union Local 22 Records, Collection 15, ILGWU Records.

50. FRC Examiner's Report no. 38, Docket no. 969, Radio Censorship Cases—2. New York, 1. Station WEVD, 1931–1933, Reel 87, Vol. 511; and Federated Press article, "Debs Radio in Fight for Life," 24 October 1930, Censorship—Radio, 1930, Reel 71, Vol. 385, ACLU Archives 1912–1950, microfilm.

51. *Federated Press* article, "Debs Radio in Fight for Life," 24 October 1930; article, "Debs Radio Permit Gets Turned Down," 17 October 1930, Censorship—Radio, Reel 71, Vol. 385, ACLU Archives 1912–1950, microfilm; *New Leader*, 27 December 1930: 1.

52. *Federated Press*, "Civil Liberties Union to Fight for WEVD," 26 December 1930, Reel 71, Vol. 385, Censorship—Radio, ACLU Archives 1912–1950, microfilm; *New Leader*, 27 December 1930: 1, 8.

53. *Labor's News* 20:2 (10 January 1931): 3; 20:4 (24 January 1931): 2; 20:5 (31 January 1931): 3; *New Leader*, 17 January 1931: 1–2; 24 January 1931: 1–2; 31 January 1931: 1.

54. FRC Examiner's Report, no. 176, Docket no. 969, Hearing 3 March 1931, 1931–1933, Reel 87, Vol. 511, Radio Censorship Cases—2. New York, 1. Station WEVD, ACLU Archives 1912–1950, microfilm.

55. *Labor's News* 20:18 (2 May 1931): 3; *New Leader*, 7 March 1931: 8; 2 May 1931: 3.

56. *New York Times*, 2 March 1931: 28; *New Leader*, 7 March 1931: 8.

57. Letter, Morris Hillquit to Norman Thomas, 27 March 1931, Box 4, folder: "1931 Jan–1931 Dec," Morris Hillquit Papers, SHSW; "Report of the Committee on the Reorganization of WEVD," attached to letter, Mary Fox to Benjamin Schlesinger, 12 June 1931, Box 171, folder 6, David Dubinsky Correspondence, ILGWU Records; *Labor's News* 20:24 (13 June 1931): 1; Letter, Roger Baldwin to Board of Directors of American Fund, 9 June 1931, folder 12, Box 29, Reel 20, American Fund Records.

58. "Report of the Committee on the Reorganization of WEVD," Letter, Fox to Schlesinger, 12 June 1931, Box 171, folder 6, Dubinsky Correspondence, ILGWU Records.

59. "Report of the Committee on the Reorganization of WEVD," Letter, Fox to Schlesinger, 12 June 1931, Box 171, folder 6, Dubinsky Correspondence, ILGWU Records.

60. "Report of the Committee on the Reorganization of WEVD," Letter, Fox to Schlesinger, 12 June 1931, Box 171, folder 6, Dubinsky Correspondence, ILGWU Records.

61. *New York Times*, 27 September 1931: II, 1; 26 October 1931: 17; *The American Labor Year Book, 1932* (New York, 1932), 96; Bernard K. Johnpoll, *Pacifist's Progress: Norman Thomas and the Decline of American Socialism* (Chicago, IL, 1970), 88; Ronald Sanders, *The Downtown Jews: Portraits of an Immigrant Generation* (New York, 1969), 438; Letter, Norman Thomas to Roger Baldwin, 13 October 1931, folder 12, Box 29, Reel 20, American Fund Records.

62. *New York Times*, 27 September 1931: II, 1.

63. FRC Examiner's Report, no. 176, Docket no. 969, FRC Decision on WEVD filed 30 October 1931, Radio Censorship Cases—2. New York, 1. Station WEVD, 1931–1933, Reel 87, Vol. 511, ACLU Archives 1912–1950, microfilm; *Broadcasting* 1 (1 November 1931): 12.

64. *Nation* 135 (12 October 1932): 321.

65. *New York Times*, 19 August 1932: 20; 29 September 1932: 44.

66. *New York Times*, 26 January 1933: 13; 5 February 1933: IX, 10.

67. Letters, Julius Gerber to Harry Davis, 12 August 1933, Gerber to B. C. Vladeck, 12 August 1933, Gerber to WEVD Station manager, 26 October 1935,

and A. Claessens to Hedwig Wachenheim, 13 December 1940, Collection 10, X:88 R2647, Reel 18, Social Democratic Federation Records 1933–1956, Tamiment Institute Library, New York University, New York, NY; Letter, Charney Vladeck to Jacob Billikopf, 19 January 1937; I-13 "V" General Correspondence, microfilm, R 1870, Baruch Charney Vladeck Papers, Tamiment Institute Library; *Variety* 125 (24 February 1937): 44.

68. Letters, Arthur Rosenberg to Walter Duncan, 19 October 1933; Phillips Carlin to Rosenberg, 29 October 1933; Carlin to Program Manager WEVD, 30 October 1933; and Morris S. Novik to Carlin, 1 November 1933, Box 19, folder 9, NBC Records; Interview with Morris S. Novik, by author, 7 December 1991, New York, NY.

69. Letters, Norman Thomas to M. H. Aylesworth, 26 May 1931, and Aylesworth to Thomas, 27 May 1931, Box 4, folder 1; Letters, Thomas to Aylesworth, 18 April 1932 and Aylesworth to Thomas, 21 April 1932; Booking Order 5 May 1932, Box 14, folder 16, NBC Records; *New Leader*, 14 May 1932: 3; 21 May 1932: 10.

70. Note, Thomas to Aylesworth, 15 August 1932, and Letter, Aylesworth to Thomas, 16 August 1932, Box 14, folder 16, NBC Records.

71. Memorandum to National Executive Committee from Clarence Senior, #3, Radio, 4 December 1932, Box 2, folder 8, Clarence Senior Papers, SHSW.

72. *New Leader*, 25 April 1931: 8.

73. Letter, Norman Thomas to M. H. Aylesworth, 2 October 1931, Box 4, folder 1, NBC Records. Thomas remained the "pet radical" of the commercial radio system until his death in 1968. The broadcast networks and independent radio stations such as WGN often placed the noted socialist against representatives from the business community. Interview with Ward L. Quaal (former president of WGN), by author, 10 August 1990, Chicago, IL.

74. Barnouw, 263–264, 279–283; Rosen, 161–174.

75. Letter, A. L. Ashby, NBC Attorney, to Miller, Mack and Fairchild, Attorneys, 17 February 1933; Memorandum, Ashby to John Royal, 24 February 1933; Memo, John W. Elwood to Phillips Carlin, 22 March 1933, Box 19, folder 9, NBC Records.

76. Herbert I. Schiller, *Communication and Cultural Domination* (White Plains, NY, 1976), 109.

9 "Education for a New Social Order": The Ideological Struggle over American Workers' Education in the 1920s

Gloria Garrett Samson

"Future historians will likely point to the men and women of the workers' education movement as the heralds of the twentieth century renaissance of labor," Marius Hansome wrote in 1931.[1] A few historians have, indeed, noted that the 1920s movement produced a cadre involved in the organization of militant Congress of Industrial Organizations (CIO) unions whose social vision surpassed the "bread and butter" unionism of the more conservative American Federation of Labor (AFL). But more often, those aware of the existence of the numerous labor colleges that waxed and waned in the 1920s view the movement as an anachronistic oddity or a misguided exercise in utopianism. Some, unable or unwilling to recognize the radical intent of most workers' education in the twenties or the ideological struggles over ultimate goals that informed the movement, prefer to describe it as a "liberal" effort intended only to help workers become more effective trade union members and better people.[2]

Most of those involved in the 1920s movement, however, recognized the "ultimate aims–education for a new social order."[3] New York's anti-subversive Lusk Committee believed that the fundamental purpose of workers' education was:

to destroy the respect of the students for the institutions of the United States. . . . To develop agitators to enter the labor field, to preach the doctrine of revolt, and to divide the people of the United States into contending classes so that they may be instrumental in hastening the social revolution.[4]

The Lusk Committee was at least partially correct. Most workers' education schools in the 1920s initially attempted to provide workers not only with the tools to make them more effective unionists, but also sought to provide information and the instillation of analytical skills that would lead to the workers' identification of their oppressors. The workers' own struggles, once subjected to analysis, would lead them to realize the need for a new social order in which economic and social oppression ceased to exist.

Education specifically for workers had its impetus in England in 1899 when Walter Vrooman, a Christian pacifist and philanthropist, worked with Charles Beard, then a graduate student at Oxford, to establish Ruskin College, named in honor of John Ruskin. They hoped to use "scientific methods" to educate workers, enabling them to "defend the interests of the working class."[5]

In all industrialized countries, the necessity of leaving school at an early age left workers ill-prepared to deal effectively with the complexities of the industrial world. According to workers' education enthusiasts, working people, in their own schools, would learn "their place in the economic world and why they occupy it, how it can be bettered." Workers' education sought "the advancement of the intellectual, moral, social, and material interests of the workers" by training "the mind to clear, calm reasoning" and by laying "a foundation for the understanding of important social and industrial problems." Workers realized that "big business prepares its lieutenants long and thoroughly from grammar school . . . to college, where their special theories of control and management are formulated." But this preparation for life and work abruptly ended for most working-class people by the age of fourteen. Advocates in all of the industrialized countries expected workers' education to fill the void.[6]

In the United States, women and Jewish workers led in the establishment of a workers' education movement. Jews in New York organized a Workers' School in 1899 to study economics, science, and socialism. In 1901 the Jewish Workers League led discussions on economic and industrial problems. Socialists organized the Rand School in 1906. The Women's Trade Union League (WTUL) initiated an education program in 1907, then established a School for Organizers in 1914. That year the International Ladies Garment Workers Union launched the Workers' University. Radical Finns established the Work Peoples College in Duluth in 1908.[7]

The surge came following World War I when labor felt strong, after winning wartime legitimation. The apparent success of the Russian workers' revolution encouraged additional confidence, and the employers' open shop, anti-union offensive initially strengthened class consciousness. State labor federations and city central labor bodies organized labor schools, in part, to prepare the workers to run the industries effectively when they became theirs. James Maurer, socialist head of the Pennsylvania Federation of Labor, feared that, if workers were not "properly prepared, we . . . will make just as big a mess out of things as the present managers are guilty of doing."[8]

Boston's Trade Union College, which opened in April 1919, was the first school established by a central labor body. It organized to realize labor's "hopes in the coming social and industrial order." While most workers' schools held only evening classes, Brookwood Labor College, founded in 1921, was a two-year residential school. It planned to "frankly challenge the prevailing system of higher education in the United States, which is dominated by men who benefit by special privilege." The school stood "for a new and better order, motivated by social values rather than pecuniary ones." Immediately after Brookwood's founding, labor progressives also organized the Workers' Education Bureau (WEB) as a coordinating agency, clearinghouse, and publicity source for the burgeoning movement. The WEB's organizers also hoped that it would be a link between conservative trade union leaders and labor progressives.[9]

The American Federation of Labor leaders had given their tentative approval to the movement, but Samuel Gompers obviously feared its consequences. AFL leaders believed that "such classes should be considered a stop gap" until the adoption of a more sympathetic attitude toward working people and organized labor by public school boards. Disregarding the fact that working people failed to receive indispensable knowledge by missing high school instruction, Gompers and his associates believed that neutral–rather than the usual pro-business–school boards would provide an adequate education during the workers' few years of school. Gompers knew that the most enthusiastic boosters of post-war labor schools were often the most militant, favored the organization of unskilled immigrant workers into industrial unions (which the skilled workers of the AFL continued to resist), and were inclined to promote a socialist new social order.

Although Gompers had been a socialist as a young man, he claimed that the repression he witnessed when police brutalized unemployed demonstrators in an 1874 Tompkins Square mass meeting made him realize that radicalism "concentrated all the forces of organized society against a labor movement and nullified in advance normal, necessary activity." Gompers also "saw the danger of entangling alliances with intellectuals who did not understand that to experiment with the labor movement was to experiment with human life."[10] He profoundly distrusted the middle-class intellectuals who rallied to the workers' education cause as instructors, administrators, writers, or funding sources.

At the second national conference of the Workers' Education Bureau, Gompers told the education enthusiasts that they had a great future if they taught "the right things." They must teach "men and women to belong to their trade or labor unions, to stand by themselves, to help improve the physical, spiritual, and mental standards and to direct the sentiments and aspirations." But, he said, "a little learning is most dangerous." Teaching "a thought that is hurtful or misdirected in its influence upon the natural and rational labor movement of your country is most hurtful and injurious in its results." Advocacy of industrial unionism and socialism was implicitly "hurtful and misdirected."[11]

Gompers's first move to ensure that no "misdirected" teaching occurred was to take over the Workers' Education Bureau. The AFL saw the need to eliminate "those conditions which were unsound," according to John P. Frey of the AFL's Metal Trades Department. Labor colleges not affiliated with the AFL were excluded from membership. The WEB disaffiliated the militant and independent Amalgamated Clothing Workers' education department, which had been a charter member.[12]

Despite the brakes that Gompers and his colleagues attempted to put on the movement, labor schools continued to proliferate in the early 1920s. Although many were called colleges, few offered genuinely college-level courses. Most schools attempted to provide instruction and materials appropriate not only to the students' actual educational levels, but also to their most urgent interests. Almost all of the schools–over ninety by 1922–offered labor history, economics, and parliamentary procedure classes. Some schools offered labor law, psychology, current events, and cultural programs. Bertram Wolfe, for a time the head of the communists' Workers' School, wanted education for workers to "abolish the class monopoly in culture along with the class monopoly in all the good things of life. Our aim is to open culture to the whole of humanity." Several labor colleges produced their own literary publications to showcase student writing and offered the opportunity for "labor players" to participate in theatre productions written by the students or by professional dramatists.[13]

Most of the labor schools offered English classes to counteract mainstream Americanization programs that promoted middle-class values and ideologies. Labor educators believed that the English lessons for immigrant children and their parents presented in public schools and industry-supported adult education promulgated a mindless jingoism as well as a virulent anti-unionism. Industries such as Goodyear Tire and Rubber Company provided their own "industrial universities"; Goodyear paid 117 teachers to train 5700 employees properly in industrial discipline and skills. Corporate schools aimed "to make loyal American citizens and productive workers out of the great mass of our foreign-born population." English class graduates at Ford Motor Company celebrated their Americanization in a pageant that dramatized their transformation from "ignorant" immigrants to flag-waving Americans who emerged from a giant melting pot stirred by their English teachers. The director of the National Association of Corporate Schools claimed that "training conducted on the premises of industrial plants decreases the chances of an invasion of Bolshevik doctrines by about ninety per cent."[14] The labor colleges, competing for the workers' ideological allegiance through rival classes in English, also offered public speaking courses to instill confidence when workers spoke to their employers or to the public.

Classes met in union halls, labor temples, or public schools, but in several locations the use of the public schools was denied them. Most of the labor schools eschewed overt propaganda, consciously promoting instead a Deweyan pragmatic investigation and testing of the facts. They sought answers to the questions enumerated by the students at the Trade Union College of Philadelphia:

We, the workers have suffered great and needless injury because we have had no place to turn for full and honest information about matters of vital concern to us . . . . What we want and need is to know about these things that directly and powerfully affect our lives. We want to know why it is that the worker who spends his life making things that are supposed to be for the use of his fellow-men so often has nothing for his own in his old age. We want to know why there is no work to be done when the workers need jobs and need the things that other workers make. We want to know why, when we are the biggest share of the voters, our elected representatives can pass [antilabor] Esch-Cummins Bills and, as judges, can get out injunctions that deprive us of all rights. We want to know whether it is necessary that the children of the workers should go to work at fourteen instead of having a chance to develop body and soul until they grow to man and womanhood. We want to learn to discuss these things, and we want to know how to get the facts about them.[15]

And when they got the facts, their conclusions, militants hoped, would point to the need for a new social order.

A representative from the Workingman's Education Institute in Roxbury, Massachusetts, vividly described the consequences of explicating the facts:

The Boston press attacked the Education work severely, recklessly due to which the Police, with its tremendous force, caused the Institute much trouble; countless raids, real Czar's pogrom that damaged the building to the amount of $1000, arrests of comrades, disturbances of many meetings; provocation and cruel actions that terrified the neighborhood were the methods of the black forces that greatly decreased the activities of the institute.[16]

Clinton Golden, an ex-machinist and Amalgamated Clothing Workers' organizer, investigated many of the labor schools in the mid-twenties, reporting their problems and potential to the left-wing American Fund for Public Service (Garland Fund), the principal financial supporter of the more militant schools. Golden was especially pleased to report that the public library in socialist-run Milwaukee not only provided a room for classes to meet, but also "purchased textbooks designated by teachers after consultation with students in whatever quantities necessary." In Portland, Oregon, "the value and necessity of the educational work is recognized in the movement and there is a degree of unity of thought and action hardly equalled in any other place visited." But a few of the labor colleges he investigated were rent by political dissension; labor conservatives, both rank-and-file and elected officials, sometimes objected to left-leaning administrators and teachers. Because the education director of the Seattle Labor College was also an organizer for the Socialist Party, right-wing unionists charged that the entire school was red. In Minneapolis, dissension within the labor movement itself led to the demise of that city's labor college.[17] Union conservatives often used more energy fighting militants within their ranks than they expended in organizing drives or struggles against the employers' open-shop movement.

In his report, Golden noted that the most effective teachers in the more successful labor schools were "those who have a labor background and whose sympathies are entirely with the movement; those whose personality and ability convince students that their knowledge is superior; those whose open-mindedness presents a 'give and take' attitude and who feel that they are learning from the students while the students are learning from them."[18]

Golden drew several conclusions from his survey. "The workers' education movement is a living, human, and growing movement," he said, but it "is still in a decidedly experimental stage." The classes he visited attracted more rank-and-file than local elected union officials; he had not decided whether the AFL's endorsement of workers' education was "a help or hindrance." He did believe that "if many of the high officials of the

American Labor Movement really were in personal contact with most of the classes and realized just how much potential dynamite there is in them, they would drop the movement like a hot potato."[19] The classes attracted those most sympathetic to industrial unionism, to organizing the unskilled unorganized, and to the need for a new social order. The potential existed for the students to coalesce and challenge AFL ideologies, policy, and leadership.

Those schools deemed sufficiently militant to receive Garland Fund assistance included one established by dissident United Mine Workers' members, the Philadelphia Labor College, Rand School, and labor colleges in Boston, Denver, Portland, Seattle, and Salem, Massachusetts.[20]

The Southern School for Women Workers received aid to initiate its annual program for southern working women ("pure Anglo-Saxons," the school's director assured AFL unionists). The school moved to various college campuses from summer to summer, but, unlike the Bryn Mawr Summer School, the host college had no control of the workers' classes. At the first session, held at Sweet Briar College in 1927, twenty-five young women who worked in the textile, tobacco, and canning industries; as telephone operators; and in other trades studied "industrial history, with emphasis on economic principles." They also learned "songs of workers' solidarity, and the poetry programs were often from the labor poetry of Sandburg or other modern writers or the social poetry of different periods."[21]

The Garland Fund turned down applications from the Bryn Mawr Summer School for Women Workers because it was initiated and controlled by the college, promoted gradualism, and hoped to bridge the economic and social classes. Further, although some unions made donations, much of the school's financial support came from John D. Rockefeller, Jr., Bryn Mawr alumnae, and the Carnegie Corporation, whose policy asserted that American workers' education should differ from that in Europe, because "there are no economic classes in the United States."[22]

The residential Brookwood and Commonwealth Colleges also received assistance from the Garland Fund. Commonwealth, after several false starts, sputtered to life in its final form in Mena, Arkansas, in 1925.[23] The Fund board advanced the school $2000 but said it would receive no more if it retained its "present basis of detachment from the organized labor movement." Former Wobbly (Industrial Workers of the World member) Covington Hall, replying from the school, reported that the students and faculty had been down to their last thirty-eight cents and were almost starving when they received the Fund's contribution. He also wrote that closer affiliation to the trade unions meant cozying up to "the bureaucracy." Commonwealth doesn't mind, he said, "if it can be guaranteed against being 'goosestepped' by a bunch of fossilized has beens and never wases."[24]

By 1926 Commonwealth had forty students from twenty states representing twenty-four occupations; the students and the ten faculty members earned their keep by working on the school's farm. The school's activities did not pass unobserved. In October 1926 the Arkansas American Legion demanded an investigation of the school because, the Legion charged, Commonwealth taught free love and revolutionary doctrines and allegedly received its support from the Soviet Union and the radical (but nearly defunct) Industrial Workers of the World.[25]

The American Legion not withstanding, a faction of the faculty demanded a *more* radical curriculum; the faction's ringleader was fired by the school's director. Eight teachers and fourteen students walked out in protest, but the school survived another decade.[26] Geographically isolated, Commonwealth did not receive the positive attention accorded Brookwood in the labor and liberal press. Commonwealth's faculty and students, who called themselves "Commoners," lived in shack-like buildings. Brookwood's classes met in a large white mansion in Katonah, New York.

Brookwood, the most favored and famous of the workers' schools, was founded by Christian pacifists Helen and William Fincke, who believed that the working class represented the only possible vehicle for radical change and the end of war. A. J. Muste, the school's first director, noted that the founders and organizers of the school "were militants, severe critics of the narrow craft unionism of the American Federation of Labor, and visionaries who believed we needed a new social order. They contended that the workers would never solve their basic problems unless they strove for a radical reorganization of society and that such an organization was possible."[27]

Students were to come from unions, which would pay their way and contribute to the support of the school, but only locals critical of AFL leadership actually contributed with much enthusiasm. The majority of the students, many of whom were socialists or communists, came primarily from the needle trades and mining unions. Len DeCaux, who attended Brookwood in its early years, said that idealistic students liked Brookwood because it resembled a quasi-utopian colony. More practical students saw it as "a step toward advancing labor from the rear end to the vanguard of progress."[28]

In 1925 Muste irritated the school's principal source of financial support by appearing to side with AFL bureaucrats at the Workers' Education Bureau conference where Scott Nearing, then president of the Garland

Fund, unsuccessfully attempted to commit the WEB to public endorsement of class conscious workers' education. "I feel that you and your colleagues from Brookwood betrayed the cause of labor education in the United States," Nearing lectured Muste.[29]

Muste replied that, while the WEB had not officially "declared for" blatantly class-conscious workers' education, it had been entirely possible "for class education . . . to go on within the trade movement in the United States." And "as a matter of fact, I venture to say that nine-tenths of the education that has actually gone on in the local labor colleges and classes has been of that type." Nearing's demand that the WEB accept only those schools that openly promulgated the class struggle and prepared their students to wage it, would have driven most schools from the organization, and we would have "another case of a radical group gloriously capturing itself." Muste said that Nearing's proposal would have killed the class education that did exist under the WEB.[30]

Muste had tried to walk a fine line to avoid upsetting AFL leaders or alienating his radical financial supporters. His faculty and students, fiercely devoted to the idea of industrial unionism, along with the prodding of Nearing, moved him to a more outspoken and militant position as the decade progressed. At Brookwood's 1928 May Day celebration Muste described the AFL as stagnant and reactionary. In June five Brookwood graduates left the North to attempt, without AFL sanction, the organization of southern mill workers. During the same year Brookwood sponsored several institutes and conferences that seemed to challenge the AFL's nonactivity in organizing the unorganized.[31]

Spencer Miller, the WEB's executive secretary, warned William Green, Gompers's successor, that Brookwood increasingly dominated and set the direction of all workers' education, that it taught radical doctrines, and accepted "a certain number of radical students" at the behest of the Garland Fund. In August 1928, after an investigation by the AFL's Matthew Woll, the executive council directed all AFL-affiliate unions to withdraw support from the school on the grounds that it taught doctrines contrary to AFL policies, that it was antireligious, and that pro-Soviet demonstrations took place there. Several unions, many former students, and prominent progressive intellectuals rose to Brookwood's defense.[32]

John Dewey charged that the AFL's goal had been to eliminate from the labor movement schools and other influences that might develop independent leaders committed to a more activist and socially concerned labor movement than that "carried on by the American Federation of Labor in its close alliance" with big business's National Civic Federation. When the WEB executive committee disaffiliated Brookwood in January 1929,

James Maurer, who had fought a lonely battle on the committee, resigned as the WEB's chair, stating that workers' education had been losing ground for two years because the AFL resisted the basic purpose of the experiment, which was to provide an "intelligent guide to the new social order."[33]

Brookwood continued to attract students and struggled on until 1937, when it succumbed to the depression and the successes of the militant unions whose cadre it had helped to educate. Many of the new industrial unions elected to initiate their own education programs. Many of the organizers and educators had received their training at Brookwood and other labor schools.[34]

Clearly then, workers' education had threatened conservatives in and out of the labor movement because it promoted not only greater labor activism, but also "action that would ultimately introduce a new social order based on service rather than on profit." David Saposs, who wrote those words, noted that the AFL had spent the decade cleansing its affiliate unions of dissidents; it then turned to Brookwood as surrogate for all workers' education it could not closely control–that it thought "misdirected." Larry Rogin, a Brookwood alumnus and leading labor educator until his death in 1988, recalled that the labor colleges with the greatest staying power were in the cities where progressive unions, critical of the AFL's labor and political policies, were strong.[35]

The several schools that did not outlast the decade of the twenties fell to low union treasuries, the fear of censure from the AFL, the fact that the militants most likely to support workers' education were often expelled from their unions, the cooptation by welfare capitalism techniques including "industrial schools" on the work premises, and sheer worker exhaustion. James Maurer had noted that "after a worker has put in eight or ten hours of work, under mechanical high pressure speed, he is not in physical or mental condition to study, or even to think seriously." Others cited changing jobs and shifts, unemployment, and long or irregular hours. Many potential students had so many other union activities that they could find no time for classes. Further, the passive entertainment and allure of the new movies, radio programs, and spectator sports competed for the attention of the younger workers, a fact noted and lamented by labor school promoters.[36]

Workers' education in the 1920s should not be considered either an idealistic failure or an anachronistic oddity. As labor educator Lois Gray wrote, "The impact of the programs was felt in succeeding decades." Many former students whose names are familiar to labor historians went on to leadership positions in their unions.[37] Although the call for a new social order was eventually muted by the Cold War and the expulsion of radicals from both AFL and CIO unions, many of the new unions in the thirties did adopt a broader social vision. Practically, workers' education kept the movement for industrial unionism alive in the "lean years" of the 1920s. Labor progressives who found ideological support in workers' educational institutions contributed to the advances made in the "turbulent years"[38] of the 1930s.

The idea of workers' education, now called Labor Studies, became entrenched. The recognition of the "potential dynamite," as Golden described it, in the 1920s movement led to the establishment of competing labor extension services attached to institutions of higher learning where curriculum and faculty could be controlled. The New Deal Workers' Education Project, although drawing on the programs devised in the preceding decade, was developed with the underlying proposition of attaining workers' rights within the existing capitalist society, rather than in an entirely new social order.[39]

NOTES

The author wishes to thank the Henry J. Kaiser Family Foundation for the travel grant to the Archives of Urban and Labor Affairs at Wayne State University, which proved helpful.

1. Marius Hansome, *World Workers' Educational Movements: Their Social Significance* (New York, 1931), 306–307.

2. Charles Howlett, "Organizing the Unorganized: Brookwood Labor College 1921–1937," *Labor Studies Journal* 6 (February 1981): 169–178; Ronald J. Peters and Jeanne M. McCarrick, "Roots of Public Support for Labor Education 1900–1945," *Labor Studies Journal* 1 (Fall 1976): 118, 120; Amy Hewes, "Early Experiments in Workers' Education," *Adult Education* 6 (Summer 1956): 217; James A. Wallace, "A New Means for Liberals: Liberal Responses to Adult and Worker Education in the 1920s," *Labor Studies Journal* 11 (Spring 1986): 27; Lois Gray, "The American Way in Labor Education," *Industrial Relations* 5 (February 1966): 56; Susan Stone Wong, "From Soul to Strawberries: The International Ladies' Garment Workers' Union and Workers' Education 1914–1950" in *Sisterhood and Solidarity: Workers' Education for Women 1924–1984*, ed. Joyce L. Kornbluh and Mary Frederickson (Philadelphia, PA, 1984), 50.

3. For only a sampling of the statements concerning the ultimate purpose of workers' education see Mark Starr in *Workers' Education in the United States*, ed. Theodore Brameld (New York, 1941), 90; James Maurer, *It Can Be Done* (New York, 1938), 367; Frank Tannenbaum, *The Labor Movement: Its Conservative Functions and Social Consequences* (New York, 1921); Lewis Mumford, "Reeducating the Workers," *Survey* 47 (7 January 1922): 567; Frederick M. Davenport, "The Educational Movement Among American Workers," *Outlook*

31 (28 June 1922): 375–378; Fannia Cohn, "The Educational Work of the ILGWU," *Second Conference on Workers Education Report* (New York, 1922): 52–53; representatives from the Rand School, Boston Trade Union College, Rochester Labor College, Amalgamated Clothing Workers of America, Cleveland Workers University, in *First Conference on Workers' Education Report* (New York, 1921): 25, 89, 112, 123–125, 135.

4. Joint Legislative Committee Investigating Seditious Activities, *Revolutionary Radicalism, Its History, Purpose and Tactics* 1 (Albany, NY, 1920), 17.

5. Al Nash, *Ruskin College: A Challenge to Adult and Labor Education* (Ithaca, NY, 1981), 4, 6–8.

6. Statements by activists in Survey of Workers' Education, n.d., Miscellaneous Reports 7, American Fund for Public Service Papers, Rare Books and Manuscripts, NY Public Library (hereafter AFPS). The crumbling papers of the AFPS have been recently microfilmed and rearranged. Therefore these citations provide only a direction rather than a guide to the collection.

7. Margaret T. Hodgen, *Workers' Education in England and the United States* (New York, 1925), 206, 211, 214; Brameld, 61.

8. Bert MacLeech, "Workers' Education in the United States," Ph.D. diss., Harvard University, 1951, 61; Hodgen, 245–246.

9. Bertha and David Saposs, *Readings in Trade Unionism* (New York, 1926), 367–368; *School and Society* 13 (9 April 1921): 437; *The Nation* 109 (30 August 1919): 298–300; Brookwood flier in Gifts 1922–1927, 2, AFPS; Hodgen, 248–249.

10. Samuel Gompers, *Seventy Years of Life and Labor*, ed., Nick Salvatore (Ithaca, NY, 1984), 34–35.

11. Hodgen, 245; Hansome, 230. For further explications of Gompers's attitude toward industrial unions and socialists see William M. Dick, *Labor and Socialism: The Gompers Era* (Port Washington, NY, 1972); Philip S. Foner, *History of the Labor Movement of the United States, vol. 8: Postwar Struggles 1918–1920* (New York, 1988), 44, 49.

12. Frey quoted in Thomas R. Brooks, *Clint: A Biography of a Labor Intellectual* (New York, 1978), 75; *American Labor Yearbook, 1923–24* (New York, 1925), 57; Hodgen, 254–255.

13. *Survey of Workers' Education*; Bertram Wolfe, *Labor Monthly* 5 (April 1926): 274–276; Jonathan Bloom, "Brookwood Labor College, 1921–1933: Training Ground for Union Organizers," M.A. thesis, Rutgers University, 1978, 76.

14. *Survey of Workers' Education*; Wolfe; David F. Noble, *America By Design: Science, Technology, and the Rise of Corporate Capitalism* (New York, 1977), 306; Stephen Meyer III, *The Five Dollar Day: Labor Management and Social Control in the Ford Motor Company 1908–1921* (Albany, NY, 1981), 160–161; Hodgen, 272.

15. *Survey of Workers' Education.*

16. *Survey of Workers' Education.*

17. Clinton Golden Report on Workers' Education Enterprises and Activities, 2 January–5 June 1925, Miscellaneous Reports 7, AFPS.

18. Golden Report.

19. Golden Report.

20. Miscellaneous Correspondence 2, AFPS; Miscellaneous Reports 1, 2, AFPS; John Brophy, *A Miner's Life* (Madison, WI, 1964), 223.

21. Miscellaneous Correspondence 2, AFPS; MacLeech, 208; Louise Leonard, "A New Summer School for Women Workers," *American Federationist* 32:2 (December 1927) 1487–1490.

22. Rita Heller, "Blue Collar and Bluestockings: The Bryn Mawr Summer School for Women Workers, 1921–1938," in *Sisterhood and Solidarity*, ed. Kornbluh and Frederickson, 109, 139–140; Moses Adam Cartwright, *Ten Years of Adult Education* (New York, 1935), 110, 198.

23. Brooks, 89. For the beginning and ensuing problems of Commonwealth College see William Henry Cobb, "Commonwealth College Comes to Arkansas, 1923–1925," *Arkansas Historical Quarterly* 23 (Summer 1964): 99–122; Cobb, "Commonwealth College: A History," M.A. thesis, University of Arkansas, 1962; Raymond and Charlotte Koch, *Educational Commune: The Story of Commonwealth College* (New York, 1972); Richard James Altenbaugh, *Education for Struggle: The American Labor Colleges of the 1920s and 1930s* (Philadelphia, PA, 1990), 81–87.

24. Cobb, 51, 61, 65; Memo, 16 June 1925; Covington Hall to Elizabeth Gurley Flynn, 25 June 1925 and 20 November 1925, Applications Favorably Acted Upon 3, AFPS.

25. Cobb, 92–93, 95, 97–99, 104, 107, 111.

26. Covington Hall, "A Short History of Commonwealth College," Raymond and Charlotte Koch Collection, Archives of Labor and Urban Affairs, Wayne State University; Koch, 13, 33, 59–60, 92, 99.

27. Brooks, 80–81; A. J. Muste in *The Essays of A. J. Muste*, ed., Nat Hentoff (Indianapolis, IN, 1967), 92–93; Bloom, 4–10.

28. Report on Brookwood submitted to the American Fund for Public Service, November 1923, Gifts 1922–1927, 2, AFPS; James O. Morris, *Conflict Within the AFL: A Study of Craft versus Industrial Unionism 1901–1938* (Ithaca, NY, 1958), 97; Brooks, 83; Lawrence Rogin, "How Far Have We Come in Workers' Education?" in *The Labor Movement: A Reexamination*, ed. Jack Barbash (Madison, WI, 1967), 124; Hentoff, 130; Len DeCaux, *Labor Radical: From the Wobblies to CIO* (Boston, MA, 1970), 95–96.

29. Nearing to Muste, 15 May 1925, Miscellaneous Correspondence 1, AFPS.

30. Muste to Nearing, 25 May 1925, Box 22, Brookwood Collection, Archives of Labor and Urban History, Wayne State University.

31. Bloom, 36, 67; Morris, 98–102; Muste to Robert Dunn, 27 January 1928, Dunn to Muste, 21 February 1928, Muste to AFPS, n.d, all Box 23, Brookwood Collection; Joann Ooiman Robinson, *Abraham Went Out: A Biography of A. J. Muste* (Philadelphia, 1981) 38; Memo, 22 April 1928, Miscellaneous Corre-

spondence 2, AFPS; Minutes, 13 June 1928, Miscellaneous Reports 8, AFPS; Israel Mufson, "Organizing the Unorganized," *Survey* 59 (15 March 1928): 757–758.

32. Morris, 114–115, 119; *New York Times*, 9 August 1928 and 31 October 1928; Brooks, 116–117; Robinson, 39, 242.

33. John Dewey, "Labor Politics and Labor Education," *New Republic* 57 (9 January 1929): 211–214; *New York Times* 6 April 1929 and 7 April 1929.

34. Folders 17–20, Box 1, Brookwood Collection; Brooks, 157; Eleanor G. Coit and Mark Starr, "Workers' Education in the United States," *Monthly Review* 49 (July 1939): 7; Howlett, 169, 175, 178; Peters and McCarrick, 118; MacLeech, 224; Morris, 99.

35. David J. Saposs, "Which Way Workers' Education?" *Survey* 62 (15 May 1929): 251; Rogin, 123.

36. Bloom, 36; Maurer quoted in Brameld, 19; *First National Conference on Workers' Education*, 103–105.

37. Gray, "The American Way," 56; Joyce L. Kornbluh, *A New Deal for Workers' Education: The Workers' Service Program 1933–1942* (Urbana, IL, 1987), 19.

38. The terms come from Irving Bernstein's *The Lean Years: A History of the American Worker, 1920–1933* (Boston, MA, 1960) and *The Turbulent Years: A History of the American Worker, 1933–1941* (Boston, MA, 1970).

39. See Kornbluh, *A New Deal for Workers' Education*.

10 "A Voice from the Forecastle": R. H. Dana's *Two Years before the Mast*

Horst Ihde

Richard Henry Dana, who lived from 1815 to 1882, received an education befitting a literary career. He interrupted his studies at Harvard, however, after suffering a bout of the measles, which left his eyes in such a bad condition that he decided to "try the effect of a voyage before the mast."[1]

The sea had attracted young Dana from childhood. Although Dana could well have afforded to travel as a passenger, with the monetary assistance of his father, an eminent poet and critic, he chose instead to sign up as an ordinary sailor before the mast. This decision, strange and whimsical as it might appear, nonetheless reflected the spirit of the time, in which Ralph Waldo Emerson was praising nature as "the beautiful asylum"[2] and urging scholars to study life directly. "Life is our dictionary," he elucidated in 1837, "Years are well spent in country labors; in town; in the insight into trades and manufactures."[3] For Dana, if his voyage as a sailor "did not cure his eyes, it would, at least, fit him for active life."[4]

The inexperienced youth embarked from Boston harbor on August 14, 1834 on the "Pilgrim," a small brig of only 180 tons, whose crew of fifteen were crowded together uncomfortably in a minimum of space. Dana's book *Two Years before the Mast* appeared in 1840, an account of his voyage from Boston around Cape Horn to California and then homeward.[5]

After returning from his voyage in 1836 with renewed health and restored vision, Dana continued his studies at Harvard, obtaining a law degree and thereafter practicing law in Boston. Among his clients were poor sailors, whose rights he defended against the wealthy ship owners and merchants of Boston. In 1867 he was appointed Lecturer in International Law at Harvard.

Dana's interest in reforms drew him into politics and in 1868 he ran unsuccessfully for Congress. When President Ulysses Grant nominated Dana Ambassador to England he was impetuously attacked by his political enemies and the Senate rejected his nomination. In 1878 Dana traveled to Europe for the last time. He died in Rome in 1882.

In writing *Two Years before the Mast*, Dana drew on his memory and on notations preserved in a brief log taken during the voyage.[6] Dana intended to elevate the sailors "in the rank of beings, and to promote in any measure their religious and moral improvement, and diminish the hardships of their daily life."[7] Written with the assistance of poet and family friend William Cullen Bryant, the volume appeared in the Harper's Family Library in 1840 and presented a realistic account of life at sea on a sailing ship.

During the 1830s, while Dana was studying, traveling, and writing, the nation experienced great economic expansion and the concomitant economic crises of 1834, 1837, and 1839. The growth of industry, the widening of markets, and the improvement of transportation created dynamic changes in the social structure of the United States. Machinery increasingly supplanted old manual processes, and the technology of travel advanced with the development of the steamship and the railroad.[8] The ruling classes of this period tried to increase their profits by extending the working day and by employing unqualified labor and children.[9] In 1830 the working day averaged twelve and one-half hours.[10] Friedrich Sorge later referred to the "noticeable" "class contrast" in this period.[11] By 1836 some three hundred thousand workers were spearheading the labor movement in the United States, although they were set back during the crisis of 1837 by the sharp deflation of wages and the steep rise of unemployment.[12]

In 1815, after the war with England, the United States had entered what was called the "golden age of American shipping." Eventually challenging British hegemony on the sea, U.S. merchant shipping became a most profitable enterprise: ship tonnage, for example, increased from five hundred thousand in 1830 to five million in 1860.[13] The demand for distribution of commodities through shipping soared as the population nearly doubled from 1820 to 1840. The striking success of the merchant marine in the United States could be achieved only by intensified exploitation of the workers at sea.[14] The success of a voyage depended almost entirely on the skill, the discipline, and the health of the sailors and sea workers. The ordinary sailors, who had remained faceless in U.S. literature before Dana's work appeared, worked the hardest, endured the greatest fatigue, and coped with the most dangerous situations.

When Dana experienced his ordeal as sea worker, no organization yet existed to defend the rights of sailors; the first one was founded in New York in March 1863.[15] With his remarkably keen insights and vivid descriptions, the young author reveals the abysmal working conditions of his fellow sailors. Dana, a gentleman's son, who until then had never been connected with the toiling classes and for whom life at sea was only a temporary expedient, tried hard to understand and sympathize with his shipmates, although the "notion that [he] was not 'one of them'"[16] surfaced and was put to test occasionally.

Dana sought primarily to discredit the romantic portrayal of maritime life and to offer instead a realistic representation of the daily hardships experienced by the sailors in their work. By exposing the most glaring evils the writer urged improvements of the economic and legal status of sea workers.

A law student and dedicated reformer when writing his book, Dana based his argumentation–as did all reformers of his age–on human rights as they had been pronounced in the Virginia Declaration of Rights (1776) or the Declaration of Independence (1776), which proclaimed equality for all people. As Karl Marx would later analyze in *Capital*,[17] these rights had a class character; they were human rights not of the socialized but of the isolated individual whose degree of freedom was determined by the quantity of his property. The bourgeois reform movement in Dana's time, far from taking any steps to change society, was designed principally to harmonize the individual with a given moral order and to elevate the individual's soul. Without ever attacking the nascent capitalist system directly, Dana vividly describes the never-ending drudgery of work promoted by that system.

Capitalism maintained the discipline and efficiency of its wage earners not only by economic measures but also by implementing a set of punitive measures, including physical violence. In Dana's day, the classes in power still used various forms of open coercion toward working people. The slave holders in the South had to rely on the application of violence to preserve their outmoded socio-economic system and to defend it against any progressive trends. Flogging with the rawhide or blacksnake whip was the usual method for punishing slaves. Racism, serving to justify the alleged 'natural' supremacy of the white ruling class in the South over their African American workers, contaminated the whole country. As Philip Foner has noted:

Thus, from the cradle to the grave, the white worker, whether native-born or foreign-born, was taught to regard the Negro as an inferior. In a society in which racial prejudice was all but universal, it is hardly surprising that he refused to work with a black craftsman or laborer, believed that no black should receive the same wages and conditions as a white worker, and excluded blacks from his union.[18]

The complex problem of slavery in the United States is reflected in Dana's book. The author devotes a whole chapter (XV) to describing the inhuman practice of flogging two of his shipmates by the sadistic ship's captain. Sam, a white victim, confirms the remarks quoted above by shouting at his torturer: "I'm no negro slave."[19] The response to this legitimate complaint, however is short and to the point: "'Then I'll make you one,' said the captain."[20]

This effective scene impressively reveals the close relationship between chattel slavery and wage slavery. Although Dana as the narrator remains a passive observer, who "would not have joined the men in mutiny,"[21] he is deeply shocked by the brutal, completely inopportune flogging and at least morally comes out strongly in favor of the culprit by commenting: "A man—a human being, made in God's likeness–fastened up and flogged like a beast."[22] And the best Dana can do as a humanist and a reformer is to vow that: "if God should ever give me the means, I would do something to redress the grievances and relieve the sufferings of that poor class of beings, of whom I then was one."[23]

Dana did not forget what he had seen and experienced on his voyage. In 1839 he published a pamphlet entitled *Cruelty to Seamen*, in which he took up the case of sailors who had been flogged to death. In *The Seaman's Friend* (1841), edited in England at the same time as *The Seaman's Manual*, Dana continued to champion the rights of his former fellow sea workers. Later, he took up the cause of the fugitive slaves with the same zeal and seriousness with which he had defended the rights of sea workers.[24]

Since Dana firmly believed that people are born equal, that the human being is divine and humanity perfectible, he wrote with great respect and sincere compassion about a group of Sandwich Islanders with whom he spent a few months in California. He does not emphasize or discuss the racial differences but treats the islanders as equals and characterizes them as "the most interesting, intelligent, and kind-hearted people that I ever fell in with."[25] The writer is not only impressed by the good manners and intelligence of his new friends, but also and especially by their "simple, primitive generosity, which is truly delightful; and which is often a reproach to our own people."[26] Dana's favorite among the Islanders was Hope, who became his special friend, or *aikane*. Encountering Hope again after several months, Dana finds he is suffering from a venereal disease, prompting him to lament the arrival of 'civilization,' of the Christian "white men with their vices."27

Although few have ever questioned the poetic power and the highly literary achievement of Dana's book, it remained a work of nonfiction. Dana's work is based on a long tradition of journey books and travel diaries. Most of the reports of expeditions and accounts of journeys that had become popular in the second half of the eighteenth century had had no literary ambitions. The travel book in the "Age of Enlightenment" had fulfilled a didactic function, skillfully combining instruction with entertainment. With the steady expansion of territory of the United States, the interest in the new regions grew. Reports of journeys and travel books began to appear, written now in the romantic vein, not only to inform or entertain their readers but also to attract and recruit new settlers for the vast but sparsely populated areas.

Before writers had developed a passion for the unknown parts of the U.S. continent, however, the minds of other travelers had been captured by the unfathomable world of the oceans. The sea played a similar role in the imagination of many U.S. Americans that the frontier was to play in the second half of the nineteenth century. According to one critic, "The sea exerted the same appeal to the individual: it offered adventure, quick profit, the chance to start anew, and the freedom from the restraints and obligations of society."28

Yet there was really no escape from the "restraints and obligations of society," if one becomes free in the positive sense of the word when one acquires the opportunity to realize one's essential powers. According to Marx and Engels, one is "free not through the negative power to avoid this or that, but through the positive power to assert his [sic] true individuality."29 One is neither free from nature nor from society and its laws, but free only within the framework provided by the operation of the laws of nature and society.

Dana, though he gave up his safe place in society temporarily to retire to nature, was to come to the painful recognition that, in a society divided into antagonistic classes, the social relations–also aboard a ship–stand opposed to people and dominate them. The young seafarer exchanged his world where freedom, beauty, and human values were supposedly cherished, for a microcosm where freedom was ignored, beauty was despised, and human values were treated with contempt.

Dana shared many of the views of romantic writers of this period. The U.S. Romanticists had become aware of internal contradictions characterizing the social order that had emerged as a result of the War of Independence. At the foundation of their writing lay an awareness of the disharmony between the democratic slogans of the newborn republic and the grim reality of the way of life, as lived by the many, not the few. Dana, brought up on the ideas of romanticism, was stimulated by William Cullen Bryant's poetry. Bryant contrasted the beauty, might, and wealth of nature to inhuman social relations, and in his well-known poem *Thanatopsis* (1817), he reveals the moral untenability of the philosophy of the man of property. Dana similarly rejected the merciless struggle for success at any cost and pitiless individualism, being attracted instead to the customs still preserved and respected by the Sandwich Islanders.

In contrast to the contemporary Romanticists, however, Dana's criticism is not restricted to a retreat to nature but is expressed in the realistic reflection of reality and in the sharp accusation of the perceived evils of his society. Dana, who had criticized the highly romanticized and distorted image of the sea as depicted by George Gordon Byron and James Fenimore Cooper, outlined his own conception as follows: "My design is . . . to present the life of a common sailor at sea as it really is,–the light and the dark together."[30]

Another point of discrepancy between Dana and other authors concerned the evident contrast between art and reality. Many romantic writers sought to save the "poetry" of life from the division of labor and the devastating effects of capitalist reality. They worshipped the individual and bestowed on the individual a universal character, thus separating the individual from the real world. The individual thus seemed free from any natural bonds that in previous periods had connected him/her with certain groups or collectives. Dana's depiction of labor relations aboard ship, however, distinguishes his work from this tendency among Romanticists.

Since oppression in society was most convincingly demonstrated by the system of slavery, Dana repeatedly referred to this sphere. From his own experience he expresses his opinion that "Jack is a slave aboard ship"[31] and he praises a day off duty emphatically as "the delightful sensation of being in the open air, with the birds singing around me, and escaped from the confinement, labor and strict rule of a vessel."[32] For Dana the voyage conjured up the idea of being enslaved, and when the time had come to bid goodbye to "the hell of California,"[33] where he had fulfilled the "disagreeable and fatiguing"[34] duties of hide-curing, he "felt as though one link after another were struck from the chain of my servitude."[35]

On board the U.S. merchant ships there existed relations of domination and cruelty. Dana underscores this situation by quoting a shipmate who lamented the years of manhood thrown away, "that there, in the forecastle, at the foot of the steps–a chest of old clothes–[was] the result of twenty-two years of hard labor and exposure–worked like a horse, and treated like a dog."[36]

The problem of nature also assumed special importance in the works and thinking of the Romanticists, and of course Dana. In turning to nature, the romantic writer searched for values not manifested in society. The writer discovered a new aspect of nature, the image of an omnipotent, mysterious friend, who, however, could easily become a troublesome, unreliable, or even cruel enemy.

Ralph Waldo Emerson challenged the contemporary romantic, sentimental thoughts, and such worn-out phrases as sublimity, grandeur, and the picturesque. In 1835 his volume *Nature* appeared, quickly becoming the manifesto of Transcendentalism and bringing about changes in the U.S. attitude toward nature. Expressing his belief in a mystical union with God through nature, Emerson saw the world of nature as a domain that can enlighten and ennoble the human being. He concluded that it was necessary to look "at the world with new eyes,"[37] that "our hunting of the picturesque is inseparable from our protest against false society."[38]

Dana, influenced by his teacher Emerson, applied Emerson's ideas in a new and unconventional way. Unlike Cooper and other contemporary writers, to whom beauty and nature seemed synonymous, and who dedicated themselves to praising the romantic features of the life at sea, Dana, though "affected by the beauty of the sea, the bright stars, and the clouds driven swiftly over them,"[39] never immersed himself in images of an ideal nature, free of compulsions and free of labor. The author's voyage narrative is indeed not a romantic vision of the glories of the sea but a realistic chronicle of a life dominated by the daily routine on board and the conflicts between the individual and nature.

The young narrator, however, did not limit himself to the revelation of the ugliness, boredom, and brutality of the sea worker's existence; he also portrayed beautiful and solemn scenes. Simple and straightforward as his report is, it is filled with profound emotion and unforgettable images. Some passages are among the finest descriptions of nature in U.S. or even in world literature. The picture he draws of a tropical thunderstorm and the image of a ship under full sail, for example, have been imitated by many other writers. The best-remembered part of the book describes his voyage home in the dead of winter, the heroic efforts of the crew to round Cape Horn. These unique episodes prompted Herman Melville to write in 1850 [*White Jacket*]: "But if you want the best idea of Cape Horn, get my friend Dana's unmatchable *Two Years before the Mast*. . . . His chapters describing Cape Horn must have been written with an icicle."[40]

For Dana, then, the sea is not just an aesthetic and natural phenomenon; it represents the vastness of the unknown, an untamed, unpredictable force, requiring human effort to cope with it. One recalls Frederick Engels's later assessment of nature in 1876:

Thus at every step we are reminded that we by no means rule over nature like a conqueror over a foreign people, like someone standing outside nature–but that we, with flesh, blood and brain, belong to nature, and exist in its midst, and that all our mastery of it consists in the fact that we have the advantage over all other creatures of being able to learn its laws and apply them correctly.[41]

After a terrific fight against a chaos of sleet and snow, icy water and icebergs, the voyager and his shipmates finally succeed in holding the ship secure against the hostile ocean. But they are not elevated by this encounter with the unrelenting forces of nature. On the contrary, they experience simple exhaustion. The account of the arduous journey around Cape Horn, then, derives its strength not only from Dana's intense portrayal of natural forces, but also from his depiction of the physical ordeal of the sea workers and their final triumph over nature.

Stylistically, Dana sought to write as suggested by Emerson, to "record truth truly."[42] Dana creates an impression of verisimilitude by drawing on the dated entries in his notebook, by piling fact upon fact, and by reporting supposedly verbatim conversations. He utilizes techniques of imaginative writing by dramatizing incidents, by shifting from past to present time narrative in scenes of action, by recalling literary quotations and allusions, and by drawing thumbnail sketches of some of his shipmates. D. H. Lawrence would later praise Dana for his "dispassionate statement of plain material facts" written from the "remoter, non-emotional centres of being."[43]

Two Years before the Mast was reviewed by the leading journals in the United States and England immediately after its publication in 1840. Dana's radically different approach toward maritime life was instantly noted and appreciated. Dana's book proved a success. When visiting California in 1864, Dana remarked that "almost . . . every American in California had read it," since his book on California had been one of the few available in 1848 at the time of the gold rush.[44]

Other sailor-writers soon followed Dana's example. Factual accounts of experiences at sea appeared by Francis Allyn Olmsted (*Incidents of a Whaling Voyage*, 1841); an anonymous author (*A Green Hand's First Cruise*, 1841); Samuel Leeds (*Thirty Years from Home or A Voice from the*

Main Deck, 1843); Nicholas Isaacs (*Twenty Years before the Mast*, 1845); and William Nevens (*Forty Years at Sea*, 1845).[45]

Cooper and Melville also were influenced by Dana's realistic approach. Cooper's *Ned Meyers: A Life before the Mast* appeared in 1843,[46] as yet another sailor's reminiscence. Melville, who became acquainted with Dana in 1847, was advised by Dana to write *White Jacket* (1850) about life on a man-of-war ship. In Melville's *Redburn* (1849) many episodes remind the reader of Dana's best seller.[47]

Inspired by the contemporary reform movement, Dana, in his innermost nature a humanitarian and philanthropist, made every effort to guarantee dignity, liberty, and justice to all. He firmly believed in the feasibility of major transformations in the social life and nature of the human being. Although *Two Years before the Mast* did not cause a direct and immediate improvement in the lot of U.S. American sea workers, its success in the United States and in other countries drew the attention of the general public to the fate of this neglected section of the working class. Without openly attacking the establishment, the author aspired to go beyond the framework of the existing system of values.

More important than his reform plans, however, was the immediate and telling effect his book had upon literature and the image of maritime life. *Two Years before the Mast* not only discredited the romantic and sentimental literature about the sea, but it also ushered in a new way of portraying human interaction with nature. Instead of romantic sentiment, superficial enthusiasm, or glamorous adventures, there were incontestable facts, a realistic style, authentic accounts based exclusively on the narrator's experience, and above all, a deep feeling for and understanding of the downtrodden and exploited.

Dana's work was original and even unique since he introduced labor as an essential part of travel literature. The writer reveals the abject conditions of physical labor under capitalism in the 1830s, while being aware of the importance of labor as a means of dominating nature and as the main condition of the specifically human existence.

Two Years before the Mast, acclaimed by many as a classic of world literature, exerted a profound influence on generations of writers. With his book Dana gave a strikingly powerful impetus to the further development of realism in U.S. literature.

NOTES

1. Richard Henry Dana's father to James Fenimore Cooper, *Correspondence of James Fenimore Cooper*, ed. James Fenimore Cooper (New Haven,

1922) 2:422. Cf. also Richard Henry Dana, *An Autobiographical Sketch (1815–1842)*, (Hamden, CT, 1953), 63ff; Robert L. Gale, *Richard Henry Dana, Jr.* (New York, 1969).

2. *The Journals of Ralph Waldo Emerson*, ed. Edward Waldo Emerson and Waldo Emerson Forbes (London, Boston, New York, 1911) 5:58.

3. Ralph Waldo Emerson, "The American Scholar" (1837), in *The Complete Essays and Other Writings of Ralph Waldo Emerson*, ed. Brooks Atkinson (New York, 1940), 54.

4. Cooper, 423.

5. In 1859, when Dana suffered a nervous breakdown, he again took refuge at sea. This time, however, he traveled around the world as a passenger in a comfortable stateroom. The tour also took him to California, where he visited people and places first encountered during his voyage of 1834. The second edition of *Two Years before the Mast*, published in 1869, contains an additional chapter with the author's observations and remarks about his second voyage.

6. The sea chest that had contained a detailed account of his adventures was lost.

7. Richard Henry Dana, *Two Years before the Mast* (New York: Harpers Family Library 106, 1840), 5. Hereafter referred to as *TYbtM/1840*.

8. Leo Marx, *The Machine in the Garden. Technology and the Pastoral Ideal in America* (New York, 1967), 191.

9. Cf. Jürgen Kuczynski, *Die Geschichte der Lage der Arbeiter unter dem Kapitalismus. Bd. 29: Darstellung der Lage der Arbeiter in den Vereinigten Staaten von Amerika von 1775 bis 1897* (Berlin, 1966), 154.

10. Philip S. Foner, *History of the Labor Movement in the United States: From Colonial Times to the Founding of the American Federation of Labor* (New York, 1947), 218.

11. *Friedrich A. Sorge's Labor Movement in the United States. A History of the American Working Class from Colonial Times to 1890*, eds. Philip S. Foner and Brewster Chamberlin (Westport, CT, and London, 1977), 54.

12. Cf. Kuczynski, 100.

13. Michael Kraus, *The United States to 1865* (Ann Arbor, MI, 1959), 391.

14. In 1824 Daniel Webster boasted that U.S. shipowners were able to meet or even overcome universal competition not "by protection and bounties, but by unwearied exertion, by extreme economy, by unshaken perseverance, by that manly and resolute spirit which relies on itself to protect itself." *Daniel Webster: Writings and Speeches, Vol. 3*, ed. J. W. McIntyre (Boston, 1903), 104, quoted in James Ford Rhodes, *History of the United States from the Compromise of 1850 to the Final Restoration of Home Rule at the South in 1877* (New York, London, 1910) 3:7.

15. Cf. Sidney Kaplan, "The American Seamen's Protective Union Association of 1863: A Pioneer Organization of Negro Seamen in the Port of New York," *Science and Society* 21 (Spring 1957): 154–159; Philip S. Foner, *Organized Labor and the Black Worker 1619–1973* (New York, 1976), 14.

16. Dana, *TYbtM/1840*, 340.

17. According to Karl Marx: "This sphere that we are deserting within whose boundaries the sale and purchase of labour-power goes on, is in fact a very Eden of the innate rights of man. There alone rule Freedom, Equality, Property and Bentham. Freedom, because both buyer and seller of a commodity, say of labour-power, are constrained only by their own free will. . . . Equality, because each enters into relation with the other, as with a simple owner of commodities, and they exchange equivalent for equivalent. Property, because each disposes only of what is his own. And Bentham, because each looks only to himself. The only force that brings them together and puts them in relation with each other, is the selfishness, the gain and the private interests of each." *Capital* (Moscow, 1978) I: 172.

18. Philip S. Foner, *Organized Labor and the Black Worker 1619–1973* (New York, 1976), 10.

19. Dana, *TYbtM/1840*, 124.

20. Dana, *TYbtM/1840*, 124.

21. Dana, *Two Years before the Mast* (New York, 1946), 83. This sentence is not in the original edition.

22. Dana, *TYbtM/1840*, 125.

23. Dana, *TYbtM/1840*, 130.

24. Cf. Rhodes, 1:500.

25. Dana, *TYbtM/1840*, 181.

26. Dana, *TYbtM/1840*, 183.

27. Dana, *TYbtM/1840*, 308.

28. Thomas Philbrick, *James Fenimore Cooper and the Development of American Sea Fiction* (Cambridge, MA, 1961), 1.

29. Karl Marx, Friedrich Engels, *The Holy Family* (1845), in Marx, Engels, *Collected Works* (Moscow, 1975), 4, 131. Cf. Marx and Engels, *The German Ideology* (1845/46) in Marx, Engels, *Collected Works* (Moscow, 1976), 5, 78f.

30. Dana, *TYbtM/1840*, 4.

31. Dana, *TYbtM/1840*, 90.

32. Dana, *TYbtM/1840*, 141.

33. Dana, *TYbtM/1840*, 323.

34. Dana, *TYbtM/1840*, 191.

35. Dana, *TYbtM/1840*, 323.

36. Dana, *TYbtM/1840*, 246.

37. Ralph Waldo Emerson, "Nature" (1835) in *The Complete Essays and Other Writings of Ralph Waldo Emerson*, 42.

38. Emerson, "Nature" (Second Series, 1844) in *The Complete Essays and Other Writings of Ralph Waldo Emerson*, 411.

39. Dana, *TYbtM/1840*, 10.

40. Herman Melville, *White Jacket* (New York, 1952), 105.

41. Friedrich Engels, "The Part Played by Labour in the Transition from Ape to Man" (1876), *Dialectics of Nature*, in Marx, Engels, *Collected Works* (Moscow, 1987), 25, 461.

42. *The Journals of Ralph Waldo Emerson*, 31 January 1841, 5:516.

43. D. H. Lawrence, *Studies in Classic American Literature* (London, 1924), 117.

44. Dana, *Two Years before the Mast* (1965), 379.

45. Cf. Philbrick, 119; Robert F. Lucid, "The Influence of *Two Years before the Mast* on Herman Melville," *American Literature* 31 (November 1959), 3, 243, n. 2.

46. Cf. *Correspondence of James Fenimore Cooper*, 2:519, 522, 604.

47. Cf. Lucid, 250.

11 Philip S. Foner at City College—Victim of the Rapp-Coudert Committee

Morris U. Schappes

The forty-four line entry on Philip S. Foner in *Who's Who in America* contains essential facts about his education, academic career, and the titles of some seventy-five volumes he had published, part of his enormous, valuable, and valued productivity as historian and researcher. But recently in the course of reading this entry, having been associated with him for almost sixty years as colleague, friend, publisher of one of my books, and reader and admirer of his works, I noted an unexpected reticence about one fact. The *Who's Who* entry included: "Began as tchr. 1933." Where? Reported on the next line is: "prof. history Lincoln U., Pa., 1967–79, Rutgers U., Camden, 1981." But what about 1933?

Out of a sense of intimacy born of joint struggle, I deem it necessary and desirable to fill in this gap sketchily. From 1933 to 1941 Philip Foner taught in the History Department of the College of the City of New York. From 1928 to 1941 I taught in the English Department of that College. Our terminal years are the same because we were among the forty to fifty members of the teaching and administrative staffs at the City College who were fired in 1941 or forced to resign or who were simply not reappointed in the absence of tenure, as a result of the invasion of that campus by the Rapp-Coudert Committee of the New York State legislature, charged, among many other things, with investigating alleged "subversive activities" in the New York City school system. There were a score or so of similar academic casualties at the three other municipal colleges—Hunter, Brooklyn, and Queens. Forty years after this academic carnage, perpetrated by the Rapp-Coudert Committee and its obedient instrument, the Board of Higher Education of the City of New York, the surviving victims (about one-third of our number had died by October 26, 1981)[1] received a formal, public apology from the Board of Trustees of the City University of New York (CUNY)[2] for the injustice done to us through the denial of our academic freedom. Aware that it was the institutional successor of the delinquent Board of Higher Education of 1941, the Board of Trustees faced up squarely to the evidence of injustice presented to it by the Faculty Senate of the City College and the University Faculty Senate, and acted honorably and courageously to rehabilitate the teachers and administrators who had been dismissed and defamed forty years earlier. More about Philip Foner's role in sparking that reinvestigation later. Now to some details about the due, but irrelevant, process by which Foner's academic teaching career was interrupted for twenty-six years—from 1941 to 1967.

On March 29, 1940, a Joint Resolution was passed by the New York State legislature, authored by upstate Republican assemblyperson Herbert A. Rapp and Senator Frederic R. Coudert, Jr., the only Republican member of the legislature from New York City, calling for an investigation into the financing of the New York City public school system, in which both the city and state were involved. The investigating committee was specifically charged with studying thirteen aspects of the situation; the eleventh of those was: "the extent to which, if any, subversive activities may have been permitted to be carried on in the schools and colleges of such educational system." Under the direction of Committee Vice-Chair Coudert, the investigation concentrated overwhelmingly on the alleged subversive activities, although in its final report released on April 23, 1942, no such activities were specified.[3] It is appropriate to record that during the period of the Committee's assault on the City College, the History Department did indeed include one teacher who could properly have been designated as "subversive," but the Rapp-Coudert Committee did not identify him; instead, after Pearl Harbor on December 7, 1941, the FBI came onto the City College campus to arrest John LeClair, who, in 1943, was convicted of being a paid agent of the Japanese government. By the time LeClair was arrested, however, the Rapp-Coudert Committee and the Board of Higher Education had dismissed from the History Department both Philip Foner and his twin brother Jack Foner (who had started teaching in the History Department in 1934), and all other victims of this academic purge.

The operation of the Rapp-Coudert Committee was accompanied by shrill red-baiting in the print media. The day after the first open hearing of the Committee on December 2, 1940, the Hearst *Journal-American* swept the European theater of war off its front page with a ninety-six-point banner headline: "100 on College Faculty Here Branded as Red." Two days after the first public hearing on the City College situation on March

6, 1941, the Taxpayers Union of New York City, representing the large realty interests, urged the mayor to cut $10 million from the budget of the four municipal colleges and demanded the closing of the City College pending the purge of all "un-American professors and students." And on March 9, Taxpayers Union president Joseph Goldsmith declared: "A majority of the [City College] students are Communists and we are in favor of closing down the college until the situation is cleared up."[4]

After I had been arrested in the offices of the College Teachers Union on March 18, 1941, and while I was awaiting a criminal trial for perjury (read: for refusing to be an informer), Senator Coudert, on June 3, according to the *New York Times*, addressed a meeting of the Republican Business Women thus:

Now, if your dog had rabies, you wouldn't clap him into jail after he had bitten a number of persons—you'd put a bullet in his head, if you had that kind of iron in your soul.

It is going to require brutal treatment to handle these teachers. . . . The first step in making it possible for American institutions to work properly is to eliminate from our public and private lives these individuals. . . . We cannot live with them nor they with us.[5]

It was in such a climate that Philip Foner approached his ordeal (as did his brother, Jack) with the Rapp-Coudert Committee. He had been "named" as a Communist at the March 6 public hearing. On April 23, Foner denied the allegation at a public hearing of the Committee. On May 19, he was formally served with charges. From August 19 to 21, he was tried before a committee of the Board of Higher Education. By that time, I had been convicted at the end of my criminal trial that began on June 18 and ended on June 28, and had been sentenced on July 11 to from one-and-one-half to two years in prison as a felon. I was out on $10,000 cash bail pending (unsuccessful) appeals to the Appellate Division of the New York Supreme Court and the Court of Appeals of New York State. By the time Foner's trial began, ten members of the teaching and administrative staffs had already been dismissed among the thirty-six who had been suspended without pay as targets of the Rapp-Coudert Committee. (Others had resigned rather than face the ordeal of a public trial in that hysterical climate.) Foner, having tenure as an instructor, was entitled to receive the "due process" of a Board trial.[6]

Tenure, it should be noted, was a recent innovation at the municipal colleges. When Foner was appointed to teach at the City College, tenure was provided only for full professors. The president of the college had full power to make all appointments, including those of deans, department heads, and members of the teaching, administrative, and janitorial staffs. By 1938 the College Teachers Union, founded in 1935, had changed all that. Foner and all the other targets of the Rapp-Coudert investigation, as members and activists in that Union, had brought about legislation that granted tenure to any teacher, in any rank, who was reappointed for a fourth year. Thus, Foner had tenure in his rank of instructor; I had tenure in my rank as tutor (after thirteen years; my radical activities had barred my promotion). Incidentally, the same legislation also provided for a democratic structure: department heads were elected for three-year terms by the vote of the tenured members of the department, and could be reelected for only one more successive term; recommendations for appointments came from a department-elected committee on appointments and promotions; and elected department curriculum committees determined the curricula. So sweeping was this law on tenure and democratic structure—the first such in any college system—that in 1938 the *Nation* magazine presented a special award to Ordway Tead, president of the Board of Higher Education, for having secured passage of the law by the state legislature. (It should be added that Jesse Mintus, a member of the Registrar's staff, helped draft the bill and was, in due time, one of those fired by the Rapp-Coudert Committee and the Board of Higher Education.)

Conducting Philip Foner's trial was a committee of the Board of Higher Education consisting of Reuben A. Lazarus, chair; Mrs. Marion A. Mack; and S. J. Woolf, the well-known artist and newspaper writer, who had only recently been appointed to the Board of Higher Education by Mayor Fiorello H. LaGuardia. The prosecution was conducted by Assistant Corporation Counsel Charles C. Weinstein. Foner's defense was conducted by two attorneys—Samuel A. Neuberger and Samuel Rosenwein. It is oddly instructive today to read the 334 single-spaced foolscap pages of the trial record, almost fifty years after the trial and almost ten years after the successor CUNY Board of Trustees had condemned the trial, conviction, and dismissal of Philip Foner.

The first charge made against Foner was that of "inculcating doctrines and principles of the Communist Party in the minds of students" and of instructing other teachers on how to so indoctrinate (*Trial Record*, 9). A few minutes after it was made, however (13), the prosecution "unconditionally" withdrew this charge. As Counsel Neuberger pointed out a few minutes later in his opening statement (23), for the trial committee to even hear the remaining charges was to "permit a flameless book-burning." The withdrawal of the charge of classroom indoctrination, he declared, meant that what was being investigated were Foner's *opinions*, which he had a constitutional right to hold and to act upon outside the classroom, in extracurricular discourse on campus, and as a citizen off campus. Yet the trial proceeded to its foregone conclusion.

The prosecution presented three witnesses, each an avowed ex-communist, who testified they knew Foner to be a communist. The first was Annette Sherman Gottsegen, a clerk in the College Evening Session Office at the 23rd Street Center. The second was William Martin Canning, an untenured history instructor in the Evening Session at 23rd Street. The third was Oscar Zeichner, a tutor in the History Department at the Main Center, where Foner taught. For the defense, Neuberger also presented three witnesses. The first was Dr. Edward Rosen, who had been teaching in the History Department for sixteen years. He testified that Zeichner had revealed to him that a Professor Walter A. Knittle, also in the History Department, had warned Zeichner that he was vulnerable not only to dismissal but also to charges of perjury, if he persisted in denying having been a member of the Communist Party at City College. Knittle, it had also been revealed, had relied on Canning's testimony in approaching Zeichner. (Incidentally, Knittle has been honored by having a college lounge named after him.)

The second witness for the defense was Allan Nevins, the Columbia University historian and Pulitzer Prize winner, under whose direct supervision Foner had written his doctoral dissertation, and for whom Foner had worked as a research assistant in the preparation of Nevins's biographies of Abram S. Hewitt and Grover Cleveland. Asked by Neuberger whether Foner had "ever asserted anything which you would describe as being subversive in character," Nevins replied (182), "I have never heard him say anything that was tendentious in character . . . and I have never known him to write anything under my supervision or for my use that was seditious in character." As to Foner's reputation for truth and veracity, Nevins had "never heard it impugned. . . . I should say that it was good. That is simply a general impression. I never heard his veracity called in question." It is relevant here to note that Foner's dissertation, *Business and Slavery*, had earlier that year been published by the University of North Carolina Press and was, in fact, favorably received in the *New York Times Book Review* of July 20, 1941, a month before Foner's trial began. (A copy of the book review was received into the trial record as Exhibit Q. When the book was published in England by the Oxford University Press, it received a highly favorable review in the *New Statesman* and the *Nation* by Harold J. Laski.)

The final witness for the defense was Professor Michael Kraus of the History Department, who testified that Foner and he, "together," had on occasion taught the same course on the Civil War, that he had found nothing subversive in Foner's writings, and that with respect to "truth and veracity," Foner's character was "good." Prosecutor Weinstein, on cross-examination, despite his earlier withdrawal "unconditionally" of the charge of classroom indoctrination, questioned why, in the course on the Civil War taught by Kraus and Foner, a book on the Civil War was listed as recommended (but not required) reading for students when, in fact, it was written by "known Communists," Karl Marx and Friedrich Engels. Professor Kraus replied (186), "It is a standard work" (consisting, one might add, of the articles written by Marx and Engels and published during the Civil War in the abolitionist daily, the *New York Tribune*.)[7]

When, finally, Philip Foner took the stand, he continued to deny membership in the Communist Party. For doing so, he was found guilty of "conduct unbecoming a teacher" and dismissed.

The most significant comment on this trial proceeding was provided by S. J. Woolf of the Trial Committee. While voting with his two colleagues to find Foner guilty and to dismiss him, Woolf filed a separate opinion in November, 1941, in which he stated: "Foner, a non-indoctrinating Communist, was not a threat to the college. Foner, lying either through shame in his beliefs or to save his job, is as unfitted to remain a teacher as the informers who spoke to save theirs." The Rapp-Coudert Committee took offense at Woolf's comparison in these last eight words. In its final report, the Committee opined that "there is grave doubt as to whether a person who expresses such views in an official capacity is fit to hold public office."[8]

Woolf's comparison, however, although perhaps perceptive on one level, is hardly adequate. More insightful was the view of Morris Raphael Cohen, the eminent philosopher and outstanding teacher of philosophy, who at that time bore City College's most honored and distinguished name. In preparing for my criminal trial for perjury, I was asked by my counsel to find an impressive "character witness" to testify that my reputation for veracity was high. As an undergraduate at City College, I had never been a student of Cohen's. When I was teaching at the college, however, I exercised my privilege of sitting in on his renowned course on Santayana. By that time, I was a professed Marxist and Cohen a professed anti-Marxist, often effective because he had read more of Marx than some of us who claimed to be Marxists. In his class, we often sparred. On the campus, our public differences of opinion on issues were known. Yet I went to his home to ask him to appear as a character witness at my trial.

At the open hearing of the Rapp-Coudert Committee on March 6, I had testified incredibly. Personally, I did not expect to be believed, but I was determined not to be an informer in a proceeding that had no basic legitimacy. How was I to say this to Cohen? As I fumbled for a rationale, he interrupted me. "Morris, I know exactly what you are doing. Why, in the old country, in Russia, we used to have a saying: 'It's no use telling the truth to the police because they wouldn't know what to do with it.' "

So this student of jurisprudence, legal philosophy, and legal practice came to court and testified, much to the discomfort of both the judge and the prosecutor—both alumni of the City College, to whom the name of Morris Raphael Cohen was intimately known. Asked by my counsel, "And from the discussion that you have had with other people about Morris Schappes, can you tell this court and jury what his reputation for honesty and veracity is?" Professor Cohen answered, "I should say very high; generally regarded as a very honorable, idealistic man; very scholarly in dealing with his students." Neuberger continued, "In other words assuming that Morris U. Schappes were a Communist, assuming that you knew it and he believed in that principle, you say it would not change your opinion?" Cohen's reply was short: "Not in the least."9

So much, then, for "telling the truth to the police who would not know what to do with it." Or, in idiomatic speech, if you ask foolish questions of Foner, Schappes, or the other fifty-two whom Canning had "named" at the Rapp-Coudert Committee's public hearing on March 6, you would possibly receive foolish answers. This is by no means intended to equate questioner and answerer, for the Board of Higher Education's apology to Foner, Schappes, and the other human targets of the Rapp-Coudert Committee in 1981 for the injustice done to them and for the violation of their academic freedom indicates quite clearly where the original sin lay.

Ten years after these events, a sober evaluation of the conduct of the Board of Higher Education was given by Lawrence H. Chamberlain, Dean of Columbia College and professor in its Department of Public Law and Government, in his book, *Loyalty and Legislative Action: A Survey of Activity by the New York State Legislature, 1919–1949* (Cornell University Press, 1951):

In retrospect the board's handling and disposition of the Communist cases is not reassuring. . . . The record suggests that the board was more intent on sloughing off an embarrassing problem than on thinking it through. It failed to establish a policy which could be defended from the standpoint of democratic institutions and upon the basis of genuine academic freedom. . . . Its real shortcoming . . . was its timorous acceptance of the Coudert Committee's conception of subversive activity. . . . Once this had occurred, there was nothing left for it to do but put its machinery of prosecution in motion. Its meticulous procedure was a poor substitute for the courageous facing up which should have preceded it. (185–186)

As for the victims, Dean Chamberlain concludes:

No one can read through the verbatim testimony . . . without being impressed with the generally superior character of the group here under scrutiny. There seems no doubt from evidence presented elsewhere that some of the group were Communists, but the impressive and inescapable fact is that *the only evidence presented by either side* points to: (1) outstanding scholarship, (2) superior teaching, (3) absence of indoctrination in the classroom. [125, emphasis in the original].

Philip Foner also played an incidental role in triggering the train of events that resulted in effecting the apology elicited from the Trustees of the City University in 1981, fully forty years after its 1941 offense. Elsewhere, I have told the story in detail (*Jewish Currents*, April 1982), but a capsule here will suffice: During the Spanish Civil War, thirteen teachers, students, and alumni of City College had been killed in action fighting against Franco, most of them members of the Abraham Lincoln Brigade. In December 1977 some of us initiated an action to raise funds for a scholarship fund at City College in memory of these thirteen, and to have an appropriate bronze plaque, naming the thirteen and citing the democratic cause for which they had died, placed in the Main Building at City College. On April 13, 1980, the unveiling of this plaque was to take place, with suitable ceremonies in the Lincoln Corridor, a spacious, marble-floored assembly point in the Main Building. Among the speakers was Philip Foner, who had been teaching at the college when its teachers and students in the 1930s had gone to Spain; also among the speakers was the Acting President of City College, Dr. Alice Chandler (now president of the State University of New York at New Paltz).

Among the 350 people who turned out for this unique function were sixteen veterans of the Abraham Lincoln Brigade and some of the victims of the Rapp-Coudert Committee. Since 1941, we had shunned the campus from which we had been unjustly ousted. However, to honor some of our colleagues who had fallen in Spain, we felt it appropriate to make this visit. Present were John Kenneth Ackley, dismissed in 1941 when he was Registrar of the College; Jack Foner, now Professor Emeritus of Colby College; David Goldway, then Professor of English at the State University of New York at Farmingdale; Jesse Mintus, already mentioned, and I. When Foner had consulted me as to what he might include in his remarks, I had suggested that he note that if the late Ralph Wardlaw, of the Public Speaking Department, and the late Alfred "Chick" Chaikin, of the Hygiene Department and coach of the wrestling team, had returned from Spain alive, they would have been fired during the Rapp-Coudert purge, just like the rest of us. In the course of his brief historical analysis of the Spanish Civil War, Foner made just that point: Wardlaw and Chaikin, he said, "would have been dismissed in 1940–41, along with over twoscore anti-fascist teachers (myself included), all victims of the Rapp-Coudert Committee—premature victims of McCarthyism." And he called on Ackley and me to stand for a bow.

Hearing this item of unremembered, unwritten history, Dr. Chandler sought out Ackley after the ceremony and asked for more information. The next day, she asked the historian (and Academic Assistant to the college provost), Dr. Stephen Leberstein (now director of the Worker Education Program at the City College), to examine the records of the Rapp-Coudert Committee and provide her with a written report of his findings.

In due course, almost a year later, on March 19, 1981, the Faculty Senate passed a resolution that stands as a landmark in the annals of academe, expressing

its profound regret at the injustice done those former colleagues on the faculty and staff of the College who were dismissed or forced to resign in 1941 and 1942 as a result of the investigations carried out by . . . the Rapp-Coudert Committee, solely on the basis of their political associations and beliefs, and their unwillingness to testify publicly about them; and be it further

Resolved, that the Faculty Senate states its determination to safeguard for the College community those fundamental American rights of association and speech . . . without which intellectual discovery and discourse is not possible; and be it further

Resolved, that the Faculty Senate requests that the Board of Trustees consider the matter of this injustice with a view toward obtaining an official resolution of regret and a pledge to safeguard in the future the Constitutional rights of the faculty, staff and students of the University.

Two months later, on May 19, this resolution of the City College Faculty Senate was endorsed, with minor semantic improvements, by the City University Faculty Senate.

Acting with much less than "all deliberate speed," the Trustees took another five months to get around to its action of October 26, 1981, responsive to the requests of the two Faculty Senates. Since the City University Trustees' meetings are public, I gathered together a few of the victims to witness this anticipated exculpation and rehabilitation: the aforementioned John Kenneth Ackley and Jesse Mintus; Anne Bernstein, widow of Dr. Saul Bernstein of the Biology Department, and their sons,

Jonathan and Peter, who had flown in from distant cities for this profoundly emotional occasion; and Minne Motz, whose husband, Lloyd, then of the City College Physics Department, now Professor Emeritus of Astronomy at Columbia University, could not be present because he was teaching a class at the New School for Social Research.

Before the Trustees adopted their resolution, a statement I had prepared for the occasion was read into the record by the secretary of the Board of Trustees. At the end of the proceedings, we were called upon to rise and received a standing ovation.

Despite advance efforts by CUNY's public relations office, not a word of this event appeared in the *New York Times*, which had been so lavish in its front-page reports of the Rapp-Coudert Committee's actions against us. Of the metropolitan press, only the *Daily News* on the next day had a story, by Sheryl McCarthy, headed, "City U Issues Apology to Red Scare Victims." The City College student weekly, *Campus*, carried the story November 2, and in December the *City College Alumnus* published a story by Professor Leberstein and his associate, Barbara Caress, including the full text of my statement to the Trustees.

As we seek to learn the lessons taught by eras of repression in U.S. history, it is fitting to recall Philip Foner's distinguished teaching record at City College, his unjust dismissal, and his ultimate vindication and rehabilitation.

In the tradition of the ancient Jewish toast: May he live in health and productivity—to 120!

NOTES

1. Since the Trustees' apology, the ranks of the City College victims of the Rapp-Coudert Committee have been rapidly thinning: Louis Lerman (15 August 1906–24 February 1988), see *Jewish Currents* (April 1988): 42; Arnold (Shukotoff) Shaw (28 June 1909–26 September 1989, *Jewish Currents* (January 1990): 18–19; John Kenneth Ackley (21 October 1905–5 July 1990, *Jewish Currents* (September 1990): 43, (October 1990): 34, (February 1991): 20–21; David Goldway (20 July 1907–24 July 1990), *Jewish Currents* (December 1990): 20–21; Jesse Mintus (19 May 1912–9 October 1990), *Jewish Currents* (January 1991): 19–20. At the Goldway memorial meeting, Philip Foner was one of the speakers. At the Ackley memorial meeting on 25 October 1990, held on the City College campus in quarters provided by the College administration, Henry Foner presided (Henry Foner and Moe Foner, younger brothers of Philip and Jack Foner, were also victims of the Rapp-Coudert Committee. A contemporary ballad, "Mrs. Foner Had Four Sons," pointed to this wholesale family purge. At the Ackley memorial, Henry Foner announced that New York City

Mayor David N. Dinkins had proclaimed that day as John Kenneth Ackley Memorial Day, thus adding official recognition of the injustice done to Ackley and his fellow victims. I delivered the main address, on Ackley as victim and victor.)

2. In 1980 the Board of Higher Education had been reorganized and enlarged as the Board of Trustees of the City University, which had been constituted in 1961, made up of four municipal colleges named above, the seventeen two-year community colleges, and the graduate school.

3. Lawrence H. Chamberlain, *Loyalty and Legislative Action: A Survey of Activity by the New York State Legislature 1919–1949* (Ithaca, NY, 1951), 70–73, 238–246.

4. Celia Lewis Zitron, *The New York City Teachers Union 1916–1964: A Story of Educational and Social Commitment* (New York, 1968), 197; Chamberlain, 162.

5. Morris U. Schappes, *Letters from the Tombs* (Schappes Defense Committee, New York, 1941), ed. by Louis Lerman, Foreword by Richard Wright, Drawings by James D. Egleson, 112; also "Personal and Political (Cont.), Prison Experiences," *Jewish Currents* (September 1982): 4–13, 32–33.

6. *Board of Higher Education of the City of New York, In the Matter of the Charges Preferred against Philip S. Foner, Instructor of History in the History Department of the City College of the College of the City of New York, August 19 to August 21, 1941,* 4; Schappes, 112–113.

7. BHE Trial Record, withdrawal of indoctrination charge, 13; Annette S. Gottsegen, 23f; W.M. Canning, 49ff; Oscar Zeichner, 166f; Allan Nevins, 182ff; Michael Kraus, 185ff; Edward Rosen, 187ff; Philip S. Foner, 275ff.

8. Chamberlain, 145–146.

9. Schappes, 114.

Selected Bibliography

This is a limited listing of sources on U.S. labor history, gender, race, and culture that may be helpful to the reader. Dexter Arnold made many cogent suggestions to enhance this bibliography and we offer him our profound thanks.

U.S. LABOR HISTORY

Books

Barrett, James. *Work and Community in the Jungle: Chicago's Packinghouse Workers 1894–1922*. Urbana, IL, 1987.

Bernstein, Irving. *The Lean Years*. New York, 1960.

————. *The Turbulent Years*. New York, 1970.

Boris, Eileen, and Nelson Lichtenstein. *Major Problems in the History of American Labor*. Lexington, MA, 1991.

Boyer, Richard O., and Herbert M. Morais. *Labor's Untold Story*. New York, 1955.

Brody, David. *Workers in Industrial America: Essays in the 20th Century Struggle*. New York, 1980.

Cahn, William. *A Pictorial History of American Labor*. New York, 1972.

Commons, John R., and Associates. *History of Labor in the United States*. 4 vols. New York, 1966 (reprint).

DeCaux, Len. *Labor Radical*. Boston, MA, 1970.

Dubofsky, Melvin. *We Shall Be All: Industrial Workers of the World*. New York, 1969.

Foner, Philip S. *History of the Labor Movement in the United States*. 9 vols. New York, 1947–1991.

Foner, Philip S., and Brewster Chamberlin, eds. *Friedrich A. Sorge's Labor Movement in the United States: A History of the American Working Class from Colonial Times to 1890*. Westport, CT, 1977.

Forbath, William. *Law and the Shaping of the American Labor Movement.* Cambridge, MA, 1991.

Ginger, Ann Fagan, and David Christiano, eds. *The Cold War against Labor.* 2 vols. Berkeley, CA, 1987.

Green, James. *The World of the Worker: Labor in Twentieth Century America.* New York, 1980.

Gutman, Herbert. *Work, Culture and Society in Industrializing America: Essays in American Working Class and Social History.* New York, 1977.

———. *Power and Culture: Essays on the American Working Class.* Edited by Ira Berlin. New York, 1987.

Keeran, Roger. *The Communist Party and the Auto Workers Unions.* New York, 1986.

Kuczynski, Jürgen. *Die Geschichte der Lage der Arbeiter unter dem Kapitalismus, Bd. 29: Die Darstellung der Lage der Arbeiter in den Vereinigten Staaten von Amerika von 1775 bis 1897.* Berlin, 1966.

Lipsitz, George. *Class and Culture in Cold War America.* South Hadley, MA, 1982.

Lynd, Staughton, and Alice Lynd. *Rank and File.* Boston, MA, 1973.

Miller, Marc S., ed. *Working Lives: The* Southern Exposure *History of Labor in the South.* New York, 1980.

Montgomery, David. *Beyond Equality: Labor and Radical Republicans, 1862– 1872.* New York, 1967.

———. *The Fall of the House of Labor: The Workplace, the State and American Labor Activism, 1865–1925.* Cambridge, England, 1987.

Moody, Kim. *An Injury to All: The Decline of American Unionism.* London, England, 1988.

Nelson, Bruce. *Workers on the Waterfront: Seamen, Longshoremen, and Unionism in the 1930s.* Urbana, IL, 1988.

Neufeld, Maurice F. et al., eds. *American Working Class History: A Representative Bibliography.* New York, 1983.

Perlman, Selig. *A Theory of the Labor Movement.* New York, 1970 (reprint).

Preston, William. *Aliens and Dissenters: Federal Suppression of Radicals, 1903–1933.* New York, 1963.

Roediger, David, and Philip S. Foner. *Our Own Time.* Westport, CT, 1989.

Saposs, David. *Left Wing Unionism.* New York, 1926.

Stephenson, Charles, and Robert Asher. *Life and Labor: Dimensions of American Working-Class History.* Albany, NY, 1986.

Articles

Dawley, Alan, and Paul Faler. "Working-Class Culture and Politics in the Industrial Revolution: Sources of Loyalism and Rebellion." *Journal of Social History* 9 (June 1976).

Fink, Leon. "Intellectuals versus Workers: Academic Requirements and the Creation of Labor History." *American Historical Review* 96 (1991).

Fitzpatrick, Ellen. "Rethinking the Origins of American Labor History." *American Historical Review 96* (1991).

Kimeldorf, Howard. "Bringing Unions Back in (Or Why We Need a New Old Labor History)." *Labor History* 32:1 (Winter 1991).

"The Limits of Union-Centered History: Responses to Kimeldorf." A collection of articles by Michael Kazin, Alice Kessler-Harris, David Montgomery, Bruce Nelson, and Daniel Nelson. *Labor History*, 32:1 (Winter 1991).

Montgomery, David. "Trends in Working Class History." *Labor/Le Travail* 19 (Spring 1987).

GENDER

Books

Abbott, Edith. *Women in Industry: A Study in American Economic History.* New York, 1910.

Balser, Diane. *Sisterhood & Solidarity: Feminism and Labor in Modern Times.* Boston, MA, 1987.

Baron, Ava. *Work Engendered: Toward a New History of American Labor.* Ithaca, NY, 1991.

Baxandall, Rosalyn, et al., eds. *American Working Women: A Documentary History, 1600 to the Present.* New York, 1976.

Beard, Mary. *Woman as Force in History.* New York, 1946; reprint 1962.

Beneria, Lourdes, and Catherine R. Stimpson, eds. *Women Households and the Economy.* New Brunswick, NJ, and London, England, 1987.

Blewett, Mary, ed. *Men, Women and Work: Class, Gender and Protest in the New England Shoe Industry, 1780–1910.* Urbana, IL, 1988.

———. ed. *We Will Rise in Our Might: Working Women's Voices from Nineteenth Century New England.* Ithaca, NY, 1991.

Chafe, William H. *American Heroine: The Life and Legend of Jane Addams.* New York, 1973.

———. *The Paradox of Change: American Women in the 20th Century.* Oxford, England, 1991.

Davis, Angela. *Women, Race and Class.* New York, 1981.

———. *Women, Culture, and Politics.* New York, 1984.

Delzell, Ruth. *The Early History of Women Trade Unionists of America.* Chicago, IL, 1919.

DuBois, Ellen C., and Vicki Ruiz. *Unequal Sisters: A Multicultural Reader in U.S. Women's History.* New York, 1990.

Dye, Nancy S. *As Equals and as Sisters: Feminism, the Labor Movement and the Women's Trade Union League of New York.* Columbia, MO, 1980.

Faue, Elizabeth. *Community of Suffering and Struggle: Women, Men and the Labor Movement in Minneapolis, 1915–1945.* Chapel Hill, NC, 1991.

Foner, Philip S. *Women and the American Labor Movement: From the First Trade Unions to the Present.* New York, 1979.

Foner, Philip S., and Sally Miller, eds. *Kate Richards O'Hare: Selected Writings and Speeches.* Baton Rouge, LA, 1982.

Henry, Alice. *Women and the Labor Movement.* New York, 1923.

Hutchins, Grace. *Women Who Work.* New York, 1934.

Kessler-Harris, Alice. *Out to Work. A History of Wage-Earning Women in the United States.* New York, 1982.

Kugler, Israel. *From Ladies to Women: The Organized Struggle for Women's Rights in the Reconstruction Era.* New York, 1987.

Lerner, Gerda. *The Majority Finds Its Past: Placing Women in History.* New York, 1979.

Levy, Anita. *Other Women: The Writing of Class, Race and Gender, 1832–1898.* Princeton, NJ, 1991.

Milkman, Ruth. *Gender at Work: The Dynamics of Job Segregation by Sex during World War II.* Urbana, IL, 1987.

―――. *Women's Work and Protest: A Century of U.S. Women's Labor History.* Boston and London, 1985.

Nestor, Agnes. *Women's Labor Leader: An Autobiography of Agnes Nestor.* Rockford, IL, 1954.

Payne, Elizabeth Ann. *Reform, Labor, and Feminism: Margaret Drier Robins and the Women's Trade Union League.* Urbana, IL, 1988.

Raineri, Vivian. *The Red Angel.* New York, 1991.

Redcliff, Nanneke, and M. Thea Sinclair. *Working Women: International Perspectives on Labour and Gender Ideology.* London and New York, 1991.

Schneiderman, Rose, with Lucy Goldthwaite. *All for One.* New York, 1967.

Shapiro, Herbert, and David L. Sterling, eds. *"I Belong to the Working Class": The Unfinished Autobiography of Rose Pastor Stokes.* Athens, Georgia, and London, 1992.

Tax, Meredith. *The Rising of the Women: Feminist Solidarity and Class Conflict, 1880–1917.* New York, 1980.

Tilly, Louise A., and Joan W. Scott. *Women, Work and Family.* New York, 1978.

Wertheimer, Barbara. *We Were There: The Story of Working Women in America.* New York, 1977.

Wolfson, Theresa. *The Woman Worker and the Trade Unions.* New York, 1926.

Zipser, Arthur, and Pearl Zipser. *Fire and Grace: The Life of Rose Pastor Stokes.* Athens, Georgia, and London, 1989.

Articles

Abbott, Edith. "Grace Abbott and Hull House, 1908–21, Part I." *Social Service Review* 24 (September 1950).

Addams, Jane. "The Settlement as a Factor in the Labor Movement." In *Hull House Maps and Papers.* New York, 1895.

Benson, Susan Porter. "The Clerking Sisterhood." *Radical America* 12 (March–April 1978).

DuBois, Ellen C. "Woman Suffrage and the Left: An International Socialist-Feminist Perspective." *New Left Review* 186 (March–April 1991).

Dye, Nancy S. "Feminism or Unionism? The New Women's Trade Union League and the Labor Movement." *Feminist Studies* 3 (Fall 1975).

Gordon, Linda. "Black and White Visions of Welfare: Women's Welfare Activism, 1890–1945." *Journal of American History* 78 (1991).

Hansen, Karen V. "The Women's Unions and the Search for a Political Identity." *Socialist Review* 16, no. 2 (March–April 1986).

Meyerowitz, Joanne. "Sexual Geography and Gender Economy: The Furnished Room Districts of Chicago, 1890–1930." *Gender & History* 2 (1990).

Scott, Joan W. "On Language, Gender and Working Class History." *International Labor and Working Class History* 31 (Spring 1987).

Walsh, Joan. "CLUW Moves out on Its Own Agenda." *In These Times* 8:18 (4–10 April 1984).

RACE

Books

Allen, James S. *Reconstruction: The Battle for Democracy.* New York, 1937.

Aptheker, Herbert. *A Documentary History of the Negro People in the United States.* New York, 1973.

———. *Anti-Racism in U.S. History: The First Two Hundred Years.* New York, Westport, CT, 1992.

Arnesen, Eric. *Waterfront Workers of New Orleans: Race, Class and Politics 1863–1923.* New York, 1991.

Asher, Robert, and Charles Stephenson. *Labor Divided: Race and Ethnicity in U.S. Labor Struggles, 1835–1960.* Albany, NY, 1990.

Bracey, John H., et al., eds. *Black Workers and Organized Labor.* Belmont, CA, 1971.

Burton, Orville V., and Robert C. McMath, eds. *Toward a New South? Studies in Post–Civil War Southern Communities.* Westport, CT, 1982.

Cantor, Milton, ed. *Black Labor in America.* Westport, CT, 1969.

Carter, Dan T. *When the War Was Over: The Failure of Self-Reconstruction in the South, 1865–1867.* Baton Rouge, LA, 1985.

Cohen, William. *At Freedom's Edge: Black Mobility and the Southern White Quest for Racial Control, 1861–1915.* Baton Rouge, LA, 1991.

Cox, La Wanda, and John H. Cox, eds. *Reconstruction, the Negro and the New South.* Columbia, SC, 1973.

Du Bois, W.E.B. *Black Reconstruction in America, 1860–1880.* New York, 1935.

———. *The Negro Artisan.* Atlanta, GA, 1902.

———. *Economic Cooperation among Negro Americans.* Atlanta, GA, 1907.

Fink, Gary M., and Merl E. Reed, eds. *Essays in Southern Labor History.* Westport, CT, 1977.

Fitzgerald, Michael W. *The Union League Movement in the Deep South: Politics and Agricultural Change during Reconstruction.* Baton Rouge, LA, 1989.

Flynn, Charles L., Jr. *White Land, Black Labor: Caste and Class in Late Nineteenth Century Georgia.* Baton Rouge, LA, 1983.

Foner, Eric. *Nothing but Freedom: Emancipation and Its Legacy.* Baton Rouge, LA, 1983.

––––––. *Reconstruction: America's Unfinished Revolution, 1863–1877.* New York, 1988.

Foner, Philip S. *The Life and Writings of Frederick Douglass.* 5 vols. New York, 1950–75.

––––––. *Organized Labor and the Black Worker, 1619–1980.* New York, 1982.

Foner, Philip S., and Ronald L. Lewis, eds. *The Black Worker: A Documentary History from Colonial Times to the Present.* 8 vols. Philadelphia, PA, 1978–84.

Foner, Philip S., and George E. Walker, eds. *Proceedings of the Black National and State Conventions, 1865–1900.* Philadelphia, PA, 1986–.

––––––, eds. *Proceedings of the Black State Conventions, 1840–1865.* 2 vols. Philadelphia, PA, 1979.

Foster, William Z. *The Negro People in American History.* New York, 1954.

Fraser, Walter J., Jr., and Winfred B. Moore, Jr., eds. *The Southern Enigma: Essays on Race, Class and Folk Culture.* Westport, CT, 1983.

Gutman, Herbert. *The Black Family in Slavery and Freedom, 1750–1925.* New York, 1976.

Harris, William H. *The Harder We Run: Black Workers since the Civil War.* New York, 1982.

Jacobson, Julius, ed. *The Negro and the American Labor Movement.* New York, 1968.

Jaynes, Gerald J. *Branches Without Roots: Genesis of the Black Working Class in the American South, 1862–1882.* New York, 1986.

Jones, Jacqueline. *Labor of Love, Labor of Sorrow: Black Women, Work and the Family from Slavery to the Present.* New York, 1985.

Kelley, Robin. *Hammer and Hoe: Alabama Communists during the Great Depression.* Chapel Hill, NC, 1990.

Kolchin, Peter. *First Freedom: The Responses of Alabama's Blacks to Emancipation and Reconstruction.* Westport, CT, 1972.

Lerner, Gerda. *Black Women in White America: A Documentary History.* New York, 1972.

McPherson, James M. *The Struggle for Equality: Abolitionists and the Negro in the Civil War and Reconstruction.* Princeton, NJ, 1964.

Marshall, F. Ray. *Labor in the South.* Cambridge, MA, 1967.

––––––. *The Negro and Organized Labor.* New York, 1965.

Montgomery, David. *Beyond Equality: Labor and the Radical Republicans, 1862–1872.* New York, 1967.

Norack, Daniel A. *The Wheel of Servitude: Black Forced Labor after Slavery.* Lexington, KY, 1978.

Northrup, Herbert R. *Organized Labor and the Negro.* New York, 1944.

Painter, Nell. *The Narrative of Hosea Hudson: His Life as a Negro Communist in the South.* Cambridge, MA, 1979.

Rachleff, Peter J. *Black Labor in Richmond, 1865–1890.* Philadelphia, PA, 1984.

Roediger, David. *The Wages of Whiteness: Race and the Making of the American Working Class.* New York and London, 1991.

Rosengarten, Theodore. *All God's Dangers: The Life of Nate Shaw.* New York, 1974.

Satcher, Buford. *Blacks in Mississippi Politics, 1865–1900.* Washington, DC, 1978.

Shapiro, Herbert. *White Violence and Black Response: From Reconstruction to Montgomery.* Amherst, MA, 1988.

Shugg, Roger W. *Origins of Class Struggle in Louisiana.* Baton Rouge, LA, 1939.

Solow, Barbara. *Slavery and the Rise of the Atlantic System.* Cambridge, MA, 1991.

Steinfeld, Robert J. *The Invention of Free Labor: The Employment Relation in English and American Law and Culture, 1850–1870.* Durham, NC, 1991.

Sterling, Dorothy, ed. *We Are Your Sisters: Black Women in the Nineteenth Century.* New York, 1984.

Synnestvedt, Sig. *The White Response to Black Emancipation.* New York, 1972.

Taylor, Arnold H. *Travail and Triumph: Black Life and Culture in the South since the Civil War.* Westport, CT, 1976.

Trelease, Allen W. *White Terror: The Ku Klux Klan Conspiracy and Southern Reconstruction.* New York, 1971.

Trotter, Joe. *Black Milwaukee: The Making of an Industrial Proletariat, 1915–45.* Urbana, IL, 1985.

Tunnell, Ted. *Crucible of Reconstruction: War, Radicalism, and Race in Louisiana, 1862–1877.* Baton Rouge, LA, 1984.

Wesley, Charles H. *Negro Labor in the United States, 1850–1925.* New York, 1927.

Wharton, Vernon L. *The Negro in Mississippi, 1865–1890.* New York, 1965.

Wiener, Jonathan M. *Social Origins of the New South: Alabama 1860–85.* Baton Rouge, LA, 1978.

Williamson, Joel. *After Slavery: The Negro in South Carolina during Reconstruction, 1861–1877.* Chapel Hill, NC, 1965.

————. *The Crucible of Race: Black-White Relations in the American South since Emancipation.* New York, 1984.

Wood, Forrest, G. *Black Scare: The Racist Response to Emancipation and Reconstruction.* Berkeley, CA, 1969.

Wood, Philip J. *Southern Capitalism: The Political Economy of North Carolina, 1880–1980.* Durham, NC, 1986.

Articles and Dissertations

Aptheker, Herbert. "Mississippi Reconstruction and the Negro Leader, Charles Caldwell." *Science and Society* 11 (Fall 1947).

Block, Herman D. "Labor and the Negro, 1866–1910." *Journal of Negro History* (July 1965).

Davis, Ronald. "Good and Faithful Labor: A Study in the Origins, Development and Economics of Southern Sharecropping, 1860–1880." Ph.D. diss., University of Missouri, 1974.

Gates, Paul W. "Federal Land Policy in the South, 1866–1888." *Journal of Southern History* 6 (August 1940).

Greene, Lorenzo J., ed. "Negro Sharecroppers." *Negro History Bulletin* 31 (February 1968).

Grob, Gerald N. "Organized Labor and the Negro Worker, 1865–1900." *Labor History* 1 (1960).

Hine, William C. "Black Organized Labor in Reconstruction Charleston." *Labor History* 25 (Fall 1984).

Matison, Sumner Eliot. "The Labor Movement and the Negro during Reconstruction." *Journal of Negro History* 33 (1948).

Meier, August. "Negroes in the First and Second Reconstructions of the South." *Civil War History* 13 (June 1967).

Moore, Howard. "Black Labor: Slavery to Fair Hiring." *Black Scholar* 4 (February 1973).

Morgan, Philip D. "Work and Culture: The Task System and the World of Low County Blacks, 1700–1880." *William and Mary Quarterly* 39 (1982).

Morris, Richard B. "Labor Militancy in the Old South." *Labor and the Nation* (May–June 1948).

Mosley, Donald C. "A History of Labor Unions in Mississippi." Ph.D. diss., University of Alabama, 1965.

Novak, Daniel A. "Peonage: Negro Contract Labor Sharecropping Tenantry and the Law in the South, 1865–1900." Ph.D. diss., Brandeis University, 1975.

Shlomowitz, R. "Transition from Slave to Freedman Labor Arrangements in Southern Agriculture, 1865–1870." *Journal of Economic History* 39 (1979).

Shofner, Jerrell H. "Militant Negro Laborers in Reconstruction Florida." *Journal of Southern History* 39 (August 1973).

Smallwood, James. "Perpetuations of Caste: Black Agricultural Workers in Reconstruction Texas." *Mid-America* 61 (1979).

Worthman Paul B., and James R. Green. "Black Workers in the New South, 1865–1915." In *Key Issues in the Afro-American Experience*, ed. Nathan I. Huggins et al. Vol. 2. New York, 1971.

CULTURE

Books

Aaron, Daniel. *Writers on the Left*. New York, 1961.

Adams, Charles F., Jr. *Richard Henry Dana*. 2 vols. New York, 1890–1891.

Ahearn, Edward J. *Marx and Modern Fiction*. New Haven, CT, 1989.

Altenbaugh, Richard J. *Education for Struggle: American Labor Colleges of the 1920s and 1930s*. Philadelphia, PA, 1990.

Angoff, Charles. *Literary History of the American People*. New York, 1935.

Bagdikian, Ben H. *The Media Monopoly*. Boston, MA, 1983.

Barnouw, Erik. *A Tower in Babel: A History of Broadcasting in the United States*. New York, 1966.

Brenkman, John. *Culture and Domination*. Ithaca, NY, 1990.

Brookeman, Christopher. *American Culture and Society since the 1930s*. New York, 1984.

Bulmer, Martin, ed. *Working-Class Images of Society*. London, England, 1975.

Cantor, Milton, ed. *American Workingclass Culture: Explorations in American Labor and Social History*. Westport, CT, 1979.

Chomsky, Noam. *Necessary Illusions: Thought Control in Democratic Societies*. Boston, MA, 1989.

Chomsky, Noam, and Edward Herman. *Manufacturing Consent: The Political Economy of the Mass Media*. New York, 1988.

Czitrom, Daniel. *Media and the American Mind: From Morse to McLuhan*. Chapel Hill, NC, 1982.

Denning, Michael. *Mechanic Accents: Dime Novels and Working Class Culture in America*. New York, 1987.

Douglas, Sara. *Labor's New Voice: Unions and the Mass Media*. Norwood, NJ, 1986.

Douglas, Susan. *Inventing American Broadcasting*. Baltimore, MD, 1987.

Downing, John. *Radical Media: The Political Experience of Alternative Communication*. Boston, MA, 1984.

Ernst, Morris L. *The First Freedom*. New York, 1946.

Foner, Philip S. *American Labor Songs of the Nineteenth Century*. Urbana, IL, 1977.

Foner, Philip S., and Reinhard Schultz. *Das andere Amerika. Geschichte, Kunst und Kultur der amerikanischen Arbeiterbewegung*. Berlin, 1983.

Fried, Marc. *The World of the Urban Workingclass*. Cambridge, MA, 1973.

Gale, Robert L. *Richard Henry Dana, Jr*. New York, 1969.

Gans, Herbert. *Popular Culture and High Culture: An Analysis and Evaluation of Taste*. New York, 1974.

Hobsbawn, Eric J. *Laboring Men.* New York, 1964.

Hodgen, Margaret T. *Workers' Education in England and the United States.* New York, 1925.

Keil, Hartmut, and John B. Jentz, eds. *German Workers in Chicago: A Documentary History of Working-Class Culture from 1850 to World War I.* Urbana and Chicago, IL, 1988.

Kornbluh, Joyce L. *A New Deal for Workers' Education: The Workers' Service Program, 1933–1942.* Urbana, IL, 1987.

Kuczynski, Jürgen. *Die Geschichte des Alltags des deutschen Volkes.* 5 vols. Cologne, Germany, 1983.

Levine, Lawrence W. *Highbrow/Lowbrow: The Emergence of Cultural Hierarchy in America.* Cambridge, MA, 1988.

Lipsitz, George. *Time Passages: Collective Memory and American Popular Culture.* Minneapolis, MN, 1980.

Marx, Leo. *The Machine in the Garden: Technology and the Pastoral Ideal in America.* New York, 1967.

Murphy, James F. *The Proletarian Moment: The Controversy over Leftism in Literature.* Burbank, CA, 1991.

Peiss, Kathy. *Cheap Amusements: Working Women and Leisure in Turn-of-the-Century New York.* Philadelphia, PA, 1986.

Philbrick, Thomas. *James Fenimore Cooper and the Development of American Sea Fiction.* Cambridge, MA, 1961.

Rosen, Philip T. *The Modern Stentors: Radio Broadcasting and the Federal Government, 1920–1934.* Westport, CT, 1980.

Rosenzweig, Roy. *Eight Hours for What We Will: Workers and Leisure in an Industrial City.* Cambridge, England, 1982.

Schiller, Herbert I. *Communication and Cultural Domination.* New York, 1976.
———. *Culture, Inc.: The Corporate Takeover of Public Expression.* New York, Oxford, 1989.

Shapiro, Samuel. *Richard Henry Dana, Jr.* New York, 1961.

Shore, Elliot. *Talkin' Socialism: J. A. Wayland and the Role of the Press in American Radicalism, 1890–1912.* Lawrence, KS, 1988.

Stegner, Wallace E., ed. *The American Novel: James Fenimore Cooper to William Faulkner.* New York, 1965.

Thompson, Edward P. *The Making of the English Working Class.* New York, 1963.

Wright, Lyle H. *American Fiction 1774–1875: A Contribution toward a Bibliography.* 2nd rev. ed. New York, 1969.

Articles and Dissertations

Dewey, John. "Labor Politics and Labor Education." *New Republic* 57 (9 January 1929).

Faler, Paul. "Cultural Aspects of the Industrial Revolution." *Labor History* 15 (Summer 1974).

Fitzpatrick, Ellen. "Carolyn F. Ware and the Cultural Approach to History." *American Quarterly* 43 (1991).

Gutman, Herbert G. "Work, Culture and Society in Industrializing America, 1815–1919." *American Historical Review* 78:3 (June 1973).

Haessler, Stephen J. "Carl Haessler and the Federated Press: Essays on the History of American Labor Journalism." M.S. thesis, University of Wisconsin, Madison, 1977.

Hewes, Amy. "Early Experiments in Workers' Education." *Adult Education* 6 (Summer 1956).

Howlett, Charles. "Organizing the Unorganized: Brookwood Labor College 1921–1937." *Labor Studies Journal* (February 1981).

Jones, Howard M. "Nature of Literary History." *Journal of Historical Ideas* 28 (1967).

————. "Working Class Women in the Golden Age: Factory, Family and Community Life among Cohoes, New York Cotton Workers." *Journal of Social History* (Summer 1972): 464–490.

Laurie, Bruce, et al. "Immigrant and Industry: The Philadelphia Experience, 1850–1880." *Journal of Social History* 9 (Winter 1975).

Lemisch, Jesse. "Listening to the Inarticulate: William Widgar's Dream and the Loyalties of American Revolutionary Seamen in British Prisons." *Journal of Social History* 3 (1969–1970).

Lipsitz, George. "The Struggle for Hegemony." *Journal of American History* 95:1 (June 1988).

————. " 'This Ain't No Sideshow': Historians and Media Studies." *Critical Studies in Mass Communication* 5 (1988).

Lucid, Robert F. "The Influence of *Two Years before the Mast* on Herman Melville." *American Literature* 31 (November 1959).

Ross, Steven J. "Struggles for the Screen: Workers, Radicals and the Political Uses of Silent Films." *American Historical Review* 96 (1991).

Saposs, David L. "Which Way Workers' Education?" *Survey* 62 (15 May 1929).

Sparks, Colin. "The Working Class Press: Radical and Revolutionary Alternatives." *Media, Culture and Society* 7:2 (April 1985).

Walkowitz, Daniel J. "Statistics and the Writing of Workingclass Culture." In *American Workingclass Culture*, ed. Milton Cantor. Westport, CT, 1979.

Index

About the Editors and Contributors

JENNIFER L. BOSCH has a Ph.D. from Miami University of Ohio. She is Assistant Professor of History, Indiana University at Indianapolis, and formerly Instructor of History at the Ohio State University. She is the author of the forthcoming biographical review article on Ellen Gates Starr in *American National Biography*.

ERIC FONER is a DeWitt Clinton Professor of History at Columbia University and author of many works on U.S. history, including *Reconstruction: America's Unfinished Revolution, 1863-1877* (1988). He is also the winner of the *Los Angeles Times* Book Award, the Bancroft, Craven, and Owsley Prizes, and other honors.

ROCHELLE GATLIN earned her Ph.D. at the University of Pennsylvania in 1978. She is Instructor at the City College of San Francisco and the author of *American Women since 1945* (1987).

NATHAN GODFRIED received his Ph.D. in History from the University of Wisconsin, Madison. He is Professor of History at Hiram College and author of *Bridging the Gap between Rich and Poor: American Economic Development Policy toward the Arab East, 1942-1949* (1987) and author of the forthcoming book *The Tragedy of Labor Radio, WCFL: Labor and American Broadcasting, 1926-1978*.

HORST IHDE was Professor of American Studies, Humboldt University in Berlin prior to his retirement.

RONALD C. KENT earned his M.S. in Industrial Labor Relations in 1973 at the University of Wisconsin, Madison. He is Education Representative for AFSCME in Wisconsin and is the editor of the International Labor History Association.

SARA MARKHAM is Lecturer of German at the University of Wisconsin in Madison, where she received her Ph.D. in 1983. She is the author of *Workers, Women, and Afro-Americans: Images of the United States in German Travel Literature, from 1923 to 1933* (1986).

ROBERT R. MONTGOMERY has an M.A. from University of Massachusetts at Amherst. He is a doctoral candidate in U.S. Labor History at the University of Massachusetts, Amherst.

DAVID R. ROEDIGER is Professor of History at the University of Missouri. His other books include *Our Own Time: A History of American Labor and the Working Day* (Greenwood, 1989). *The Wages of Whiteness: Race and the Making of the American Working Class* (1991), and *Fellow Worker: The Life of Fred W. Thompson* (1992).

ALLEN RUFF received his Ph.D. in History at the University of Wisconsin, Madison, in 1987. He works as an activist historian in Madison. He is also the author of "The Socialist Press and Repression in the World War I Era: The Case of Charles H. Kerr & Company," *Journal of Newspaper and Periodical History* (Spring 1989), and a forthcoming book on Charles Kerr.

GLORIA GARRETT SAMSON earned her Ph.D. at the University of Rochester in 1987. She teaches labor history at Cornell University's Industrial Relations School in Rochester and U.S. history courses at several area colleges.

MORRIS U. SCHAPPES received his M.A. from Columbia University in 1930. He is Editor-in-Chief of *Jewish Currents* and author of several works on U.S. Jewish history, including *A Documentary History of the Jews in the U.S.A.: 1654-1875* (3d ed., 1971).

HERBERT SHAPIRO is Professor of History at the University of Cincinnati. His other books include *White Violence and Black Response: From Reconstruction to Montgomery* (1988) and (with David L. Sterling) *"I*

Belong to the Working Class": The Unfinished Autobiography of Rose Pastor Stokes (1992).

ELIZABETH ANN SHARPE has a Masters of Social Sciences (University of Colorado, 1986) and an M.A. in History (Jackson State University, 1992). She is presently Lecturer in History at Jackson State University. She is the author of "The Legacy of Slave Labor in Mississippi," *Proceedings of the 1990 Annual Meeting of the American Political Science Association* (1990).

JOHN SHERMAN earned his M.A. from the University of Toledo in 1989. He is currently a doctoral candidate in Latin American History at the University of Arizona at Tuscon.